The Economic Status
of Women
Under Capitalism

The Economic Status of Women Under Capitalism

Institutional Economics and Feminist Theory

Edited by
Janice Peterson
Assistant Professor of Economics
State University of New York, College at Fredonia
and
Doug Brown
Associate Professor of Economics
Northern Arizona University

Edward Elgar

Published by
Edward Elgar Publishing Limited
Gower House
Croft Road
Aldershot
Hants GU11 3HR
England

Edward Elgar Publishing Company
Old Post Road
Brookfield
Vermont 05036
USA

British Library Cataloguing in Publication Data
Economic Status of Women Under Capitalism:
Institutional Economics and Feminist
Theory
  I. Peterson, Janice II. Brown, Douglas M.
  330.122082

Library of Congress Cataloguing in Publication Data
The Economic status of women under capitalism: institutional
  economics and feminist theory/edited by Janice Peterson and Doug
  Brown.
      p.   cm.
  Includes bibliographical references and index.
  1. Women — Economic conditions. 2. Feminist theory — Economic
aspects. 3. Institutional economics. 4. Capitalism. I. Peterson,
Janice. II. Brown, Douglas M., 1947–   .
  HQ1381.E24 1994
  305.42—dc20

                                                                    93–8713
                                                                      CIP

ISBN 1 85278 894 1

Printed and bound in Great Britain by
Hartnolls Limited, Bodmin, Cornwall

Contents

List of Contributors   *vii*
Acknowledgements   *ix*
Introduction   *x*
Janice Peterson

PART I: EXPLORING CONNECTIONS: INSTITUTIONALISM
AND FEMINISM

1. Institutionalism and Feminism   3
    William M. Dugger
2. Institutionalism: A Useful Foundation
    for Feminist Economics?   19
    Charles Whalen and *Linda Whalen*
3. Radical Institutionalism and Postmodern
    Feminist Theory   35
    Doug Brown

PART II: EXTENDING OUR ANALYSIS

4. Technology and Gender in Institutional
    Economics   55
    William Waller
5. Feminism and Science Reconsidered:
    Insights from the Margins   77
    Paulette Olson
6. Cultural Contours of Race, Gender,
    and Class Distinctions:
    A Critique of Moynihan and Other
    Functionalist Views   95
    Ann Jennings and *Dell Champlin*

PART III: EXAMINING THE ISSUES OF GENDER

7.   Traditional Economic Theories and Issues
       of Gender:
       The Status of Women in the United States
       and the Former Soviet Union   113
       Janice Peterson
8.   Equality and the Women's Movement:
       What's Missing?   128
       Gladys Parker Foster
9.   Radical Institutionalism, Sociology,
       and the Dual Career Couple   142
       Jacqueline Bloom Stanfield
10.   The Status of Women in Japan   157
       Bernadette Lanciaux

Conclusion   177
Doug Brown

Index   182

List of Contributors

Doug Brown is professor of Economics at Northern Arizona University. He is the author of *Towards A Radical Democracy,* and his publications include articles in the *Journal of Economic Issues* on postmodernism, Marxism, and democratic theory.

Dell Champlin received her Ph.D. in Economics from the University of Utah in 1990. Her research interests include work organization and structure, and feminism.

William M. Dugger is professor of Economics at the University of Tulsa. He is the author of *An Alternative to Economic Retrenchment, Corporate Hegemony, and Underground Economics.* He is the editor of *Radical Institutionalism,* the first volume of an ongoing series of collected essays in radical institutionalism. He is coeditor, with William T. Waller, Jr., of *The Stratified State*, the second volume of the ongoing series. He has also published numerous articles on institutionalism and corporate capitalism. He is past President of the Association for Institutional Thought, and past President of the Association for Social Economics.

Gladys Parker Foster is currently adjunct assistant professor of Economics at the University of Colorado, Denver. At the age of sixty-four she received a Ph.D. in Economics from the University of Colorado in Boulder. She has published a number of articles and book reviews on institutional economics and feminism.

Ann Jennings is professor of Urban and Regional Studies and Economics at the University of Wisconsin, Green Bay. She is active in the Association for Evolutionary Economics, the Association for Institutional Thought, and the International Association for Feminist Economics. Her current research interests include economic methodology, the articulation of race, gender and class distinctions, and feminist macroeconomics.

Bernadette Lanciaux is professor of Economics and Coordinator of Asian Studies at Hobart and William Smith Colleges, Geneva, New York. She has been the recipient of several grants to travel to Japan and has participated in several interdisciplinary workshops on various aspects of Japanese history and society.

Paulette Olson, professor at Wright State University, teaches in the Departments of Economics and Women's Studies. Her interests include Third World feminism, environmental issues and the confluence of racism and poverty in America. Her articles have appeared in the *Journal of Economic Issues* and the *International Review of Applied Economics*.

Janice Peterson is professor of Economics at the State University of New York, College in Fredonia. Her interests include institutional economics, feminist theory, and public policy. Her articles have been published in the *Journal of Economic Issues* and *The Social Science Journal.*

Jacqueline Bloom Stanfield is currently professor of Sociology, at the University of Northern Colorado, Greeley, Colorado. She received her Ph.D. in Sociology from Colorado State University, Fort Collins, Colorado. Her current research interests include gender inequality, family process, dual career couples and family policy.

William Waller is professor of Economics at Hobart and William Smith Colleges, Geneva, New York. He has written many articles on institutional economic theory and methodology appearing in the *Journal of Economic Issues* and is the coeditor of *Alternatives to Economic Orthodoxy* with R. Albelda and G. Gunn, and *The Stratified State* with W. Dugger. His current research interests include the intersection of feminist theory, critical rhetoric and institutional economics.

Charles J. Whalen is professor of Economics at Hobart and William Smith Colleges. He has published widely on economic thought, macroeconomics, and labor relations.

Linda B. Whalen is a regional public health nutritionist with the New York State Department of Health. Her specialization is community nutrition and public policy.

Acknowledgements

Because this volume is a collaborative effort involving a dozen individual contributors, the thanks we owe to many of our friends, colleagues, and supporting academic institutions is collectively given here. The help we have received from so many different people and groups is greatly appreciated, and all of us whose names are listed as contributors want to express our gratitude for the vital role played by the others whose names remain unstated. We are humbled by the awareness that books such as this are a social, not individual outcome. We also recognize that what insights and understandings are communicated here are only part of a broader social and evolutionary process. The thanks and appreciation go to many people and to many places.

We want to especially thank Kate St. Germain for her outstanding work in the preparation of the camera-ready copy of the typescript. Without her excellent skills, diligence and patient tenacity, the book would not have been completed. Additionally, we express our appreciation and thanks to Dean Joseph Walka and the Northern Arizona University, College of Business Administration for support of the summer conference that brought us together for this volume.

Introduction

Janice Peterson

One of the essential features of institutional economics is its activist approach to social inquiry. Institutional economists share the conviction that for social inquiry to be meaningful it must be addressed to solving the socio-economic problems of the day.[1] This commitment to meaningful, relevant inquiry is reflected in the purpose of this volume. Our purpose is to explore the usefulness of institutional economics in analyzing the subordination of women and in promoting progressive social and economic change.

The contributors to this volume belong to a group of scholars dedicated to the ideal of socially relevant economic inquiry. Many of our views differ, reflecting different life experiences and different areas of professional interest and academic training. We share, however, a concern over the economic status of women and a belief that the dominant approaches to economic analysis are limited in their ability to analyze the subordination of women and to prescribe policy responses. We believe that for economic inquiry to provide support for the struggles of women it must incorporate the insights of feminist scholarship and activism.

This volume does not intend to make a definitive statement on what 'feminist institutionalism' must be. There are important differences among both institutionalist and feminist scholars on the appropriate focus and method of inquiry. Our purpose is to show that institutional economics can provide the foundation for a more feminist economics. It is our hope that this volume will provide the impetus for continuing discussions on the meaning and purpose of feminist economic inquiry.

The contributors to this volume have been informed and inspired by the ideas and ideals of 'radical institutionalists'.[2] Radical institutionalism is the branch of institutional economics most explicitly concerned with sexism and the economic status of women. The following section provides a very brief overview of radical institutionalism and its relationship to feminism. The last section introduces the major themes of the volume and the chapters that address these themes.

Radical Institutionalism and Feminism

Radical institutionalism has its roots in the work of Thorstein Veblen, who provided a scathing critique of American capitalism at the turn of the century, as well as an alternative methodology for the study of economic systems and social change. According to William Dugger, radical institutionalism is, 'a processual paradigm focused on changing the direction of cultural evolution and changing the outcome of social provisioning in order to promote full participation of all' (Dugger 1989, 126). Radical institutionalism is dedicated to the goals of social and economic equality; it is unabashedly political.

Radical institutionalists view the economy as a process, not a set of equilibrium conditions (Dugger 1989, 4). They reject the neoclassical vision of economics as merely a study of individual choice under conditions of scarcity. They also reject the economic determinism of classical Marxism. Radical institutionalists argue that the focus of economic inquiry should be on the processes by which societies provision and reproduce themselves.

Radical institutionalism stresses the importance of culture in shaping societal value systems and economic processes. The choices and behaviors of individuals are influenced by the culture and belief system of the society they live in. Radical institutionalists recognize that individual rationality can be distorted by myths, the ceremonial justifications for exploitative behavior (Dugger 1989, 6). Individual behavior is far too complex to be explained in terms of abstract rationality or maximization. Nor can it be explained entirely in terms of property ownership and one's relationship to the means of production. Individual choice is only meaningful within the cultural context of the decision maker.

Radical institutionalism stresses that economic systems are human creations, continually subject to change and amenable to reform. Radical institutionalism is democratic, stressing the necessity of full participation in social and economic life. It is through the full participation of all individuals and groups that the 'imbecile institutions' promoting invidious distinctions, such as those embodied in racism and sexism, are combatted.

There is a literature emerging within radical institutionalism that focuses on issues of gender and the prospects of engaging in feminist economic inquiry. William Waller and Ann Jennings, for example, have argued that institutionalists and feminists share a rejection of traditional approaches to scientific inquiry. Most fundamentally, they reject the Cartesian conception of knowledge as 'the objective ordering of facts' (Waller and Jennings 1990, 615). This leads both feminists and institutionalists to the recognition that knowledge itself is socially constructed. Knowledge is 'a product of the culture that generated it' and cannot be separated from 'cultural preconceptions and prejudices' (Waller and Jennings 1990, 617).

Waller and Jennings argue that the rejection of traditional views of 'objective knowledge' leads institutionalists and feminists to the rejection of dualistic constructions of reality, such as those embodied in gender distinctions. The dualistic categorization of human activities ignores the cultural continuity of the life process, falsely separating behaviors that constitute an interrelated whole. Dualistic categories are not ideologically neutral, but lead to hierarchy through the creation of ranked comparisons (Waller and Jennings 1990, 616–18).

The dualistic categorization of human activities has played an important role in traditional social and economic thought. Of particular importance to the study of the economic status of women is the public-private dualism. This dualism separates human activity into 'separate spheres', one which is 'public' in the sense of being connected to social life, and one that is 'private' in the sense of being removed from social life, untouched by cultural values. The public sphere has typically been associated with those activities carried out by men; the private sphere with those activities carried out by women (Waller and Jennings 1990, 618–19).

In traditional economic theories of capitalism and socialism the public-private dualism is reflected in definitions of the economy that exclude many activities performed by women. Work and production have been defined as activities that take place within the public sphere; activities that take place in the private sphere are not defined as work and are not examined as economically relevant. This has had serious implications for the economic status of women. It has distorted our perceptions of women's activities and the nature of the economy. It has reinforced the view of women as non-economic, unproductive beings and provided the basis for policies that ignore the needs of women and are detrimental to their social and economic wellbeing.

Most studies of the economic status of women have taken place within this context. Often, attempts to incorporate gender into economic inquiry have simply resulted in the addition of women to the existing categories of analysis. Given the bias in existing modes of inquiry, this is not enough. Simply adding women to existing categories of analysis, such as the labor force or the working class, does not explain why women have previously been ignored. It is necessary to reevaluate and redefine existing categories from the perspective of women's experiences. Without such a reevaluation, economic analysis and policy will continue to work within and reinforce the existing biases.

Radical institutionalism and feminism share a devotion to equality and full participation. The experiences of women all over the world suggest, however, that it is critical to carefully consider the meaning of these concepts. For increased participation to end the subordination of women it must mean the transformation of existing institutions. Simply adding women into existing structures is not sufficient and may even result in further exploitation.

Increasing women's participation in paid labor, for example, has been viewed by many as the road to liberation and a sign of increased equality. Yet without accompanying institutional change, this has led many women to bear a double burden of work in and outside the home. While this has increased the work they must perform, it has not always increased their status or wellbeing. In addition, for many women the type of wage labor available limits the liberating potential of their participation. Liberation must imply more than the mobilization of women as economic resources; it must bring with it a more equitable distribution of power.

The following chapters address these issues in the context of three major themes. First, we explore the connections between radical institutionalism and feminist theory. This section seeks to answer the questions: 'Why is institutionalism relevant to feminism'? and 'What can institutionalism contribute to feminist research in economics'? Second, we examine ways of extending our analyses to more fully address issues of gender and the problems faced by women. Third, we examine various issues of importance to the economic status of women in different economic systems.

Major Themes

Exploring Connections

The writings of Thorstein Veblen provide the starting point for our exploration of feminist institutionalist scholarship.[3] Veblen saw women's position in economic society as a reflection of the prevailing system of status and values. He argued that in early predatory societies the contributions of women were depreciated because they lacked the requisite elements of prowess and exploit. In modern capitalist societies, the predatory and acquisitive instincts are refined and are manifested in the behavior of the leisure class, where women are relegated to the role of conspicuous consumption and vicarious leisure.

According to Veblen, the downgrading of women's work is a reflection of the dominance of disserviceability over workmanship in modern society. It also reflects a fundamental flaw in orthodox economic theory: the emphasis on market relations as the source of value. Thus, orthodox economics can provide no solution to the oppression of women; it only serves to mask the real issues at hand.

In chapter 1, William Dugger begins with Veblen's institutionalism and applies his model to the study of gender inequality. Dugger argues that gender inequality is a major concern to radical institutionalists because it distorts the direction of cultural evolution away from democratic politics and participatory economics. Gender inequality is supported by myths of inferiority and superiority that must be exposed and refuted. Dugger discusses several of the myths of gender inequality, including those of the 'feminine mystique' and the 'super mom'. He concludes that the cultural, processual method of radical institutionalism provides feminists with a framework for analyzing inequality and developing strategies to combat it.

The connections between feminist and institutionalist methodology are explored in chapter 2 by Charles Whalen and Linda Whalen. They examine feminist and institutionalist considerations in three areas of methodology: ontology, epistemology and axiology (the studies of the nature of reality, knowledge, and values, respectively). Whalen and Whalen find that institutionalism and feminism both reject the atomistic and static view of traditional science and share a holistic and processual view of reality. Institutionalism and feminism also share a pragmatic and instrumentalist theory of knowledge and a multifaceted view of values. Whalen and Whalen conclude that institutionalism has a great deal to offer feminist inquiry and is ready to provide a foundation for building a feminist economics.

In chapter 3, Doug Brown continues the discussion of methodology, arguing that the important commonality between institutionalism and feminism is their postmodern epistemology. Brown argues that Veblen's institutionalism, with its rejection of 'universal truths', and 'fundamental principles', is consistent with the writings of contemporary postmodern feminists, who reject excessive reliance on 'totalizing categories' that are presumed to be universal. He observes that, over time, the lives of individuals are becoming increasingly diverse and sources of oppression increasingly varied. Thus, feminist institutionalist scholarship must recognize this diversity and strive for the development of a political movement based on building alliances that respect differences across groups while at the same time uniting them through the process of democratic reform.

Extending Our Analysis

The chapters in Part II build on the theoretical foundation presented in Part I. They critique aspects of institutionalist and feminist thought and offer ways to extend our analyses to be more inclusive and progressive.

In chapter 4, William Waller examines an issue of critical importance to institutional analysis: technology. Waller argues that it is essential for us to view technology holistically, as a social construct and a cultural process. He illustrates how dualistic, hierarchical distinctions have driven what is defined as technology and he examines how these distinctions have been linked to dualistic gender hierarchies. Waller argues that institutionalism must come to terms with the gendered meanings traditionally associated with technology if it is to become a feminist economics.

In chapter 5, Paulette Olson examines feminist scholarship from the perspective of the struggles of Third World women. Olson seeks to extend the boundaries of radical institutionalism through an examination of the postcolonial critique of western humanism. She illustrates the role of enabling myths in constructing inequality between the 'the West' and 'the East' as well as between men and women. She argues that the use of universal categories, even in the context of wellmeaning analyses, has distorted our views of the lives of Third World women. She argues that a feminist economics must move beyond the 'hegemonic discourse' found in the economics and feminist literatures of the West and respect the voices of those who have been previously ignored.

The practice of universalizing the experiences of white Europeans to all people has marginalized women of color in the United States as well as in the Third World. In chapter 6, Ann Jennings and Dell Champlin examine how the concept of the 'universal family' invoked by functionalist analyses of the poverty of black Americans has distorted our understanding of the problem and contributed to misguided policies. Jennings and Champlin argue that functionalist analyses have led to the conclusion that black poverty in the United States is caused by the family breakdown and 'improper' gender roles, ignoring the role of racism and lack of economic opportunity. Jennings and Champlin call for the development of a noninvidious social theory which accounts for racism and its interaction with other forms of oppression. They suggest the

writings of black feminist scholars and Thorstein Veblen as the foundation
for such a theory.

Examining Issues of Gender

As the world experiences social and economic changes, the status of
women becomes an increasingly important issue and traditional theories
become less and less relevant. Social and economic change may improve
the economic status of women, providing them with new resources and
opportunities. At the same time, it may produce new insecurities and
sources of oppression. The chapters in Part III examine the economic
status of women in several different societies experiencing important
changes.

In chapter 7, Janice Peterson examines the economic status of women
in the United States and the former Soviet Union. She examines trends in
several of the traditional indicators of economic status, finding both
interesting similarities and differences in the position of women in these
two very different economic systems. She argues that the dominant
economic ideologies — neoclassical economics and classical Marxism —
have failed to overcome traditional gender ideology and dualistic
conceptions of 'public' and 'private' activities, and thus, have failed to
provide the basis for progressive policy in each system.

In chapter 8, Gladys Parker Foster explores the meaning of 'equality',
a concept that has played an important role in both the institutionalist and
feminist literatures. Foster argues that it is not enough to fight inequality;
one must be clear on what equality means and how it will be obtained.
She focuses on how equality has been defined in the United States and the
problems that have been encountered in its pursuit. She argues that
traditional notions of equality have been deficient as guidelines for
organizing society to include women and children in a reasonable way.
She argues that the instrumental value theory of institutional economics
provides a viable alternative.

In chapter 9, Jacqueline Bloom Stanfield examines the characteristics
and operation of an increasingly important type of family — the family
with a dual career couple. Social scientists have been slow to move away
from the notion of the 'universal family', assuming the traditional family
with the male breadwinner and female homemaker. Stanfield illustrates
how, in fact, the American family is not static, but has undergone
significant change and evolution over time. She examines how the dual
career couple has emerged from changes in society since the industrial
revolution and illustrates how this type of family has been treated in the

sociology literature. She suggests important variables that need to be considered in our analyses of modern families.

In chapter 10, Bernadette Lanciaux examines the status of women in another society experiencing rapid change: Japan. She examines the historical evolution of the roles of Japanese women as well as their current economic status. Western observers have been quick to conclude that the status of women in Japan is changing rapidly and that Japanese women will become more and more like their Western counterparts. Lanciaux disagrees, arguing that the institutions that most affect the status of Japanese women have changed very little. She concludes that the direction of change that is taking place is not toward a Western model, but reflects the many unique aspects of Japanese culture.

These chapters illustrate many of the issues raised in Parts I and II. They show the need to recognize changing family structures and the operations of real-life families. They illustrate the fact that increased labor-force participation is not equal to liberation and has not necessarily improved the status of women. They stress the need to carefully define equality in such a way that its pursuit truly improves the wellbeing of women. It is toward the development of a feminist economics, an approach capable of addressing these issues, that this book is dedicated.

Notes

1. For an introduction to the fundamentals of institutional economics, see Petr 1984.
2. For a more detailed discussion of radical institutionalism and its relationship to the institutional economics literature, see Dugger 1989.
3. Two of the most well-known discussions of the status of women in Veblen's work are in *The Theory of the Leisure Class* (1899) and *Essays in Our Changing Order* (1934).

References

Dugger, William, ed. (1989), *Radical Institutionalism: Contemporary Voices*, New York: Greenwood.

Petr, Jerry (1984), 'Fundamentals of an Institutionalist Perspective on Economic Policy', *Journal of Economic Issues*, 18 March: 1–17.

Veblen, Thorstein (1899), *The Theory of the Leisure Class*, New York: Macmillan.

Veblen, Thorstein (1934), *Essays in Our Changing Order*, New York: The Viking Press.

Waller, William and Ann Jennings (1990), 'On the Possibility of a Feminist Economics: The Convergence of Institutional and Feminist Methodology', *Journal of Economic Issues*, 24 June: 612–22.

PART I

Exploring Connections:
Institutionalism and Feminism

1. Institutionalism and Feminism

William M. Dugger

Introduction

In sexist societies like mine, men should refrain from writing about women so as to avoid making fools of themselves. We write foolishness, not because of what we do not know, but because of what we know that just is not so. According to Ashley Montagu, 'To listen to most men dilating authoritatively on the subject of women is to suffer a positive increase in one's ignorance' (Montagu 1974, 49). Being a man, and agreeing with Montagu, I proceed with real trepidation. Nonetheless, also being a radical institutionalist, I claim license to proceed because feminism forms the very heart of radical institutionalism. The founder of institutionalism, Thorstein Veblen, was a feminist of the first order. And his feminist-inspired dichotomy is a foundation of institutionalist thought.

From the very beginning, Thorstein Veblen was profoundly interested in women's issues. His early interest in feminism formed the foundation of his later economic and social critique of business civilization. Four of his best early articles dealt sympathetically and knowledgeably with feminism: 'The Economic Theory of Women's Dress' (1894), 'The Instinct of Workmanship and the Irksomeness of Labor' (1898), 'The Beginnings of Ownership' (1898), and 'The Barbarian Status of Women' (1899). In these four essays he worked out the foundations of the Veblenian dichotomy. According to Veblen, two sets of human activities and their corresponding values, beliefs, and meanings form the point and counterpoint of human existence. On one hand is male personal exploit and on the other hand is female social industry. Male exploit is aimed at seizure of wealth (ownership), capture of slaves and servants (ownership/marriage) and display of status (conspicuous consumption and conspicuous leisure). Female industry is aimed at production of serviceable items (the instinct of workmanship), care of children and the infirm (parental bent), and the increase and sharing of arts and crafts (idle

3

curiosity). In his later books he referred to male personal exploit as pecuniary employment and female social industry as industrial employment. By bringing into his analysis the impacts of different kinds of work (the incidence of the machine process) he also firmly connected his feminism to his socialism, enriching them both.

Gender issues played a crucial role in Veblen's systematic critique of the wastefulness of business civilization. Pecuniary employments based on male exploit and on getting something for nothing sabotaged the potential of the industrial system. To realize our full industrial potential, a fundamental institutional transformation was required; a new value standard based on peaceful service was needed to replace the business values based on predatory acquisition. However, Veblen did not look to the middle-class women's movement of his time to provide the new values. Instead, he looked to the working-class strata of rootless and iconoclastic industrial workers that he called 'the engineers' (Veblen 1965 and 1919, 279–323). Nonetheless, Veblen fully integrated the significance of gender into his radical branch of institutionalism.

In an earlier volume, a predecessor to this one, radical institutionalism was defined as 'the processual paradigm focused on changing the direction of cultural evolution and the function of social provisioning in order to promote the full participation of all' (Dugger 1989c, 132). Inequality is anathema to institutionalism because it restricts the full participation of all and it distorts the direction of cultural evolution. Inequality is not a state, not a stable equilibrium between the top dogs and the under dogs. It is a cumulative process that does not stand still. It either gets worse, or it gets better. When it gets worse, it becomes a vicious circle of cumulative causation in which the under dogs fall further and further in status, income, and power. The vicious circle of inequality corrodes social bonds and strengthens enabling myths — racist, sexist, and other elitist beliefs become more and more widespread and entrenched in the culture. The culture then moves further and further away from participatory practices and also further and further away from instrumental values, replacing warranted knowledge with the edicts of authority and the rationalizations of arrogance. In addition to being the very heart of Veblen's thought, feminism is important to radical institutionalism as an ally in the effort to change the direction of cultural evolution toward the full participation of all.

Radical institutionalism is also important to feminism because it provides an effective framework for analyzing gender inequality and for reducing its distorting effects on women. Unlike classical Marxism, institutionalism does not reduce inequality down to class and then interpret gender inequality in class terms. Furthermore, unlike neoclassical economics, institutionalism does not explain inequality in terms of the individual's subjective tastes for discrimination. Institutionalism emphasizes the role of cultural myth instead of the role of optimal individual choice.

The Importance of Gender

The best way to begin a study of gender inequality is to understand what it means to be a female born into our male-dominated society. As Simone De Beauvoir defined her, woman is 'a human being in quest of values in a world of values, a world of which it is indispensable to know the economic and social structure' (De Beauvoir 1989, 52). The same definition applies to man. However, De Beauvoir emphasized, a man is the One while a woman is Other. Her quest for values in a world of values, if it takes her beyond her narrow woman's role, is not judged in terms of authentic excellence. Instead, her quest is judged as a pale mimicry of male accomplishments and her drive is interpreted as a sublimated desire to be a man. She is not understood in light of her own experience, but in light of the experience of men. She is the subject of a twisted invidious distinction. If she likes to climb trees when a girl, it is because she is a 'tomboy'. If a boy likes to climb trees, no questions are asked and no answers must be given. While a young man who likes to paint nude women has no explaining to do, a young woman who likes to paint nude men has quite a lot of explaining to do — she must explain why she is not merely sublimating her alleged desire to be a man. While a young man struggling to advance his professional career has no explaining to do, a young woman doing the same has quite a lot of explaining to do — she must explain why she is putting off having children. And so on, and on.

Distorting a woman's 'quest of values in a world of values' is the central fact that the values are not supposed to be hers. Her values are supposed to be Other, and so when she achieves excellence, she also tastes the bitterness of defeat. It is not so with him, with man, with the One. When he achieves excellence, it is true excellence, and he tastes the sweetness of success. De Beauvoir explains, 'woman's independent successes are in contradiction with her femininity, since the "true woman" is required to make herself object, to be the Other' (De Beauvoir 1989, 162, quotation marks in the original).

The Otherness of woman is not 'natural,' but 'artificial'. It is determined by her culture, not her biology. Her culture, unlike her biology, is a product of human action, of human artifice rather than natural law. Culture can be changed; is constantly being changed.

Nonetheless, the implications of Otherness for women's identity and for their full participation in the economy outside the family are truly profound. Otherness and the motivational ambiguity it invokes makes it difficult for women to perform nontraditional roles with the joy and creativity that men can easily bring to bear on them. Man is not divided against himself when he participates in public life outside the family, but woman is. Herein lies a very real handicap for women, a disease caused by their cultural conditioning, a deep ambiguity in their psyche about what values to pursue and about what it means to them when those values are pursued. When woman pursues values outside the traditional family ones she has been taught, does it mean she loses a part of her self-identity as a vital female person? When man pursues values outside the narrow realm of the family, there is no such ambiguity. He can give himself to the quest wholeheartedly. He is not handicapped by self-doubt. She is. And, no other victim of inequality is handicapped in just this way, for the self-identity of no other victim of inequality is so closely wrapped up in the culturally-defined values that delineate the contours of their self-worth.

The effort required to overcome the gender handicap imposed on females by patriarchy explains the importance of consciousness raising. It also explains why gender inequality cannot be reduced to class or race or ethnic inequality. For many contemporary American feminists these insights came in a series of frightening flashes that occurred when women tried to take their rightful places as leaders in the protest movement of the 1960s. For example, one feminist describes the response of movement men at a 1969 peace demonstration in Washington, D.C. when a woman got up to speak about feminism:

> The men go crazy...They yell and boo and guffaw at unwitting double entendres like 'We must take to the streets'. When S., who is representing the New York group...announces that women will no longer participate in any so-called revolution that does not include the abolition of male privilege, it sounds like a spontaneous outburst of rage...(Hymowitz and Weissman 1978, 348).

The feminist observer of this male outburst reflected, 'If radical men can be so easily provoked into acting like rednecks, what can we expect from others' (Hymowitz and Weissman 1978, 348)? Indeed, and so the women feminists rightly refused to allow their movement against gender inequality to be reduced down to a movement against racism, classism, or jingoism. Instead, their painfully acquired insights led to the development of consciousness-raising among women. By the early 1970s, consciousness-raising groups had become an important part of women's liberation. In their consciousness-raising groups the women invented a new form of collective action, a very fruitful form. Consciousness-raising groups focused their attention on gender inequality itself and made great strides in their understanding both of the larger issues confronting them from the outside culture, and of the deeper ambiguities confronting them from inside their own psyches. From the consciousness-raising efforts of women acting collectively came the most important contribution to evolve out of the 1960s — the idea that the personal is political. The idea had been around for a long time, but the consciousness-raising activities of the women's liberationists brought the truth home to many, even to those who did not participate in consciousness-raising itself. And also from the consciousness-raising groups came a new self-confidence for the women who participated. They came to realize that they could be creative, disciplined, and aggressive without losing some allegedly important part of their own female identity. Through collective action, they learned how to overcome the crippling ambiguity in the self-identity of women who search for values in a male-dominated society.

Domination: Power, Status, Income, and Invisibility

Men have more power than women, more income than women, and higher status than women. These three measures of inequality — power, income, and status — are not separate dimensions that offset one another, but mutually reinforcing dimensions of inequality. We all know that men occupy most of the higher positions in the corporate, educational, military, religious, and political worlds. We all know that men earn more than women, even in the same occupations. And we all know that men are looked up to more than women. In fact, we honor men so much that we incorrectly believe that if a woman tries to raise children without a man in the house, the children will suffer from not having someone to look up to. (Why not look up to your mother? What is wrong with her as a role model?)

We realize all these things, dimly. But what we do not realize even dimly is how power, income, and status mutually reinforce male dominance and female subservience. The political power of men in the state is not offset by the alleged status of women in the family. The higher income of men in the workplace is not offset by the alleged power exercised by the wives' expertise at shopping. Instead, all the advantages that men gather to themselves make men the center of existence and push women out onto the margin, making women almost invisible in the lofty world of men. Not only are they not recognized as someone in the family that children can look up to, but their traditional work at home is not even recognized as a part of the Gross National Product. In fact, the GNP would rise dramatically if all of the wives divorced their husbands and then hired on as their former husbands' personal accountants, maids, cooks, nannies, chauffeurs, nurses, and prostitutes. Then, at least, the market value of most of the work the women did in the family would no longer be excluded from the GNP. Women would no longer be invisible.

Furthermore, if women were really no longer invisible, the hand-wringing about young women trying to raise children without fathers at home could stop. Then we could see that single women often do a very good job of building a network of supporting sisters, aunts, grandmothers, and girlfriends for raising children without men. What these creative, even heroic young women need is not someone else to take care of — the young man who biologically fathered the children — but enough income to pay the bills. This means equal pay for equal work and adequate state support for families with children, not financial dependence on men. After all, upper-class women — mainly women whose husbands work in the higher levels of corporate management — have been raising their children for several generations now with very little real help from their husbands. What their husbands provide is money. Their husbands are totally absorbed in their corporate careers and have little time to 'waste' with children. But, these husbands still lend their status to their family, so they are not considered to be absent *de jure* even though they are absent *de facto*. Upper-class fathers are handy, to pay the bills and lend legitimacy. But the invisible wives do the real parenting.

Sexism: The Feminine Mystique and Supermom

Because woman is Other, her contributions to the life process are invisible. But also because woman is Other, the onerous responsibilities assigned her are highly visible. She has duties to perform, but she gets no recognition for performing them, only criticism for not performing them. The duties assigned her by her culture are of a mythical quality. No mere mortal can perform them, only a goddess. She is expected to be Supermom, to be mysteriously and passively feminine for her husband, to be the exclusive caretaker and parent of her young children, and to have a challenging job in the paid workforce. If she fails to do so, if she fails in her quest for values, the myths that keep her in a fog also make it hard for her to see that the values were set by men. The myths also lead her to blame herself rather than to band together with other women and take collective action to overcome her problems — at least the myths tended to do so before women began practicing consciousness raising. The mythical duties imposed upon her and the negative sanctions applied to her should she fail in her duties, severely cripple her full participation in the life process.

The Feminine Mystique

Betty Friedan explained that the feminine mystique puts woman on a pedestal:

> Beneath the sophisticated trappings, it simply makes certain concrete, finite, domestic aspects of feminine existence — as it was lived by women whose lives were confined, by necessity, to cooking, cleaning, washing, bearing children — into a religion, a pattern by which all women must now live or deny their femininity (Friedan 1983, 43).

A woman's meals for her husband and children must be tasty, nutritiously sound, cholesterol free, served on time and brought in smiling and under budget. Her hardwood floors must be squeaky-clean and her carpets smell like a pine forest in spring. Her children must be happy and on the educational path to graduate work at Harvard. Her husband must be sexually aroused and satisfied according to the latest findings published in the women's magazines. Both Friedan and De Beauvoir emphasized that this culturally-defined role for woman is not just something near and dear to the hearts of unsophisticated male bullies and undeconstructed patriarchs. Rather, it was strongly reinforced by more than a few sophisticated intellectuals who passed off their biases as the findings of science. The most egregious male biases were promoted by many of the early Freudians, who blithered and blathered about penis envy in women and about Electra Complexes. Thanks to Friedan and De Beauvoir, we have freed ourselves from much Freudian idiocy (Friedan 1983, 103–25, De Beauvoir 1989, 38–52).

But we have not freed ourselves from housewifery. The over-emphasis placed on housewifing wastes and misdirects human effort. The quest for clean floors and satiated husbands is a quest far below the potential of aspiring women. If we are to plan for a better life, says Friedan, 'The first step in that plan is to see housework for what it is — not a career, but something that must be done as quickly and efficiently as possible' (Friedan 1983, 342).

Instead of freeing women from culturally imposed household drudgery, we have added more content to the feminine mystique. Now, in addition to being a housework whiz, women are expected to be successful in outside careers as well. Her professional career must be personally rewarding and financially lucrative. And, of course, it cannot interfere with her real job — housewife and mother. In the 1990s, the feminine mystique has become even more impossible to fulfill than it was in the 1960s. Now women are also expected to have careers, to be supermoms. The so-called 'liberated woman' seems to have fallen victim to the old speed up.

Supermom: The Myth of Motherhood

The myth of motherhood is a part of the feminine mystique. Being a mother is not a myth, but a very real challenge. However, motherhood has been instituted in a particular way and a particular set of myths have grown up around the institution of motherhood. In the twentieth century, motherhood in advanced countries has been instituted in such a way as largely to isolate young children and their mothers from the rest of society. This social isolation in the nuclear or single-parent family living in the suburbs or living in the disintegrating urban centers has left most mothers as the sole adults responsible for their pre-school children. (Some men have found themselves in the same situation, as the sole adult responsible for children, and the problems they face are similar to those faced by women. The men are expected to be Superdad instead of Supermom. But Superdad often earns higher income and enjoys higher status than Supermom. Furthermore, Superdad is widely congratulated for taking on his 'extra' responsibility while Supermom is vaguely condemned for losing her children's father). Rather than the state stepping in with expensive day-care programs and expensive redesigns of urban and suburban living spaces that make communities child and parent friendly, we have saved a great deal of money by meeting the challenge of raising children with myths instead of supportive programs. Society has abandoned its children to the exclusive care of their mothers and has provided almost no real support for either.

As Ann Dally points out in her *Inventing Motherhood* (1983), before the industrialization and bureaucratization of western economies, mothers and children were integral parts of daily adult life. Among the peasantry and small farmers, mothers and children participated in work, leisure, and spiritual life. The same was largely true for the handicraft activities of the towns. But now, there is no place for children in the factory, the store, or the office. The children have become segregated, and in the absence of appropriate child-care programs, their mothers have become segregated with them. This is not meant to idealize the good old days. Those days were not so good, not with the high infantmortality rates, high childbirth death rates, and widespread poverty of the preindustrial era. Instead, this is merely to state two facts — children and their mothers have been segregated from the larger society and the larger society has not provided new support systems for them. Instead, we have insisted that small children need the exclusive care of their mothers. In spite of the fact that until very recently small children were not under the exclusive care of their mothers, we now insist that this be the case. We have created the exclusive care myth — the myth that small children will not develop into healthy adults unless they have the exclusive and uninterrupted care of their biological mothers. Dally explains:

> The idea that a young child should have the constant and exclusive attention of his mother (supplemented perhaps by his father during evenings and weekends) has replaced the acceptance of a much more usual and traditional situation. This is and has always been that mothers are usually the most important people in their children's lives but to some extent they share their children, right from birth, with others — not only with fathers and grandmothers but with aunts and older siblings, neighbors, workmates, servants and friends (Dally 1983, 278, parentheses in original).

The myth of exclusive maternal care serves a political purpose. It has not been consciously designed and propagated by an elitist conspiracy, but it has saved the state a great deal of money and it has imposed a heavy burden upon the mothers of small children. We have not spent money on redesigning our lives to make them mother and children friendly. Instead, we believe in a myth about the exclusive dependence of young children on their mothers. The myth is a self-fulfilling prophecy. Dally explains that our society:

> has been trying to condition babies to become attached to their mothers exclusively and, having done that, we (that is, academics and research workers) proceed to do research which reveals the undoubted distress caused when an infant who has been conditioned in this way is suddenly separated from his mother...This research is then used by academics and politicians to 'prove' that young children should be tied even more totally and exclusively to their mothers, which leads either to further measures to induce this or to failure to take measures to assist mothers who

are not able or willing to conform to it (Dally 1983, 278–9, parentheses and quotation marks in original).

Of course, children need to be sheltered from situations and from challenges that are too much for them at their young age. Of course, children need loving, warm relations with adults, mainly their parents. Of course, children need a sense of security, a sense that their needs will be met by the adults in their world. But these needs do not have to be fulfilled exclusively, solely, and continually by their biological mothers. In fact, in the modern world of segregated mothers and children, it has become very difficult for biological mothers to meet these needs. Rather than come to their aid, however, society has built up the myth of exclusive maternal care. If children develop a problem, it must be the fault of their exclusive care-giver, a fault of their mother. She is not up to being Supermom. In her quest for value in a male-dominated world, she blames herself when she fails. She does not question the value for which she strives — the impossibility of being Supermom. And, most importantly, she does not join together with other women — some mothers and some not — to demand that the state begin redesigning the workplace and the community and to demand that good child care programs be provided for all. Enabling myths keep us thinking that what are really political problems are not that at all, but personal failures.

The enabling myth of motherhood lets the state ignore the need for building new institutions. The role of the state in the economy is not and has not been one of simply leaving it alone. Instead, progressive states have always moved to fill gaps in the social provisioning process (Dugger 1993 and 1989a). Such a gap now clearly exists. The children and those who parent them have been left out of the social provisioning process. The state should bring them back in, should fill the gap opened up by unplanned urbanization and industrialization. Not only do children and those who parent them suffer from a lack of income, they also suffer from a lack of social space. We have not designed our industrialized and urbanized life with them in mind. Instead, we segregate them from the mainstream of our activities and stigmatize them for not thriving. But the state will not bring parents and mothers back into the mainstream as long as myths about motherhood hide the pressing needs of parents and children and blame parents (mothers) for personally failing. Only when the personal has been made political, can the state be brought into the process in a positive way.

Feminism: The Desperately Needed Antidote

In the 1960s and 1970s, however, feminists made it clear to anyone who would listen that the personal problems of women were not just personal. The problems were shared by far too many women. The personal was actually political. That simple message can help debunk the myths, can help women understand that no human being can be Supermom and that failing to do so is not due to their unworthiness (which is inculcated into them by the sexist myths of female inferiority). Feminism is the antidote we desperately need to rid us of sexist inferiority myths and of impossible values like Supermom and the feminine mystique. Feminism is the movement to put realistic values into women's lives and into men's lives and to create new institutions for putting these values into practice. Feminism is based on warranted knowledge about the equality of women. But feminism also is based on the knowledge that ours is a patriarchal society that denigrates the capabilities of women, that supports the domination of women by men, and that makes it difficult for women to participate fully in the life process. Feminism is the push that we need to politically weaken the vicious circle of domination and passivity and to strengthen the virtuous circle of liberation and participation.

The Vicious Circle

Inequality is not a state; it is a process. The process is circular and cumulative, not stable and counterbalanced. It is either increasing in a vicious circle, or decreasing in a virtuous circle. In the United States, gender inequality was losing its legitimacy throughout the 1960s and into the 1970s. Women's liberation made significant headway during those tumultuous years of racial and sexual revolt, even gaining the right to abortion. But a strong reaction set in and during the Reagan–Bush years, women lost much ground. Cumulative decline set in as the forward push of feminism began losing its cumulative force against patriarchy and misogyny. Sexist myths began spreading once again.

Sexism is a complex of enabling myths and enabling myths always lead the under dogs (women) to blame themselves for their low-status, low-income, and lack of power. Enabling myths also lead the top dogs (men) to think they are personally worthy of their high status, high income, and power. Enabling myths also lead people to interpret the problems that grow out of inequality as personal ones, not political ones. With their psyches distorted by enabling myths, the under dogs lack self-confidence and are far less productive and assertive than they could be. So they are stuck in low-status positions, stuck in low-income jobs, and pushed out to the margins of power. This pushes their self-confidence, productivity, and assertiveness even lower, which in turn reduces even further their status, income, and power. The circle continues: the low status, income, and power of the under dogs seem to verify the negative myths about them and to verify the positive myths about the top dogs. And so they fall and are pushed even further below the top dogs. De Beauvoir described how the vicious circle of inequality begins in the childhood of a typical girl:

> She is treated like a live doll and is refused liberty. Thus a vicious circle is formed; for the less she exercises her freedom to understand, to grasp and discover the world about her, the less resources will she find within herself, the less will she dare to affirm herself as subject (De Beauvoir 1989, 280).

After childhood, most women marry and even those who resisted the vicious circle in their childhood and applied themselves seriously to discovering the world around them and to cultivating a career for themselves, find their marriage brings an end to all that. De Beauvoir remarks, 'it is often astounding to see how readily a woman can give up music, study, her profession, once she has found a husband' (De Beauvoir 1989, 369). The vicious circle is hard to break, on one's own. After the gains made by women in the 1960s, the vicious circle of domination began to work against them once again. Reaganism, retrenchment, patriarchy and misogyny began sweeping across the United States. But women are acting collectively against the reactionary tide, organizing numerous political campaigns and putting many women into political office.

The Virtuous Circle

Even in reactionary times, positive processes remain at work. During the 1980s and 1990s two processes have been particularly significant. Both processes mean that individual women are no longer simply on their own in their struggle. The first social process has been the women's movement itself, in particular the change in public opinion that the women's movement has been able to bring about. The second social process has been the dramatic rise in the number of women working for pay outside the home. Feminism — the women's movement — has made millions of women aware of their potential and although the battle for the Equal Rights Amendment in the United States was lost, other political battles were won. Overall, feminism has been remarkably successful and its success should not be forgotten in times of retrenchment and reaction.

Feminism has set a new, much higher ideal for us to live up to. Although we backslide from the ideal, the ideal is still strong. In addition to the change in public opinion, (weakening sexist myths) the basic way that more and more women live their lives has also changed (weakening sexist practices). More and more women are attaining a significant degree of economic independence from their husbands and fathers as they move out of the home and into the paid workforce. Moving from the home to the office or factory is not a panacea. Working-class women still suffer from inequality. But the move does replace the direct personal domination of the patriarchy with the impersonal job discrimination of the bureaucracy. It gets women out of their isolation in the home and it gets them an income of their own.

The best indicator of this movement out of the home is given by the employment/population ratio. This ratio is more informative than the simple labor force participation rate for women because it shows the proportion of civilian, noninstitutionalized women who are actually employed and does not include women who are just looking for employment. In the United States, 35.5 percent of civilian, noninstitutionalized women 16 years old and older were employed outside the home in 1960. That percent has gradually increased until it stood at 53.4 percent in 1988 (US Bureau of the Census 1990, 380). Most women — more than half — are now employed outside the home. They are not just looking for work, but are actually working. Although they are still underpaid and although many of their families are dependent on their earnings, more than half of the women in the United States have established at least a toehold on economic independence. And, every indication is that women will soon attain more than just a toehold.

An important indication of woman's continued rise is the educational efforts of young women. In the United States, for every female attending college in 1960, there were two males attending. But by 1988, for every female attending college, there were only 0.81 males (US Bureau of the Census 1990, 131). More women attend college now than men. This is not to say that the quality of the education they get there is acceptable, for it is not. I have criticized higher education at length elsewhere (Dugger 1989b, 55–80). But at least a college education provides them some time in their life for thinking and for questioning. Furthermore, more women getting the education needed for professional careers means that not only are more women working outside the home, but it also means that more women are qualified for good careers than ever before. Women are rapidly approaching a kind of critical mass in the workforce. Higher educational credentials and stronger commitments to outside work both make it harder and harder to maintain the myths of female inferiority and harder and harder to convince women that they should devote the best years of their life to keeping their floors shiny and to being the exclusive care-giver to their husband's children. Women will continue to want more and women will continue to prepare themselves for more, in spite of the seemingly dreary prospects facing us at the close of the twentieth century. They have acquired an economic toehold and they are doing their homework. Their efforts are about to be rewarded with another cumulative improvement in their condition. But not just yet.

As women continue moving out of the home and into the political arena, the office, factory and store, their struggle will increasingly focus on the bureaucratic rules that discriminate against them. The well-educated women of the coming generation have a good chance of changing those rules, particularly if they apply the principle of collective action that they learned in their consciousness-raising groups to their struggles to get the state to take political action on their behalf and perhaps even to get the labor movement to do the same.

Conclusion

When the vicious circle of cumulating inequality of the Reagan–Bush years turns into a virtuous circle of cumulating equality in future years, as I am convinced it will, what should women demand? Friedan, in writing down the statement of purpose for the National Organization for Women, had the simple answer: 'full participation in the mainstream of American society now, exercising all the privileges and responsibilities thereof, in truly equal partnership with men' (Friedan 1983, 384). It is almost the same answer that radical institutionalists give — full participation for all. However, it is also necessary to change what we all are participating in. It is also necessary to change the patriarchal mainstream into an egalitarian mainstream. That is what the women want, and that is what we want. That is what any group victimized by inequality wants. And, the radical institutionalist framework for analyzing inequality can help us to understand not only why they want it, but also how they might try to get it. Institutionalism does not reduce gender inequality down to class inequality and then treat women as if they were merely a special part of the working-class (original Marxism). We recognize that gender inequality and class inequality are not the same so they cannot be understood or eliminated with reductionistic thought and abstract slogan. Only thorough, detailed, institutional analysis is adequate. Only analysis that stays as close to the content and meaning of everyday life as possible can hope to be fruitful.

Radical institutionalism does so and it incorporates into its analytical concepts the cumulative causation of process, rather than the counter-balancing state of equilibrium. The vicious circle and the virtuous circle are both cumulative processes, not offsetting forces. In the radical institutionalist paradigm, cultural processes, particularly myth-making, are used to explain human behavior. Subjective individual choice (neoclassical economics) is inadequate as a foundation for theory. Furthermore, the noninterventionist view of the state is inadequate as a foundation for policy. The personal is political. The state cannot be neutral. Instead, its pretended neutrality allows existing forms of inequality to remain entrenched and legitimated.

References

Ardzrooni, Leon, ed. (1964), *Essays in our Changing Order,* New York: Augustus M. Kelley.

Dally, Ann (1983), *Inventing Motherhood,* New York: Schocken Books.

De Beauvoir, Simone (1989), *The Second Sex,* translated and edited by H.M. Parshley, New York: Random House.

Dugger, William M. (1989a), 'The State: Power and Dichotomy' in Samuels, Warren J., ed. *Fundamentals in the Economic Role of Government,* New York: Greenwood Press.

Dugger, William M. (1989b), *Corporate Hegemony,* New York: Greenwood Press.

Dugger, William M. (1989c), *Radical Institutionalism,* New York: Greenwood Press.

Dugger, William M. (1993), 'An Evolutionary Theory of the State and the Market' in Dugger, William M. and Waller, William, Jr., eds. *The Stratified State,* Armonk, New York: M.E. Sharpe.

Friedan, Betty (1983), *The Feminine Mystique,* 10th anniversary edn, New York: Dell.

Hymowitz, Carol and Michaele Weissman (1978), *A History of Women in America,* New York: Bantam Books.

Montagu, Ashley (1974), *The Natural Superiority of Women,* revised edn, New York: Macmillan.

US Bureau of the Census (1990), *Statistical Abstract of the United States,* Washington, DC: US Government Printing Office.

Veblen, Thorstein (1894) 'The Economic Theory of Woman's Dress' reprinted in Ardzrooni, Leon, ed. *Essays in Our Changing Order.*

Veblen, Thorstein (1898a) 'The Instinct of Workmanship and the Irksomeness of Labor' reprinted in Ardzrooni, Leon, ed. *Essays in Our Changing Order.*

Veblen, Thorstein (1898b) 'The Beginnings of Ownership' in Ardzrooni, Leon, ed. *Essays in Our Changing Order.*

Veblen, Thorstein (1899) 'The Barbarian Status of Women' in Ardzrooni, Leon, ed. *Essays in Our Changing Order.*

Veblen, Thorstein (1919) *The Place of Science in Modern Civilization and Other Essays,* New York: B.W. Huebsch.

Veblen, Thorstein (1965) *The Engineers and the Price System,* New York: Augustus M. Kelley.

2. Institutionalism: A Useful Foundation for Feminist Economics?

Charles Whalen and Linda Whalen

The movements of feminism and institutionalism each contain much diversity. Nevertheless, feminists seem united in a commitment to understanding and eliminating gender-based domination, while institutionalists appear to adopt a common approach to economic methodology. The purpose of this chapter is to suggest that the institutionalist methodology may be a useful foundation for feminist economics.[1]

A recent article by William Waller and Ann Jennings examined feminist and institutionalist views on epistemology. They found that scholars within both movements 'share noncartesian (i.e., holistic) epistemological roots that lead to a recognition of knowledge as socially constructed'. Thus, they concluded that 'institutionalism is both congenial and equipped to become a feminist economics' (Waller and Jennings 1990, 614, 620).

This chapter builds on the work of Waller and Jennings. It also extends their analysis beyond epistemology. In particular, institutionalist and feminist considerations in three methodological areas will be discussed: ontology, epistemology and axiology.[2]

Ontology

The Dominant Perspective

According to the prevailing ontological perspective in most disciplines, reality is conceptualized as a set of logically and analytically separable structures and processes. Economics is no exception. Consider, for example, Yngve Ramstad's description of the ontology accepted by mainstream (or 'neoclassical') economists:

> It is taken for granted by the neoclassical economist that there lies submerged within the social totality a logically separable mechanism known as 'the market system' which allocates resources and distributes income. In other words, 'the market' is assumed to operate according to a logic independent of the principles determining the operation of the social system in which it is embedded. This presumption permits the economist to mentally dissever the economic sphere — 'running in its own groves and governed by its own laws' — from the larger entity, society. The operation of this analytically independent subsystem — and only its operation — constitutes the appropriate subject matter for economics as a social science (Ramstad 1985, 16).

Moreover, the ontological view that dominates in modern science does not merely define disciplinary boundaries. It also shapes work *within* disciplines. The fundamental unit of analysis in conventional economics, for instance, is the individual, an actor considered separate from — indeed, 'analytically prior to' — his/her society. In fact, mainstream economists view society and its various groups of humans as mere 'aggregations' of individual desires and activities (Ramstad 1985, 12–13).[3] This perspective is what might be called an 'atomistic' approach to the economy and society.

The Feminist Critique

Many modern feminists reject the 'atomistic' viewpoint of traditional scholarship in favor of a 'holistic' successor science (Waller and Jennings 1990, 618; Ferguson 1989). In particular, they 'assert a unity of science' *across* disciplines, and prefer a 'relational rather than individual' approach *within* disciplines (Harding 1986, 250; Dornbusch and Strober 1988, 4). As Jennings writes, 'In recent years feminist research had expanded beyond accounts of women's history and women's experiences to challenge the legitimacy of social theories that either ignore women or *have treated women's issues as separable from men's issues*' (Jennings 1989, 2, emphasis added). Similarly, Sanford M. Dornbusch and Myra H. Strober opened a 1988 work by stating that 'feminist scholarship is ready for a new stage of development in which women are perceived as part of organic working wholes' (Dornbusch and Strober 1988, 3).[4]

But what makes holism more 'feminist' than atomism? Moreover, doesn't the attention to 'wholes' cause feminist concerns to vanish, as women — indeed all individuals — leave center stage and get replaced by an emphasis upon groups? In response, many feminists would maintain that their perspective denies neither the existence nor the significance of individuals. As Dornbusch and Strober note, it would be inappropriate to discuss their organic 'wholes' as 'homogeneous units without regard to the individuals who compose them' (Dornbusch and Strober 1988, 3). In short, instead of intending to suggest that individuals are insignificant, feminists are seeking to argue that individuals *cannot be adequately understood in isolation*. Further, it is precisely holism's ability to offer a more thorough understanding of reality — including the reality of androcentrism and sexism — that makes it 'feminist'.[5]

Institutionalist Ontology

Institutional (or evolutionary) economics seems well prepared to support feminist 'relational' analyses and the study of 'organic working wholes'. Institutionalism is holistic in nature; it views social reality as a unified historico-cultural whole. Thus, by today's standards, evolutionary economics is 'interdisciplinary' in nature.[6] Indeed, instead of defining its scope of analysis so as to permit a focus upon only market activities, institutionalism seeks to encompass the entire process of social provisioning. While markets are certainly important, institutionalists must also consider other social structures involved in this provisioning process — including, for example, states and families.[7]

Further, the various elements within the scope of evolutionary economics cannot be considered independently. As Charles K. Wilber and Robert S. Harrison have stated, institutionalism 'is rooted in the belief that the (social) whole is not only greater than the sum of its parts but that the parts are so related that their functioning is conditioned by their interrelations' (Wilber and Harrison 1978, 73). In short, 'reality is of a whole piece' (Waller and Jennings 1990, 616).[8]

Finally, institutionalists recognize the economy as an *ongoing process*. While reality is a unified 'whole', institutionalists maintain that this whole is *not* an unchanging one. Rather, social systems, institutions and processes are all dynamic, ever-developing entities. Thus, the ontology of institutionalism requires holism but it also requires a 'processual' perspective.

Epistemology

The Dominant Perspective

Turning to the realm of epistemology, we find that many conventional scientists — including most economists — adhere to a belief in both scientific 'objectivity' and a sharp distinction between 'positive' and 'normative' analyses. As Campbell R. McConnell and Stanley L. Brue write in their popular economics text:

> Positive economics deals with facts (once removed at the level of theory) and is *devoid of value judgments*. Positive economics attempts to set forth *scientific* statements about economic behavior. Normative economics, *in contrast*, embodies someone's *value judgments* about what the economy should be like or what particular policy action should be recommended on the basis of some given economic generalization or relationship (McConnell and Brue 1990, 6, emphasis added).

Moreover, the most popular epistemological statement among mainstream economists is Milton Friedman's (1953) 'The Methodology of Positive Economics', a work widely read as allowing economists to both incorporate false assumptions in their theories and ignore explanation (in favor of prediction) as a reason for economic analysis. In fact, Friedman wrote that 'truly important and significant hypotheses will be found to have "assumptions" that are wildly inaccurate . . . , and, in general, the more significant the theory, the more unrealistic the assumptions' (Friedman 1953, 14).

The Feminist Critique

Even a cursory examination of the feminist literature will indicate that most feminists would reject Friedman's 'positive economics'. But many feminists also reject the notion of scientific objectivity and the related positive/normative dichotomy. In their view, science is both an ongoing and fully social activity, and *all* social activities and processes are *value-laden* (Harding 1986, 24–57). As Sandra Harding indicated in *The Science Question in Feminism*, many contemporary feminists recognize 'the hypothetical character of all scientific claims' and maintain 'a profound skepticism regarding universal (or universalizing) claims about . . . reason, progress, science' and the like (Harding 1986, 27–8).[9]

Since androcentrism and sexism are cultural — and thus value-laden — phenomena, a view of knowledge (including 'scientific' knowledge) as value-laden is an appropriate part of the methodological foundation of feminist scholarship. But there are also other reasons why feminists insist upon a pragmatic, rather than positivist, approach to science.[10]

For example, as a result of undertaking research designed to expose implicit assumptions about gender, feminists have become aware of, and unable to ignore, the various types of preconceptions — andocentric and otherwise — embedded within approaches to science that claim to be value-free (Harding 1986, 30–57 and 82–110). This fact alone seems to lead many feminists toward pragmatism.

Finally, some feminists are seeking to move beyond traditional epistemology because they are critical of the asymmetric gender symbolism associated with its dualistic constructs. As Harding writes:

> The androcentric ideology of contemporary science posits as necessary, and/or as facts, a set of dualisms — culture vs. nature; rational mind vs. prerational body and irrational emotions and values; objectivity vs. subjectivity; public vs. private — and then links men and masculinity to the former and women and femininity to the latter (Harding 1986, 136).

Moreover, the 'masculine' categories are often held in high esteem while the 'feminine' ones are treated with disdain (Jennings 1989; Waller and Jennings 1990, 616; Jennings 1991). Thus, Harding adds: 'Feminist critics (of mainstream science) have argued that such dichotomizing constitutes an ideology in the strong sense of the term: in contrast to merely value-laden false beliefs that have no social power, these beliefs structure the policies and practices of social institutions, including science' (Harding 1986, 136).

Institutionalist Epistemology

As in the case of ontology, the epistemology of evolutionary economics seems to suit the needs of feminists. In particular, consistent with the institutionalist notion of a dynamic and evolving social reality is an epistemology that emphasizes the absence of absolute certainty from human understanding. While institutionalists recognize that neither verification nor falsification procedures will produce unambiguous truth, their pragmatic approach to knowledge demands that they continually reevaluate economic theories against all available evidence.[11] Further, since institutionalism is seeking to *understand* social reality, institutional economists strive for theories with logical consistency, testable predictions, *and* realistic assumptions.

Of course, feminists and institutionalists are not interested in merely *understanding* the real world; they seek also to change it.[12] In particular, they seek to solve practical social problems and enable individuals to realize their full personal potential. Indeed, another aspect of the institutional approach to knowledge is acceptance of the 'instrumentalist' belief (one that can be traced to the work of institutionalists influenced by

John Dewey) that problem solving is 'the guiding factor' behind the entire process of economic inquiry (Gruchy 1987, 51).[13]

In addition to pragmatism and instrumentalism, institutionalist epistemology is rooted in a rejection of the belief that economic systems have inherent tendencies. Since institutionalists see such systems as cultural creations, they reject both the neoclassical preconception of economic self-regulation and the traditional Marxist notion that capitalism is — by its very nature — self-destructive. This does not mean that institutionalism cannot conceive of economic order or systemic tendencies. Rather, both are viewed as products of the parties within a particular social system. As Allan G. Gruchy has stated the position for institutionalists, '(A)ctual economic systems exhibit *cultural* coherence, rather than the equilibrating forces of a *mechanistic* system' (Gruchy 1987, 4–5, emphasis added).

Finally, institutionalists recognize that economics is not — and cannot be — a value-free science. As Harding (1986, 102) writes, '(O)bservations are theory-laden, theories are paradigm-laden, and paradigms are culture-laden: hence there are and can be no such things as value-neutral, objective facts'. While orthodox and Marxist scholars argue over whose analysis is positive and whose is not (McConnell 1987, 825), institutionalists — along with many contemporary feminists — instead accept Joan Robinson's statement:

> [An economist's] attempt to be purely objective must necessarily be either self-deception or a device to deceive others. A candid writer will make his [sic] preconceptions clear and allow the reader to discount them if he [sic] does not accept them (Robinson 1970, 122).

Axiology

The Dominant Perspective

A third category of methodology (beyond ontology and epistemology) is axiology. The belief in 'positive' science, however, leaves few modern scholars with an interest in this realm. Yet it is also true — indeed it is unavoidable — that these scientists have an approach to values, even if it is accepted only tacitly. Moreover, as in the case of ontology and epistemology, it is an approach that many of today's feminist philosophers and theorists find troubling.

In orthodox economics, for example, a focus on market transactions causes economic 'value' to be equated (assuming no externalities) to the price at which items are exchanged. Further, since economic efficiency is defined in terms of a competitive equilibrium in a decentralized, individualistic economy, 'equilibrium' becomes a standard against which the real-world is compared. In short, instead of removing value judgements from economic science, what these economists have chosen to remove from their discipline is the following: (a) any reason to consider other approaches to valuation (beyond valuation by the market); and (b) the need to identify the values of economic actors and understand how such values are shaped and modified.

The Feminist Critique

While it should be clear from our earlier discussion (of epistemology) that many feminists reject the veil of 'objectivity' that modern science uses to dismiss axiology, the tacit approach to values adopted by neoclassical economists is unacceptable as well. Indeed, just as these feminists acknowledge the importance of valuations, they also recognize the possible existence of *many valuation methods* — and the unavoidable element of subjectivity associated with the making of value judgements (Harding 1986, 87–92: Jennings 1990, 36–7). In fact, on the matter of how individual values may differ, Harding — drawing on the works of Marcia Millman, Rosabeth Moss Kanter and Jessie Bernard — writes:

> Social science often assumes a 'single society' with respect to men and women, in which generalizations can be made about all participants, yet men and women may actually inhabit different social worlds and this difference is not taken into account. Jessie Bernard has argued, for example, that the same marriage may constitute two different realities for the husband and the wife; this fact invalidates generalizations about marriage and family life that do not identify and account for the differences in position and interests (Harding 1986, 87).

Moreover, contemporary feminists often find that the particular 'field-defining' approach adopted by orthodoxy (i.e., the focus on market prices) allows too many truly important aspects of economic life to be overlooked (Harding 1986, 85–92; Jennings 1991, 35–6). Such matters are often considered 'private', 'personal', or 'familial' in nature, and thus outside the realm of study and/or policy. Finally, by ignoring the nature and development of values held by economic actors, gender cannot be 'taken into account as a factor in behavior', even though it 'may be among the most important explanatory variables' (Harding 1986, 89–92).

Institutionalist Axiology

There are three important elements of institutionalist axiology. Together they indicate that the entire human valuation process is an integral part of the subject matter of evolutionary economics. As with the methodological realms previously discussed, institutionalism seems to have developed a foundation appropriate for feminist theorizing on economic issues.

First, institutionalism considers the concept of 'value' to be multifaceted. Once the narrow focus of orthodoxy is replaced with a holistic view of provisioning, it becomes clear both that the market is only one institution offering insight into human values and that the notion of 'price' is only one type of valuation in a world of many alternatives.[14] Indeed, as Harding (1986, 87) notes in the passage quoted above, the same experience — even the same relationship — may constitute entirely different realities for different individuals. Thus, an institutionalist decision to analyze a particular form of values must be shaped by the particular problem being addressed — and this decision must be a conscious one, not one made merely on the basis of past practice. Moreover, where individual values differ regarding a particular phenomenon, institutionalists — like feminists — must strive to identify and account for the differences.

Second, since institutionalism acknowledges the value-laden nature of economic science, institutional economists recognize that both their own judgements and those of government officials are important elements in public-policy analysis. Of course, by now it should be clear that both institutionalists and many feminists would recognize that economists' values influence *all* economic analyses. Nonetheless, policy discussions introduce the need for an entirely new set of value judgements — ones that shape an individual's view of what 'ought' to be. In addition, such discussions place new attention upon actors in the public sector. Indeed, a public official is often *much more* than an umpire (i.e., one who coordinates, or settles disputes arising from, existing needs and desires). As many institutionalists — including Neil Chamberlain and Philip Klein — have observed, the state commonly plays a *creative* role in society by helping to shape community preferences.[15]

Finally, since institutionalism maintains a processual ontological perspective, it must also view valuation as an ongoing activity. In other words, evolutionary economists recognize that individuals are, over time, *continually reappraising* their opinions of both economic means and ends. Thus, quite unlike neoclassical researchers, institutionalists emphasize the need to investigate the various influences that determine and modify human values.

Gender and the Veblenian Dichotomy

A Methodological Convergence?

In recent years, feminists 'have begun to formulate clear and coherent challenges to the (standard) conceptual frameworks of their disciplines' (Harding 1986, 19). As Harding writes of these efforts to 'reinvent' science, much feminist attention has shifted from 'the "woman question" in science . . . (to) the "science question" in feminism' (Harding 1986, 9, 251). Moreover, what is particularly interesting from an evolutionary economist's perspective is that feminists seem to be moving toward the pre-analytic viewpoint that has defined the institutionalist alternative to economic orthodoxy for nearly a century.[16]

In short, both institutionalism and feminism (at least as viewed by many contemporary scholars) seem to share the following: a holistic and processual ontology; a pragmatic, instrumentalist and non-teleological epistemology; and a multifaceted and comprehensive view of values. Thus, institutionalism appears ready to provide feminist economics with a coherent and useful foundation.

Gender

Readers of the preceding discussion might have noted — perhaps with some surprise — the absence of an explicit role for gender. But methodology is not analysis; *methodology provides only a frame of reference for understanding what is going on.* Thus, although gender is not explicitly present in what has been outlined, an institutionalist 'frame of reference' may still be the approach most capable of allowing economists to produce feminist analyses.

Jennings suggests that a feminist economics should be 'gender conscious' (Jennings 1990, 15; 1989, 49). By that she means it should be 'one which takes gender as a form of social inequality that affects the process of social provisioning in fundamental ways and abandons the economism (i.e., market focus) of most other types of economic theory'. The feminist–institutionalist methodology presented above seems entirely capable of serving as the foundation for such an economics.

While gender does not play an explicit role in the realm of *methodology*, in feminist economics it *must* clearly play an important role both at the level of *theory* and in *applied research*. Unfortunately, although institutionalism is capable of producing 'gender conscious' work, 'institutionalists have, with a few notable exceptions, ignored gender in their analysis' (Waller and Jennings 1990, 613). If institutionalism is to contribute more than a methodological foundation to feminism, institutionalists must do more to expose androcentrism and gender-based domination than they have in the past.[17]

The Veblenian Dichotomy

A well-known feature of much institutional thought is Thorstein B. Veblen's ceremonial–instrumental dichotomy. Nonetheless, like gender, there has been no reference to this dichotomy in the methodological discussion above. Indeed, the previous discussion has been quite critical of other dualisms, including 'positive versus normative' science, 'masculine versus feminine' gender symbolism, and the strict 'economic (read market) versus noneconomic (nonmarket)' conceptualization of neoclassical economics.

While institutionalists may recognize that 'reality is of a whole piece', the creation of dualisms is an important intellectual act. As Waller and Jennings have noted, dichotomies play a significant role in how 'human beings conceptualize and systematize their understanding of the world' (Waller and Jennings 1990, 616–17). In fact, the Veblenian dichotomy actually plays *two* roles in evolutionary economics. First, the dichotomy represents categories found in institutionalist theories and policy analyses. Thus, it is understandable that a consideration of the dichotomy, like gender, would be absent from our discussion of pre-theoretic (i.e., methodological) elements.

Second, the dichotomy clearly defines two types of values. Consequently, there *is* a role for the dichotomy at the level of methodology. In particular, this role is implicit in the multifaceted nature of the institutionalist approach to values. While economic orthodoxy equates value and price, it is institutionalism's broader view of this methodological component that permits it to both recognize pecuniary valuation as only one manifestation of 'ceremonialism' and consider the alternative of 'instrumental' valuation.

Of course, use of the Veblenian dichotomy is not without difficulty. As Waller and Jennings write:

> The problem with dualisms is in their reification. The unified reality ceases to be the object of inquiry and instead the bifurcated conceptual apparatus becomes the reality (Waller and Jennings 1990, 617).[18]

Moreover, employing the dichotomy has often led to its use in the evaluation of social structures. As Waller explained in *Radical Institutionalism,* this is inappropriate:

> Structures are socially organized behavior generated *by the interaction of both ceremonial and instrumental cultural processes* that reproduce and modify these structures. . . . It is clear that *structures are not ceremonial (bad and nonprogressive) or instrumental (good and progressive)* (Waller 1989, 46, emphasis added).

Nonetheless, if these pitfalls are avoided — and they can be if the methodology outlined above is taken seriously — the Veblenian dichotomy may be a useful part of future institutionalist and feminist research.[19]

The Creative State

In recent years, feminism has become, in part, a philosophical and scholarly movement for intellectual change.[20] But feminism *still* remains a '*political* movement for *social* change' (Harding 1986, 24, emphasis added). Thus, this chapter closes with a brief discussion of some implications that the institutionalist approach has for the economic role of the state.

Institutionalism and the State

Methodological preconceptions shape analyses, but they also affect an economist's conception of the state. In orthodox economics, the state (except when it is 'interfering' with the market) plays a corrective role in the economy. In traditional Marxism, meanwhile, the (capitalist) state is given a protective role. In particular, the former see public policy as a way to correct market failure (or accelerate market adjustment), while the latter see it as a way to protect the interests of the capitalist class. In contrast, institutionalists see the state as having a *creative* role.

According to this (evolutionary) perspective, the state plays a role in creating social order. It also helps shape the social preferences that permit a society to both define 'order' and determine which methods are most appropriate for establishing it. Finally, the state, unlike the capitalist state in traditional Marxism, is considered capable of being an oppressor or emancipator — and is likely to often be a bit of both.[21]

This view is derived largely from institutionalist methodology. According to that foundation, the state is an inseparable part of the economy, and institutional adjustment — not the price system — is the 'balancing wheel' of the social-provisioning (i.e., economic) process. But this view is also derived partly from empirical study and observation. The feminist-institutionalist work of Janice Peterson on women and the state, is one example of such research (Peterson 1989).

Although the notion of a state capable of acting as both an emancipator and liberator may seem insignificant, it is not. It is significant because when investigators seek to understand and evaluate a *particular* public action, this notion directs them toward the only sort of work that institutionalism believes can shed light on such matters — toward empirical and historical analyses of actual economic activity.[22]

Conclusion: Toward Intellectual and Social Change

In a recent work, one of the present authors has outlined the social values, contemporary economic problems, and policy suggestions discussed in the institutionalist literature (Whalen 1990). While we will not review these matters here, it should be noted that the positions of institutionalists are quite similar to those found in much of the feminist literature. In fact, in her 'Afterword' to *Families, Politics, and Public Policy: A Feminist Dialogue on Women and the State,* Mary Lyndon Shanley, a feminist political scientist, offers a discussion of public policy that seems thoroughly compatible with the institutionalist view of contemporary problems, social values, and necessary state action (Shanley 1983).

Moreover, in discussing the 'theoretical task' facing those seeking to offer a foundation for such action, Shanley seems to be calling for precisely the sort of theories that could be developed with the methodology of evolutionary economics (Shanley 1983, 361). Thus, it appears that institutionalism can indeed provide feminist economics with a useful foundation — a foundation that can contribute to feminist attempts at securing both intellectual and social change.

Notes

1. According to H. H. Liebhafsky, 'methodology' does not mean technique or method. Rather, it refers to the logic that justifies a particular analysis or procedure. Thus, economic methodology refers to the pre-analytic, belief system implicit in applied economic research and upon which an economist constructs theories (Liebhafsky 1968, 7–8).

2. Ontology, epistemology, and axiology examine the nature of reality, science (and knowledge), and values, respectively.

3. As Ramstad writes, 'From this perspective of methodological individualism, causality, at least when "doing" economics, is seen by the neoclassical economist to run *from* the individual *to* outcomes. The reciprocal...causal link from society/groups to individual desires typically is ignored' (Ramstad 1985, 13).

4. As Harding notes approvingly, Jane Flax has expressed a view similar to Dornbusch and Strober:

> Gender (according to Flax) should be understood as relational; gender relations are not determined by nature but are social relations of domination, and feminist theories 'need to recover and write the histories of women and our activities *into the accounts and self-understanding of the whole of social relations'* (Harding 1986, 154, emphasis added).

5. Moreover, as Jennings explains in some detail, in economics an atomistic perspective has narrowed the focus of mainstream practitioners in a way that largely excludes women, and gender concerns in general, from analysis (Jennings 1989; 1990).

6. In other words, institutionalism, like Harding's feminism, asserts 'a unity of science' (Harding 1986, 250).

7. In contrast, orthodox (and, to some extent, even Marxian) economists view nonmarket institutions and structures as 'noneconomic'. Thus, such elements are considered to be beyond the scope of their analyses. On this, see Jennings (1989).

8. As Waller and Jennings write, 'Institutionalism...does not recognize bifurcation of reality or accept the existence of isolated cultural forms. The compartmentalization of cultural meanings, values, and behavior must...be seen by institutionalists as artificially imposed boundaries on our understanding of the interrelatedness of social life' (Waller and Jennings 1990, 618).

9. Our discussion of feminist methodology relies heavily upon works written in the 1980s by Harding (a feminist philosopher). After the present chapter was well under way, we became aware of a new volume published by Harding, *Whose Science? Whose Knowledge? Thinking from Women's Lives*. In that book, Harding develops her views beyond what has been offered previously (Harding 1991). There is also a different approach taken toward various feminist labels, and an attempt to resuscitate *a form* of 'objectivity'. Nonetheless, we find the substance of her methodological outlook still compatible with both her earlier works and the views expressed in this essay.

10. 'Pragmatic' (and 'pragmatism', a term that will appear shortly) in this chapter refers to the philosophical perspective developed by John Dewey, William James and Charles Peirce.

11. As Marc R. Tool has written, the fruit of inquiry is 'tentative truth'—'the provisional removal of doubt' (Tool 1979, 38–9). In John Dewey's words, the closest we can come to absolute truth is 'warranted assertibility'.

12. According to Harding, feminism — like institutionalism — is ultimately a 'movement for social change' (Harding 1986, 24).

13. Thus, institutionalism has no interest in recent conventional economic developments that have sought to transform economics into merely a *good game* with no intended real-world relevance. It is likely that most feminists take a similar view toward these developments.

14. Like the orthodox focus on price, the Marxist preoccupation with labor exertion — i.e., the labor theory of value — prohibits this group from offering the flexible approach to values needed by feminist economics. For more on the methodological differences between institutionalism, neoclassicalism and Marxism, see Charles J. Whalen (1990). For more on the incompatibility of feminism and traditional Marxism, see Jennings (1989).

15. See Whalen (1988, 69).

16. In addition to the works cited in the previous sections, see Bleier (1984) for evidence supporting this point.

17. Some of the best conceptual work on gender has been done by Jennings and Waller. See, for example, Jennings (1989; 1990; 1991); Jennings and Waller (1990); and Waller and Jennings (1990; 1991). Excellent applied work, meanwhile, has been done by, among others, Paulette I.

Olson (1990); Janice Peterson (1989; 1990); and Bernadette Lanciaux (1989). See also Greenwood (1984; 1988) for work that addresses both conceptual and applied matters.

18. In clarifying their point about the reification of dualistic conceptual apparatuses, Waller and Jennings add:

> We do not mean this in the trivial sense of the dualistic conception becoming the object of inquiry, although this also occurs in the process of reification. But for the inquirer, and for the society as a whole, if this dualistic conception reflects the common conceptual construct of that society, *the dualism becomes the reality we see* because all processes of inquiry will view reality through the lens of the dualism (Jennings and Waller 1990, 617, emphasis added).

19. It is not clear *a priori*, however, that a simple extension of Veblen's work is always appropriate. This is a point explored further by Waller in his contribution to this volume.

20. On this point, see (in addition to the Harding works cited in the subsection above on 'methodological convergence') Jennings (1991).

21. For more on this, see Peterson (1989). Also see Whalen (1990, 16), who notes that this view is similar to that of John R. Commons.

22. Harding seems to agree with institutionalists on this point when she notes that feminist theorizing must recognize the diversity of human experience. As she wrote in 1987:

> In trying to develop theories that provide the one true (feminist) story of human experience, feminism risks replicating in theory and public policy the tendency in the patriarchal theories to police thought by assuming that only the problems of *some* women are human problems and that solutions for them are the only reasonable ones. Feminism has played an important role in showing that there are not now and never have been any generic 'men' at all — only gendered men and women. Once essential and universal man dissolves, so does his hidden companion, woman. We have, instead, myriads of women (and men) living in elaborate historical complexes of class, race, and culture (Harding 1987, 284).

References

Bleier, Ruth (1984), *Science and Gender,* New York: Pergamon Press.

Dornbusch, Sanford M. and Myra H. Strober (1988), *Feminism, Children, and the New Families*, New York: Guilford Press.

Ferguson, Ann (1989), 'A Feminist Aspect Theory of the Self' in Garry, Ann and Marilyn Pearsall, eds. *Women, Knowledge, and Reality: Explorations in Feminist Philosophy*, Boston: Unwin Hyman.

Friedman, Milton (1953), 'The Methodology of Positive Economics' in his *Essays in Positive Economics*, Chicago: University of Chicago Press.

Greenwood, Daphne (1984), 'The Economic Significance of "Women's Place" in Society', *Journal of Economic Issues*, 18, September.

Greenwood, Daphne (1988), 'A Comment on Evolutionary Economics I', *Journal of Economic Issues* (22) March.

Gruchy, Allan G. (1987), *The Reconstruction of Economics: An Analysis of the Fundamentals of Institutional Economics*, Westport, Connecticut: Greenwood Press.

Harding, Sandra (1986), *The Science Question in Feminism*, Ithaca, New York: Cornell University Press.

Harding, Sandra (1987), 'The Instability of the Analytical Categories of Feminist Theory' in Harding, Sandra and Jean O'Barr, eds. *Sex and Scientific Inquiry*, Chicago: University of Chicago Press.

Harding, Sandra (1991), *Whose Science? Whose Knowledge? Thinking from Women's Lives*, Ithaca, New York: Cornell University Press.

Jennings, Ann L. (1989), 'Not the Economy: Feminist Theory, Institutional Change, and the State', presented at the Hobart and William Smith Colleges Conference on Institutionalism and the State.

Jennings, Ann L. (1990), 'Feminism, Labor Market Theory and Economics', presented at the Annual Meeting of the Association For Institutional Thought (Portland, Oregon).

Jennings, Ann L. (1991), 'Public or Private? Institutional Economics and Feminism', manuscript (revised June 1991) of a chapter prepared for *Beyond 'Economic Man': Feminist Theory and Economics,* (Forthcoming), Marianne Ferber and Julie A. Nelson, eds.

Jennings, Ann L. and William Waller (1990), 'Constructions of Social Hierarchy: The Family, Gender, and Power', *Journal of Economic Issues,* 24, June.

Lanciaux, Bernadette (1989), 'The Role of the State in the Family', presented at the Hobart and William Smith Colleges Conference on Institutionalism and the State.

Liebhafsky, Herbert Hugo (1968), *The Nature of Price Theory*, Homewood, Illinois: Dorsey Press.

McConnell, Campbell R. (1987), *Economics*, New York: McGraw–Hill.

McConnell, Campbell R. and Stanley L. Brue (1990), *Macroeconomics,* New York: McGraw–Hill.

Olson, Paulette I. (1990), 'Mature Women and the Rewards of Domestic Ideology', *Journal of Economic Issues,* 24 June.

Peterson, Janice (1989), 'Women and the State', presented at the Hobart and William Smith Colleges Conference on Institutionalism and the State.

Peterson, Janice (1990), 'The Challenge of Comparable Worth: An Institutionalist View', *Journal of Economic Issues,* 24, June.

Ramstad, Yngve (1985), 'What is Institutional Economics?' University of Rhode Island Working Paper, Number 87– 04.

Ramstad, Yngve (1991), 'A Chapter in the "Compulsive Shift to Institutional Analysis"' manuscript of a chapter prepared for a forthcoming volume, Warren J. Samuels and Marc R. Tool, eds.

Robinson, Joan (1970), *Freedom and Necessity*, New York: Pantheon.

Shanley, Mary Lyndon (1983), 'Afterword: Feminism and Families in a Liberal Polity' in Diamond, Irene, ed. *Families, Politics, and Public Policy: A Feminist Dialogue on Women and the State*, New York: Longman.

Tool, Marc R. (1979), 'The Discretionary Economy: A Normative Theory of Political Economy', Santa Monica, CA: Goodyear Publishing Co.

Waller, William (1989), 'Methodological Aspects of Radical Institutionalism' in Dugger, William, M., ed. *Radical Institutionalism: Contemporary Voices*, Westport, Connecticut: Greenwood Press.

Waller, William and Ann Jennings (1990), 'On the Possibility of a Feminist Economics: The Convergence of Institutional and Feminist Methodology', *Journal of Economic Issues,* 24, June.

Waller, William and Ann Jennings (1991), 'Feminist Institutionalist Reconsideration of Karl Polanyi', *Journal of Economic Issues,* 25, June.

Whalen, Charles J. (1988), *Beyond Neoclassical Thought: Economics from the Perspective of Institutionalists and Post Keynesians*, PhD Dissertation, The University of Texas at Austin.

Whalen, Charles J. (1990), 'Schools of Thought and Theories of the State: Reflections of an Institutional Economist' presented at the Hobart and William Smith Colleges Conference on Institutionalism and the State.

Wilber, Charles K. and Robert S. Harrison (1978), 'The Methodological Basis of Institutional Economics', *Journal of Economic Issues*, 12, March: 61–89.

3. Radical Institutionalism and Postmodern Feminist Theory

Doug Brown

Not surprisingly, institutional economics as a male-dominated discipline for the last 100 years has neglected issues of sexism, gender-based domination, and patriarchy. Like Marxism, the fact that institutionalism has had a leftist, critical edge has not prevented it from neglecting gender-based domination. This point has been made in the *Journal of Economic Issues* (see Greenwood 1988; Jennings and Waller 1990). Institutional economics has contributed more in the area of research on sex discrimination and the economic effects of patriarchy and capitalism than in the development of feminist theory.

However, as we know, institutional economics is broad enough that it should be considered an intellectual paradigm and consequently contains an epistemology of its own. The remarks in this chapter are concerned with institutionalist epistemology and its relationship to feminist theory. This chapter is an answer to the question, 'What kind of feminist theory can properly be derived from the epistemology of institutional economics'? More specifically institutionalism has a consistent and coherent 'postmodern' character, and because of this its methodology dovetails with what is being developed in feminist literature under the heading of 'postmodern feminist theory'. Thus, the connecting link between institutionalism and feminist theory is postmodernism.

Postmodern feminist theory, unlike earlier theoretical developments in feminism, suggests that an appropriate epistemology for recognizing differences between women while building unity among them must be one that abandons excessive reliance on totalizing categories and broad commonalities based upon 'essences' that are themselves presumed to be universal. Unity-through-diversity requires an epistemology that accepts particular differences within broad and unifying theoretical categories like 'humanity' and 'woman'.

The epistemology that sought 'original unity', and believed in 'universal essences' is that associated with what is now called modernism (see Harding 1986, 193). It began with the Enlightenment. But the epistemology of postmodern feminist theory is leery of the use of such universals as 'humanity' and 'woman'. Institutionalism, postmodernism, and postmodern feminist theory share a rejection of the modernist Enlightenment claims of universal truths, common 'essences', teleological processes and cartesian dualism.

Postmodern feminist theory is situated by the observation that not only is life becoming more pluralized, differentiated, particularized and individualized, but this forces limitations in our ability to fully comprehend the world. Rather than bringing women together through life experiences that are more homogeneous with shared commonalities, the direction seems to be the opposite. There are 'diverse axes of identity' (Bordo 1990, 139). Postmodern feminist theory is nonessentialist and nonuniversalizing. Its 'proposals for more adequate approaches to identity begin from the invaluable insight that gender forms only one axis of a complex, heterogeneous construction, constantly interpenetrating, in historically specific ways, with multiple other axes of identity' (Bordo 1990, 139).

Postmodern feminist theory relies on an epistemology suggesting that not only is there a multiplicity of causes for male domination, but there is a multiplicity of forms of domination in general. Its epistemology says that there are no teleological forces operating behind the scenes; that the knower is always part of the object of investigation; that there are no universal essences or unifying tendencies in today's capitalism. In these important respects and others, this is also the epistemology of institutionalism.

Finally, postmodern feminist theory and institutionalism imply a common theory of political mobilization derived from the extension of democratic rights, both collective and individual. Both view the process of progressive social change as one involving the full democratization of economic and political decision-making. This will have to take place through the building of a mass-based, majoritarian and popular movement to subordinate the profits-first logic of capitalism to the broader imperative of the equal right to participate in social decision-making. Since their epistemologies, unlike orthodox Marxism, rule out any inevitability of growing unification based upon class commonalities that override race, gender and ethnicity, the movement will have to be one that uses coalition-building. Or as Anna Yeatman says, 'postmodernism enjoins a new and qualitatively distinct stage of democratization. It is this implication of postmodernism which feminist theories in the 1980s begin to discover and to celebrate' (Yeatman 1990, 290; see also Cronin 1990, 24). So, postmodern feminist theory recognizes age, class, ethnic and racial differences between women but is not nihilistic nor subversive of the activism necessary to build the majoritarian movement (Haraway 1985, 72–3).

Postmodernism and Technological Change

There are two dimensions to postmodernism that are frequently confused in the literature. The first refers to the *experience* of everyday life in contemporary capitalist societies. The second dimension concerns epistemology and is, in effect, our *intellectual reaction* to the new and somewhat frightening conditions of postmodern living. When we state that postmodernism has its origins in the capitalist, high-tech revolution of the past two decades and is consequently a description of our fragmented, de-centered lives, we are referring to experiential and cultural changes in daily life. The resulting awareness of these changes has caused social theorists and philosophers to rethink their epistemological foundations and begin to reformulate theories of knowledge. Intellectually, this process took the form of rethinking many of the premises, assumptions and conclusions of the *modernist, Enlightenment tradition.* Also, today's postmodern critics have their precursors. Nietzsche and Veblen were such people.

Today, David Harvey has described the technological changes in some detail and his notion of 'time–space compression' is an accurate term for them (see Harvey 1989; Harvey 1991). Essentially, the high-tech revolution in communications, computerization and transportation has allowed corporations to tailor production toward highly customized, specialized and individualized consumption. Firms face a highly integrated, accelerated, intensified and mobile world economy. People in both their roles as producers and consumers have found their lives to be towed in its wake. Time and space get compressed by these changes. Fredric Jameson states that although these technological changes are significant, 'postmodernism *really expresses multinational capitalism*' (Jameson 1988, 14). The system is still consumerist capitalism, but market forces are quickened, operate over greater distance and with greater intensity. Capital and labor are more mobile as we know, and corporate planning horizons are shortened (Harvey 1989, 147).

The source of these technological changes is both the corporate restructuring that has resulted from the 1960s profit-squeeze on US corporations and the emergence of intense global competition. For Harvey, 'flexibility' of capital accumulation is the key development:

> Corporations undertook an extreme adjustment process involving technological change (computerization, telecommunications), reorganization of production techniques (such as the development of 'just-in-time' systems), financial restructuring, product innovation, and massive expansion into cultural and image production. They emphasized flexibility in production systems and highly targeted or 'niche' marketing as new goals for capitalist endeavor (Harvey 1991, 67).

These technological changes, because they have occurred within the parameters of our previously-existing, mass-consumption capitalism, and because they have not altered the basic ideological underpinnings of the system (that the 'good life is the goods life') have only now received the attention they deserve. We still face a system of mass production and mass consumption, but it is simultaneously one that is geared towards *customization* in both spheres. In effect it is now a system of 'mass customization'. Pam Rosenthal suggests that:

> of all the new 'post'-words, post-Fordism is the one most directly concerned with technology. Theorists of post-Fordism interpret the contemporary world in light of a movement away from large-scale mass production and toward production under conditions that are often called 'flexible specialization'. The Fordist model of production was Henry Ford's assembly line, where a mass work force produced large batches of goods using large-scale machinery designed for only that purpose. The post-Fordist model, by contrast, implies an insecure, retrainable work force, producing smaller batches of goods in computerized, reprogrammable machinery, in response to a variegated and unpredictable consumer market (Rosenthal 1991, 80–81).

Mass customization requires flexibility and speed, and the high-tech revolution has produced the necessary means.

Obtaining flexibility in production involves outsourcing, subcontracting, temporary contracts, two-tiered wage structures and a variety of other mechanisms such as electronic funds transfer and infinite varieties of computerization in production and finance. As workers and consumers, we are subjected to these forces. Yet it is a mistake to conclude that business is doing this as part of a grand scheme to manage or channel our lives down predetermined avenues of consumerism. Firms are increasingly subordinated to globalized market mechanisms that, although they may not be totally self-regulating, are intensely competitive and integrated. The postmodern world is one of insecurity — capital is no exception. With time–space compression, American businesses are as de-centered as both their workforce and their consumers.

Postmodernism and Its Epistemology

The technological changes *within* consumerist capitalism have accelerated, diversified, fragmented, multiplied, pluralized, differentiated, individualized and ultimately de-centered the way we experience life. Under modernist conceptions it was once thought that life in mass society was becoming 'one-dimensional', homogenized, standardized and routinized. This is not so. Postmodern living is of course stressful and anxiety-ridden, but more importantly, we experience tremendous diversity and heterogeneity. The encounters we have with others whose lives and cultural backgrounds are different than our own also increase. This is a result in part due to our increased mobility. However, even for those whose lives are less mobile, the diversity is brought to them through the media and the effects of high-tech communication. David Harvey states that we have experienced 'these last two decades, an intense phase of time–space compression that has had a disorienting and disruptive impact' (Harvey 1989, 284).

Likewise, Fredric Jameson suggests there is 'discontinuity' in our lives as 'the psychic subject has been decentered by late capitalism' (Jameson 1988, 14). Thus, 'the shifting social construction of space and time as a result of the restless search for profit creates severe problems of identity: to what space do I as an individual belong?' (Harvey 1991, 77).

Postmodern living creates a profound identity crisis. Our traditions are destroyed, our lifestyles are diversified, heterogeneous and pluralized. In such a milieu we find less basis for shared experiences and common meanings with others. We find ourselves going different places, doing different things and defining ourselves in different ways than those around us. Rather than becoming more alike we feel ourselves increasingly different from others. Communication becomes more important in the remaining ability we have to relate to others, because our experiences appear different and unique (Aronowitz 1988, 48).

Additionally, consumerism is not of the homogeneous, standardized form. Production is increasingly customized and tailored to highly differentiated needs. As Ferenc Feher and Agnes Heller note:

> The specter of 'mass society' in which everyone likes the same, needs the same, practices the same, was a short intermezzo in Europe and North America. What

has indeed emerged is not the standardization and unification of consumption, but rather the enormous pluralization of tastes, practices, enjoyments and needs (Feher and Heller 1988, 142).

It is the pluralistic character of this stage of capitalism that postmodernism emphasizes.

The technological changes of the postmodern world are creating time–space compression of the two driving forces of the market economy: freedom and insecurity. These are the two fundamental experiential attributes of capitalism. As Karl Polanyi suggested, they have been the driving forces of the disembedded economy for over two hundred years. The de-centeredness and identity crisis correspond to heightened insecurity. The pluralization of lifestyles, needs and self-expression that the system simultaneously produces corresponds to the inherent individual freedom of the disembedded economy. Postmodernism is a cultural transformation in which the momentum of freedom and insecurity has accelerated (see also Huyssen 1990, 234–77). Postmodern capitalism is producing a smorgasbord of lifestyles under the maxim of 'self-expression', yet the 'self-expression' is riddled with insecurity!

De-centered postmodern living produces a feeling that subjectivity has lost its mooring. Meanings seem diverse, relative and relational. For postmodern philosophers like Michel Foucault, Jean-Francois Lyotard and Richard Rorty not only are life experiences and the meanings associated with them destabilized, but more importantly, knowledge and truth are called into question.

The epistemology of modernism suggested that the phenomenal world could be represented in *one* fundamental way, and that knowledge was ultimately grounded in an identifiable 'essence' lodged in 'humanity' itself. It maintained that underneath the seemingly irrational and anarchic surface of daily life in industrial capitalism, there was an essence of universal validity that could be discovered by the methods of science. Explanations of history were not only possible but could discover common truths that all people would eventually accept.

In part these notions rested upon a premise that the drift of history was not only teleological but that people's experiences *and their consciousness* were gradually becoming more and more alike, that is, that there was a universalizing tendency occurring throughout the world. This is a view implicit in both neoclassical economics and classical Marxism. Progress was not only possible but probable. Postmodernism disputes this confidence in progress and knowledge (see Aronowitz 1988, 46).

Modernism implied the possibility that a totalizing knowledge derived from a 'view from nowhere' could be achieved. Somehow, through cartesian dualism, we could step outside what we were trying to examine and capture an essential and total truth. The observer is able to get outside of the observed, and thus fully comprehend its essence. Linda Nicholson suggests that postmodernism is then a 'view from everywhere' (Nicholson 1990, 9). It is an epistemology situated from within the observed, because we are always part of whatever we examine. This makes our knowledge partial and somewhat particularistic rather than universal. It rejects the modernist idea of a 'God's eye view' of the world (Nicholson 1990, 3).

Thus, 'postmodern discourses are all deconstructive in that they seek to distance us from and make us skeptical about beliefs concerning truth, knowledge, power, the self, and language that are often taken for granted within and serve as legitimation for contemporary western culture' (Flax 1990, 41). Likewise, as Susan Bordo states, 'in theory, deconstructionist postmodernism stands against the ideal of disembodied knowledge and declares that ideal to be a mystification and an impossibility' (Bordo 1990, 142; see also Benhabib 1990, 110).

So our experience of postmodern living suggests to us that common meanings are increasingly difficult to obtain. As life becomes more and more different for more and more people, who also in the course of their lives have more and more diverse experiences, it may be 'impossible to say anything of solidity and permanence in the midst of this ephemeral and fragmented world' (Harvey 1989, 291).

Ernesto Laclau, among others, argues that postmodern living implies a multiplicity of meanings in any given experience. This calls into question human emancipation based upon total knowledge. 'The collapse of the myth of foundations deprives history and society of an ultimate meaning, of an absolute point of departure for political reasoning in the sense of a Cartesian cogito. Society can then be understood as a vast argumentative texture through which people construct their own reality' (Laclau 1988, 78–9). The 'argumentative texture' means that we are bound together not by hidden universal essences but by language. Lyotard remarks that 'the social subject itself seems to dissolve in this dissemination of language games. The social bond is linguistic, but it is not woven with a single thread' (Lyotard 1984, 40).

As a result of the linguistic bond, postmodern epistemology according to Rorty means that 'theory' becomes a huge conversation among a variety of 'fractured participants' (Rorty 1979). The 'grand narratives' of liberalism and Marxism were global theories of emancipation and were based on presumed homogenizing tendencies of industrial capitalism. By contrast, they developed 'systems' of interrelated ideas and 'essences'.

However, the problem with postmodern epistemology is not with its critique of modernism and Enlightenment reason. The issue is how to legitimize knowledge when there is no ultimate foundation other than the experiences of people themselves. As Nicholson argues, 'modern ideals of science, justice, and art, *are* merely modern ideals carrying with them specific political agendas and ultimately unable to legitimate themselves as universals' (Nicholson 1990, 4).

Additionally, if we cannot appeal to anything beyond or external to our own limited human experience and our linguistic bonds, then moral relativism is a problem. As Ludwig Wittgenstein stated, under these conditions, 'philosophy leaves everything as it is' (Wittgenstein 1965, 124). What is the point of theorizing when knowledge is impotent for social change?

Postmodern epistemology results from the awareness that society is going nowhere in particular — at least in any predictable fashion; that the knower is part of the known; that knowledge is provisional and partial; and that we have to be our own foundation — nothing beyond us exists. In many respects existential humanists have been saying this for decades. Left postmodernists do not want to abandon theory altogether but accept its bounded and partial character. They do not want to 'lapse into irrationality or into apocalyptic frenzy', nor succumb to moral relativism (Huyssen 1990, 268). For this they must do 'social criticism without foundation', and this is where postmodernism and institutionalism connect (Fraser and Nicholson 1990).

Postmodern Character of Institutional Economics

Understanding what we do about postmodernism leads to the conclusion that institutional economics is postmodern in character. The postmodern character of institutionalism concerns its epistemology and its underlying methodology. These are the foundation for its economic critique of neoclassicism and capitalism.

Beginning with Thorstein Veblen and his 'science' articles in the *Quarterly Journal of Economics,* we recognize that his epistemology, implicit in his critique of neoclassical and Marxist methods, was postmodern. In the 'Karl Marx' articles, in 'Why is Economics not an Evolutionary Science' and in the three 'Preconceptions of Economic Science' articles, Veblen's critique is aimed at the modernist nature of Marxism and neoclassicism. He critiques from what would now be called a postmodern perspective.

The following comment by Veblen is not only suggestive of his postmodern epistemology but also implies that for him, 'evolutionary science' is *post*modern, while classical economics is modern. Classical economics, he says, 'is not an exception to the rule, but it still shows too many reminiscences of the "natural" and the "normal," of "verities" and "tendencies," of "controlling principles" and "disturbing causes" to be classed as an evolutionary science' (Veblen 1919, 64). Veblen's above statement is quite similar to Lyotard's view in the *Postmodern Condition,* because both recognize how postmodern epistemology is a search for 'instabilities' and for 'bounded knowledge' (Lyotard 1984, 60).

Also with respect to the unstable and tentative character, Veblen states that, 'by its own nature the inquiry cannot reach a final term in any direction. So it is something of a homiletical commonplace to say that the outcome of any serious research can be to make two questions grow where one question grew before' (Veblen 1919, 33). Lyotard and other contemporary postmodernists would undoubtedly agree.

With respect to the postmodern notion (which is clearly noncartesian) that the knower is always situated within the object of investigation, that is, that we cannot achieve a 'God's eye view' of the world, Veblen says 'the question of tendency in events can evidently not come up except on the ground of some preconception or prepossession on the part of the person looking for the tendency' (Veblen 1919, 76). Ann Jennings and William Waller, in their *Journal of Economic Issues* article on institutionalism and feminism, say essentially the same thing: 'the epistemological observation made by institutionalists and feminists that knowledge is as much a product of the culture that generated it as any other cultural artifact and therefore cannot be free of cultural preconceptions and prejudices is significant' (Jennings and Waller 1990, 617).

Then regarding legitimizing knowledge that is grounded in a 'God's eye view', Lyotard says, 'but the fact remains that knowledge has no final legitimacy outside of serving the goals envisioned by the practical subject, the autonomous collectivity' (Lyotard 1984, 36). This, of course, is consistent with institutionalism and points toward reliance on instrumental value theory and John Dewey's pragmatism. In a similar vein, Veblen states that 'this ultimate term or ground of knowledge is always of a metaphysical character. It is something in the way of a preconception, accepted uncritically, but applied in criticism and demonstration of all else with which the science is concerned' (Veblen 1919, 149).

Veblen, like postmodern contemporaries, is suggesting that knowledge is both provisional and 'socially constructed' (we are within the object of our investigation). Jennings and Waller argue similarly, 'that institutionalism and feminism share noncartesian epistemological roots that *lead* to a recognition of knowledge as socially constructed' (Jennings and Waller 1990, 614).

For Veblen and postmodernists, knowledge is not obtained through representation of reality by grand systems, but is provisional and processual. Of evolutionary science, that is postmodern epistemology, Veblen says that 'the inquiry converges upon a matter of process; and it comes to rest *provisionally*, when it has disposed of its facts in terms of process' (Veblen 1919, 33).

In the following comment Veblen, in characteristically postmodern fashion states that:

> In order to search for a tendency, we must be possessed of some notion of a definitive end to be sought, or some notion as to what is the legitimate trend of events. The notion ot a legitimate trend in a course of events is an extra-evolutionary preconception, and lies outside the scope of an inquiry into the causal sequence in any process. The evolutionary point of view, therefore, leaves no place for a formulation of natural laws in terms of definitive normality (Veblen 1919, 76).

Postmodern epistemology, as Veblen suggests above, rejects 'natural' laws, universal truths, and teleology. Veblen's criticism of Marxism is postmodern as well. Karl Marx was a 'left modernist', whose view of history was essentialist, universalist and reductionist.

Finally, 'social criticism without foundation', in other words, Veblen's postmodern epistemology, implies the use of instrumental value theory and Dewey pragmatism. Postmodern philosophers like Cornel West have been increasingly drawn to pragmatism, a vital part of the institutionalist tradition, because it derives its purpose from both its awareness that ultimate foundations cannot be identified and from the commitment to *not* let philosophy 'leave things as they are'. It is committed to humanist democratic values, in part derivable from the Enlightenment project, and yet humble enough to recognize that humans must be their own foundation (West 1988, 269).

Institutionalists, postmodern feminist theorists, and postmodern philosophers all have the same basic epistemology. Nancy Fraser, a postmodern feminist theorist states that, 'one gives up the foundationalist metainterpretation of humanist values: the view that such values are grounded in the nature of something...But one does not give up the substantial critical core of humanism' (Fraser 1985, 171–2).

For institutionalists, postmodern feminist theorists and postmodern philosophers, the challenge is to contribute to legitimately changing the world for the better without sinking into moral relativism. As Lyotard suggests, 'most people have lost the nostalgia for the lost narrative. It in no way follows that they are reduced to barbarity. What saves them from it is their knowledge that legitimation can only spring from their own linguistic practice and communicational interaction' (Lyotard 1984, 41). The *postmodern epistemology of institutionalism* recognizes heterogeneity of life, foundationless critique, and commitment to justice, and because of these features postmodern feminist theory is what can be derived from it.

The Development of Postmodern Feminist Theory

Feminist theory has gone through several stages of development in the last three decades, and today there continue to be competing theories and epistemologies, some of which are modernist. But there is also the emergence of postmodern feminist theory (see Irigaray 1985, for a defence of modernist theory and critique of postmodernist theory; see also Marks and de Courtivron 1980 and *Signs* 1981 for early defence of the feminism–postmodernism connection).

However, postmodern feminist theory is partially a consequence of difficulties discovered through the refinement of earlier modernist theories. Modernist theories of patriarchy/male domination sought universally-valid and essentialist explanations. They generally criticized androcentric epistemology, arguing that the category of 'humanity' concealed a fundamental difference — that between male and female. They argued that gender was important yet not validated by the broader category of 'human'.

The effort to reveal how 'woman' is different and must be recognized separately from 'human' took on essentialist and universalist characteristics. As Patricia Waugh says:

> Certainly, for women in the 1960s and early 1970s, 'unity' rather than dispersal seemed to offer more hope for political change. To believe that there might be a 'natural' or 'true' self which may be discovered through lifting the misrepresentations of an oppressive social system is to provide nurturance and fuel for revolutionary hope and practice (Waugh 1989, 13).

A search for ultimate causes of male domination, for universal features of gender-based domination, and for an *essence* of being women that could show an *inherent unity of interests* among all women, was initially very important for movement-building.

To what extent is the category 'woman' universalizing and therefore unable to adequately represent the diversity of life experiences and the multiplicity of forms of women's subordination to men? Sandra Harding states that 'there is no "woman" to whose social experience the feminist empiricist and standpoint justificatory strategies can appeal; there are, instead, *women:* chicanas and latinos, black and white, the "offshore" women in the electronics factories in Korea and those in the Caribbean sex industry' (Harding 1986, 192). Such diversity of women's experiences and the degree to which particularity is important in attempting to reveal sources of domination, spill over into feminist theory and have been at the root of postmodern feminist theory.

Harding, in her development and defence of postmodern feminist theory, argues that there are two types of modernist theory, the limitations of which led ultimately to postmodern theory. The first she calls 'feminist empiricism' and the other, 'feminist standpoint' (Harding 1986 and 1990). In the 1960s these theories 'emphasized the ideological production of "femininity" as the "other" of patriarchy and the need, therefore, for women to become "real" subjects and to discover their "true" selves. Thus, with a search for a *coherent and unified feminine subject*, began the destruction of the myth of woman as absolute Other and its exposure as a position within masculine discourse' (Waugh 1989, 9).

The problem of feminist empiricism is that it is essentially cartesian or dualistic in nature and argues that sexism and androcentrism are biases that can be corrected by 'better' analysis — yet analysis of the traditional cartesian variety (Harding 1986, 24). This approach is essentialist like the rest of modernist philosophy. But, she continues, 'can there be *a* feminist standpoint if women's (or feminists') social experience is divided by class, race, and culture?' (Harding 1986, 26). As Christine Distefano argues, 'feminist postmodernism goes even further to challenge the assumptions of feminist empiricism and feminist standpoint theories. It embraces a skepticism regarding generalizable and universal claims of *any* sort, including those of feminism' (Distefano 1990, 74).

Postmodernism and institutionalism have an epistemology that rejects single-cause, essentialist and totalizing explanations for social change. Craig Owens states, '"no single theoretical discourse..." — this feminist position is also a postmodern condition' (Owens 1983, 64). Likewise, Veblen criticized Marxism for relying excessively on a 'single theoretical discourse'.

Postmodern feminists began to say this, because of the realization that there is an increasing heterogeneity of life experiences, a pluralizing and diversifying trend occurring for women globally. There is an identity crisis in postmodern living in which women's lives are criss-crossed by differences in race, class, age, ethnicity, sexual preference and parenting. Each of these dimensions is a source of identity and can be a cause of oppression and marginalization.

Postmodern feminist theory suggests that no one sphere is necessarily or essentially more important or more a source of identity than any other. This is feminist theory that does not rely on anything fundamental, essential or universal about being a 'woman' (see Butler 1990, 324). Gender does make a difference and is the basis for domination, but it is not the only nor most basic cause. As Jean Grimshaw states, 'the experience of gender, of being a man or a woman, inflects much if not all of people's lives...But even if one is always a man or a woman, one is never *just* a man or a woman' (Grimshaw 1986, 84).

There is a complex relationship between the multiplicity of axes of identity. Which is more important — being black, being young, being poor, or being female? Is there an inherent unity of interests between white middle-class women, Third World peasant women and urban black teenage women? Some would say, yes, because they are all 'oppressed'. But this is something we attribute *to* them and is not *inherent* in the fact that they are all women. Postmodern feminist theory as well as institutionalist epistemology would agree that there is no inherent unity of interests (Meese 1986, ix). Again, this is precisely what Veblen had to say about Marxism.

On the other hand, the major criticism of postmodern feminist epistemology (and institutionalism as well) is that if accounting for all of the differences and particularities is necessary then, with the continued pluralization of life, broad theories have no place. Have we ended up with 'sheer plurality and elusiveness of cultural forms wrapped in the mysteries of rapid flux and change?' (Harvey 1991, 65; see also Feher and Heller 1988, 142). The relevant question for postmodern feminist theory is whether gender 'is so thoroughly fragmented by race, class, historical particularity and individual difference, as to self-destruct as an analytical category'? (Bordo 1990, 133).

Yet, Yeatman also adds that the project of social justice is no less compelling simply because our epistemology no longer assures progress nor emancipation. Also, in Yeatman's words, 'it is at this point that feminists, as others who are committed to developing the democratic implications of postmodernism, need to firmly distinguish their position from those who take postmodernism to imply an anomic relativism'

(Yeatman 1990, 291–2). So postmodern feminist theory is clearly partial. But it does exist. Also, postmodern feminist theory implies that epistemology itself deserves proportionately less emphasis than instrumentally-valid political action (see Fraser and Nicholson 1990, 35; Harding 1986, 251).

Conclusion

Postmodern epistemology in institutionalism and in postmodern feminist theory, by rejecting the 'grand narratives' of Hegelianism and Marxism, argues that there is no '*inherent* unity of interests', among women and other subordinate social groups. What they have in common — human beings and victims of social injustice — are commonalities that we *attribute* to them. For these to become progressive social forces leading to change, there has to be a new awareness created from within the victims. This new awareness can only come about through language-based articulation in the process of struggle by each group and person involved.

Yet, there appears to be nothing inherent in the development of capitalism at this stage that will automatically create this change of awareness. In fact, the technological forces seem to be divisive rather than unifying. It is as likely that victims will be increasingly pitted against each other as it is that they will find common cause.

Consequently, we can say that there is nothing *inherent* in being women, blacks, wage-workers, poor, or Third World peasants that would tend to generate a unified majoritarian social movement. The unity has to be constructed and articulated through both language and social activism. There is no reason, according to postmodern epistemology in feminism and institutionalism, to believe that a common interest in social change will be forged by developments in technology or capitalism. Therefore, we need to move in the direction of building alliances and coalitions, in which each group retains some of the particularity of its interests and some decision-making autonomy, or what Iris Young calls a 'politics of difference'.

The 'politics of difference' suggests that various subordinate social groups *can* develop a consensus based upon the classical liberal Enlightenment principles of equal rights and democratic decision-making. It is a politics of mobilization that accepts the reality of the postmodern world in which pluralization of lifestyles, meanings, interests and cultural values is a fact. It does not say that growing heterogeneity of capitalist life makes broad progressive movements impossible, nor that because there is no tendency toward revelation of common human essence and universalization, that common concerns cannot be achieved.

This should strike institutionalists as instrumental value theory; it is simply stated differently. To embrace the value of pluralism without simultaneously slipping into absolute individualism and moral relativism requires the collective commitment to democracy and equal rights (see Laclau 1988, 81). This commitment carried to its logical extreme can bring diverse groups together and take us beyond capitalism to a type of radical democracy. We commit to democracy *and* pluralism (see Young 1990, 319; Ross 1988, xvi).

We want to construct broad-based coalitions that respect autonomy and pluralism while communicating to one another the mutual recognition that a socially just society based upon principles of equal rights and democracy is instrumentally valid. Certainly preserving difference while building unity is problematic. For Harding, 'this approach requires embracing as a fruitful grounding for inquiry the fractured identities modern life creates: black-feminist, socialist-feminist, women-of-color, and so on' (Harding 1986, 28).

In the end postmodern epistemology in institutionalism and feminist theory suggests that nothing is for certain, and to a great extent building the majoritarian democratic movement of unity through diversity is a problem of communication. We cannot escape the communication character of postmodern life.

Yet this coalition-based movement that is capable of bringing people in marginalized groups together, is one in which democratizing decision-making in the economy will undoubtedly subordinate profit-led growth and consequently lead us beyond our traditional type of capitalism.

The postmodern world is one in which institutionalist and feminist epistemology recognizes that the techno-induced growth of pluralism, heterogeneity, and mass customization is part of a 'non-zero sum game'. Postmodernism has expanded pluralism, that is, expressions of individual freedom, while not reducing institutional domination and repressive marginalization for large blocks of people. The 'non-zero sum' condition of postmodern life has increased freedom without reducing domination. It has increased freedom and also simultaneously increased insecurity.

The 'politics of difference' suggests that we admit to the increased pluralization of life, to the increase in forms of self-expression, and thus to the freedom that this demonstrates. Yet, the 'politics of difference' embedded in institutionalism and postmodern feminist theory requires that we not only admit to increased freedom but fight domination as well.

Modernism, for example in both neoclassical economics and Marxism, tended to view the world as a zero-sum game. Postmodernism suggests otherwise. The world is not so much driven by a dialectic as Hegel and Marx said, but by a multiplicity of interest conflicts revolving around the fundamental forces of insecurity and freedom (as Karl Polanyi stated).

In Polanyi's terms, the disembedding of economy from society over one hundred years ago, initially set the stage for the anxiety, stress, confusion and pluralization/self-expression of the postmodern world we face. The full democratization of society, based upon equal rights and democracy, is an effort to retain the freedom/pluralism of capitalism, and of course, advance it for oppressed and marginalized social groups such as women, while also using democracy to assure security. The best we can hope for is to maximize freedom and security within an institutional framework that will always remain provisional and subject to reevaluation.

References

Aronowitz, Stanley (1988), 'Postmodernism and Politics' in Ross, Andrew, ed. *Universal Abandon*, Minneapolis: University of Minnesota Press: 46–62.

Benhabib, Seyla (1990), 'Epistemologies of Postmodernism: A Rejoinder to Jean-Francois Lyotard' in Nicholson, Linda, ed. *Feminism/Postmodernism*, New York: Routledge: 107–30.

Bordo, Susan (1990), 'Feminism, Postmodernism, and Gender-Scepticism' in Nicholson, Linda, ed. *Feminism/Postmodernism*, New York: Routledge: 133–56.

Butler, Judith (1990), 'Gender Trouble, Feminist Theory, and Psychoanalytic Discourse' in Nicholson, Linda, ed. *Feminism/Postmodernism*, New York: Routledge: 324–99.

Cronin, Jim (1990), 'Western Socialism after the Cold War', *Socialist Review*, 20 (2) June: 20–30.

DiStefano, Christine (1990), 'Dilemmas of Difference: Feminism, Modernity, and Postmodernism' in Nicholson, Linda, ed. *Feminism/Postmodernism*, New York: Routledge: 63–82.

Feher, Ferenc, and Agnes Heller (1988), *The Postmodern Political Condition*, New York: Columbia University Press.

Flax, Jane (1990), 'Postmodernism and Gender Relations in Feminist Theory' in Nicholson, Linda, ed. *Feminism/Postmodernism*, New York: Routledge: 39–62.

Fraser, Nancy (1985), 'Michel Foucault: A "Young Conservative"?' *Ethics*, 96, October: 165–84.

Fraser, Nancy, and Linda Nicholson (1990), 'Social Criticism Without Philosophy: An Encounter Between Feminism and Postmodernism' in Nicholson, Linda, ed. *Feminism/Postmodernism*, New York: Routledge: 19–38.

Greenwood, Daphne (1988), 'A Comment on Evolutionary Economics I: Foundations of Institutionalist Thought', *Journal of Economics Issues*, 22 (1) March: 249–51.

Grimshaw, Jean (1986), *Philosophy and Feminist Thought*, Minneapolis: University of Minnesota Press.

Haraway, Donna (1985), 'A Manifesto for Cyborgs: Science, Technology, and Socialist Feminism in the 1980s', *Socialist Review*, 15(2) March: 65–108.

Harding, Sandra (1986), *The Science Question in Feminism*, Ithica, NY: Cornell University Press.

Harding, Sandra (1990), 'Feminism, Science, and the Anti-Enlightenment Critiques' in Nicholson, Linda, ed. *Feminism/Postmodernism*, New York: Routledge: 83–106.

Harvey, David (1989), *The Postmodern Condition: An Enquiry into the Origins of Cultural Change*, Cambridge, MA: Basil Blackwell.

Harvey, David (1991), 'Flexibility: Threat or Opportunity', *Socialist Review*, 21 (1) March: 65–78.

Huyssen, Andreas (1990), 'Mapping the Postmodern' in Nicholson, Linda, ed. *Feminism/Postmodernism*, New York: Routledge: 234–77.

Irigaray, Luce (1985), *The Sex Which is Not One*, Porter, Catherine (translator), Ithaca, NY: Cornell University Press.

Jameson, Fredric (1988), 'Regarding Postmodernism — A Conversation with Fredric Jameson' in Ross, Andrew, ed. *Universal Abandon*, Minneapolis: University of Minnesota Press: 3–30.

Jennings, Ann and William Waller (1990), 'On the Possibility of a Feminist Economics: The Convergence of Institutional and Feminist Methodology', *Journal of Economic Issues*, 24 (2) June: 613–22.

Laclau, Ernesto (1988), 'Politics and the Limits of Modernity' in Ross, Andrew, ed. *Universal Abandon*, Minneapolis: University of Minnesota Press: 63–82.

Lyotard, Jean-Francois (1984), *The Postmodern Condition: A Report on Knowledge*, Minneapolis: University of Minnesota Press.

Marks, Elaine, and Isabella de Courtivron, eds. (1980), *New French Feminisms*, Amhurst, MA: University of Massachusetts Press.

Meese, Elizabeth (1986), *Crossing the Double-Cross: The Practice of Feminist Criticism*, Chapel Hill, NC: University of North Carolina Press.

Nicholson, Linda (1990), 'Introduction' in Nicholson, Linda, ed. *Feminism/Postmodernism*, New York: Routledge: 1–16.

Owens, Craig (1983), 'The Discourse of Others: Feminists and Postmodernism' in Foster, Hal, ed. *The Anti-Aesthetic*, Port Townsend, WA: Bay Press: 57–82.

Rosenthal, Pam (1991), 'Jacked In: Fordism, Cyberpunk, Marxism', *Socialist Review*, 21 (1) March: 79–103.

Ross, Andrew (1988), 'Introduction' in Ross, Andrew, ed. *Universal Abandon: The Politics of Postmodernism*, Minneapolis: University of Minnesota Press: i–xx.

Rorty, Richard (1979), *Philosophy and the Mirror of Nature*, Princeton: Princeton University Press.

Signs: Journal of Women in Culture and Society (1981), 'Special Issue on French Feminism': 7 (1) March.

Veblen, Thorstein (1919) 1961, ed. *The Place of Science in Modern Civilization,* New York: Russell and Russell.

Waugh, Patricia (1989), *Feminine Fictions: Revisiting the Postmodern*, New York: Routledge.

West, Cornel (1988), 'Interview with Cornel West' in Ross, Andrew, ed. *Universal Abandon*, Minneapolis: University of Minnesota Press: 269–86.

Wittgenstein, Ludwig (1965), *Philosophical Investigations*, New York: Macmillan.

Yeatman, Anna (1990), 'A Feminist Theory of Social Differentiation' in Nicholson, Linda, ed. *Feminism/Postmodernism*, New York: Routledge: 281–99.

Young, Iris (1990), 'The Ideal of Community and the Politics of Difference' in Nicholson, Linda, ed. *Feminism/Postmodernism*, New York: Routledge: 300–23.

PART II

Extending Our Analysis

4. Technology and Gender in Institutional Economics

William Waller

Technology and Institutionalism

The term technology is very important in institutional economics. Its definition can be very simple, a favorite of mine was coined by David Hamilton: 'organized intelligence in action'. While this definition is both simple and suggestive, it lacks sufficient explicative detail to be of much use to those unfamiliar with the term's usage in institutional economics. Technology is usually described by institutionalists as an aspect of behavior and as a social process. This aspect or process is socially organized and socially learned tool-oriented behavior associated with people securing a livelihood (Hamilton 1986, 529). The technological process is identified with science and the development of matter-of-fact knowledge, but is not special or different from other social processes by virtue of providing 'objective' or certain knowledge. Instead it offers a process of knowledge-seeking that is inherently corrigible, through a self-correcting process of continuous reevaluation in the face of new or changed circumstances — the outcome is not knowledge which is certain, rather it is tentative knowledge with warranted assertability.

Technology as a Cultural Process

An important issue to begin with is the clarification of the ontological status of technology. What is it? I have already noted that it is used as an abstract concept, a social process, and an aspect of behavior. Technology is a category, constructed for the purpose of making holistic human behavior comprehensible for analysis. Human behavior is continuous and culturally integrated, it is not separable into distinct parts. The life process of the individual has no meaning except as an ongoing stream of behavior within

55

a social-cultural context. In order to do social analysis this ongoing social-cultural life process has to be made analytically tractable. The way we do this is to construct categories that divide up the whole into analytically manageable parts.

The term technology refers to a conceptual category that is constructed by the analyst, in order to describe or analytically separate certain social processes that represent aspects of human behavior. The responsibility of the analysts who construct and subsequently use this category include identifying the aspects of behavior the construct is designed to employ and describing how these aspects constitute a cultural process. Then this cultural process must be reintegrated into an overall understanding of the society.

Our understanding of the world is made of organized structures of categories and constructs. The structuring of these categories affects not only how we understand the world, but how we experience it. In other words, we live in the existential world, but we comprehend it through the linguistic constructions that constitute our understanding. It is our comprehension of how our world works that we use to solve problems and acquire the necessities of life. Thus we live in a world that we understand in terms of intellectual and linguistic constructs and we act on that understanding; thus we live our lives in a world we continuously reconstruct in terms of these constructs. 'Man makes himself' (to use the gendered title of V. Gordon Childe's famous book) in more than the material sense.

The point I wish to emphasize here is not only that technology is a construct, but more importantly the technological process is lived. It is part of our culture, it is part of our understanding, it is part of us. This is crucial in this analysis of technology and gender, because the category gender shares this ontology with technology. Gender and technology are constructs, part of a schema of categorization, but gender and technology are also lived.

Technology as Tools

This understanding of technology as a social process is different from the common usage of this term. Technology is commonly identified with things such as hammers, wrenches, computers — material things that are manipulated. Technology as useful stuff, or even as the skills to manipulate useful stuff, is a static understanding of a cultural process. This static understanding of technology is what orthodox economists understand as technology, thus they cannot understand why technology is so important in the institutional paradigm. To them it is part of the furniture of the economy — to be rearranged, used, replaced, or disposed of, but of no causal or dynamic importance.

To clarify this misunderstanding Jim Swaney has suggested the following taxonomy: the term technology should be used to refer to current knowledge and skills-cum-tools (which he calls skilcut), the term technological process should be used to refer to human activity characterized by the application of technology, and instrumental valuation (to be discussed later) refers to the human activity that develops new knowledge during the technological process — making it a subset of the technological process (Swaney 1989, 570). This paper will adopt Swaney's usage to avoid confusion.

Technology and Science

The relationship between technology and science is a complicated one. Historians of technology and science note that the tendency to identify science and the technological process as part of the same activity is a recent development (White 1968, 161). This identification of technological process and science is not historically comprehensible in terms of the purpose of the activities. It is the recognition that the method of knowing employed in both activities is similar (epistemologically and methodologically) that leads to the contemporary identification of the two. As a result it is scientific research and the technological process that are currently categorized together, not the end results of the behaviors, except in the sense that both define their end result as an attempt to solve a problem — a speculative one in the case of science and a practical one in the case of technology. The growth of applied science and theoretical engineering make obvious the falseness of this dualistic schema of differentiation.

This transformation of the conceptual categories of science and technology from a focus on teleological outcome to a focus on behavioral processes, represents a step away from thinking of human activity in a static way towards understanding it in terms of ongoing cultural processes. This chapter will explore if other human activities and behaviors currently identified and categorized on the basis of their teleological outcomes, should be categorized with science and technological processes as behaviorally similar in terms of epistemology and methodology.

But equally important is the recognition that these categorizations have social significance. White identifies the presence of a hierarchical relationship between the highly valued theoretical science and the lower valued practical achievements of technology (that White calls inspired empiricism) (White 1968, 163). Dualistic categorizations almost always imply status hierarchies. We now recognize the similarity — possibly even the unity — of science and the technological process. But the dualistic categorization of science and technology leads not only to the activities being related hierarchically, but the people — in this case scientist and engineers — are socially ranked in hierarchical relations as well. I will explore whether there are other behaviors that should be included within this category, on the basis of the same similarities identified between science and technological processes, that are held in lower regard and in a dualistic relationship to science and technology. If so, I will try to identify the status relationship vis-a-vis science and technological processes of the persons who perform these similar activities. I will also address the question of whether these behaviors are undervalued because of their association with the dualistic understanding of hierarchical gender relationships in our society.

Technology and the Veblenian Dichotomy

So far I have addressed what technology means in institutional economics, but not its significance within institutional thought. When Thorstein Veblen adapted and metaphorically extended the concept of evolution from biology to economics he meant to construct a description and theoretical formulation of the life process, explainable in terms of cumulative causation with no teleological preconception with regard to direction (improvement or decline) and no tendency to approach a meliorative trend or attain static equilibrium (Veblen, 1990). He was calling for economics to become a science of cultural evolution. The human processes that cause change were of central importance to this transformation of economics. Veblen's work often focused on the differential impact of animistic habits of thought versus matter-of-fact habits of thought, this distinction later becoming known as the Veblenian dichotomy among institutionalists.

Warren Samuels has argued convincingly that matter-of-fact habits of thought in Veblen's work are self-referential (Samuels 1990, passim). By this I take him to mean that Veblen constructed a category called matter-of-fact habits of thought to describe and analyze a cultural process, yet the process it describes and analyzes is the same process that generated the category in the first place. This category is a product of inquiry — itself cultural behavior subject to the same analysis. This category was constructed by Veblen to describe cultural behavior through which knowledge is attained, the behavior is identified as matter-of-fact, and the knowledge attained through this behavior is matter-of-fact, moreover it is desirable because it is matter-of-fact. This means that matter-of-fact behavior–knowledge–preconceptions (Samuels and Veblen use each of these terms) is a category of cultural processes constructed for the purpose of analysis by a fully acculturated human being. The status of matter-of-fact knowledge is neither objective or more deserving of consideration than knowledge or behavior resulting from other cultural processes.

This understanding of the status of matter-of-fact habits of thought is important for this paper because the Veblenian dichotomy continued to evolve. The archetypal form of the dichotomy became a contrast between ceremonial aspects of behavior, corresponding to Veblen's animistic-teleological habits of thought, and technological aspects of behavior, corresponding to Veblen's matter-of-fact habits of thought. Thus we return to the role of technology in institutionalist thought (Waller 1982,1991).

In the Veblen-Ayres tradition technological aspects of behavior are seen as promoting the growth in technology (tools and tool skills) and through this effecting other behavior. Technology's effect on cultural behavior is generally to create opportunities for changes in the culture's behavioral norms. It creates the potential for change and thus the potential for improvement in the ways and means of provisioning. Technological aspects of behavior are seen as important causal elements of change and thus it creates or increases evolutionary potential. Up to this point in my description of technology in institutional thought, the role of technological aspects of behavior on cultural evolution is largely descriptive. To fully understand the concept's role in institutional thought valuation processes must be considered.

Technology and Instrumental Valuation

In the work of C. E. Ayres, technological aspects of behavior were closely linked to John Dewey's instrumentalism. Ayres identified the technological aspects of behavior with the valuation behavior in Dewey's instrumentalism.

Ayres, Dewey and others have argued that the usefulness of technology can be recognized across cultures. The whole notion of diffusion of technology from one culture to another depends on this recognition. It is a short jump, but a very significant one, from cross-cultural recognition of the usefulness of technology to the treatment of technology as transcultural. Through inadvertent and careless use of language, some institutionalists occasionally make this short jump. When Dewey's notion of instrumental valuation is identified as being the type of valuational process associated with technological aspects of behavior, and technology is treated as a transcultural process, the technological process is elevated to a pancultural form of behavior and instrumental valuation a pancultural standard of value (Mayhew 1987).

This treatment of instrumental valuation and its relationship to technology would be profoundly at odds with the description of the technological process and Veblen's notion of matter-of-fact behavior and knowledge. These are cultural processes categorized by the analyst — they have no independent existence beyond the description and analysis as understood by the analyst and his/her audience. Human behavior is. It is not technological or ceremonial or traditional or good or bad — it just is. We place behavior in these culturally constructed categories. The meaning of the categories is created by the interaction of the acculturated analyst(s) who construct them and the acculturation of his/her audience. This process of category construction, analysis, consideration and discussion of analysis, response, and revision is a process and it is what we mean by knowing — if knowing has a larger meaning than belief and a larger frame of reference than the individual.

If one is serious about the concept of culture and cultural analysis, then all knowledge is cultural and understanding is achieved through discourse within and/or between cultures, and thus the meaning of technology, technological processes and instrumental valuation is relative, culture-bound and hermeneutically determined (Waller and Robertson 1991).

Technology and Progress

Many institutionalists, like many historians of science and technology, see in science and technology the path to progress. Since the usefulness of tools is often comprehensible across cultures, many have thought that more tools, that can do more useful things or are of increased complexity, indicate progress. More tools that can do more useful things are just that; more and useful — if this constitutes progress within a particular culture it will be so decided and categorized within that cultural context. Increased levels of usefulness and complexity in tools and the understanding of tools does create opportunities for application and further development. It may even have the potential, though not necessarily recognized, for solving important societal problems. Instrumental valuation does suggest the use of the value principle articulated by Marc Tool:

> ...that direction is forward which provides for the continuity of human life and the noninvidious re-creation of community through the instrumental use of knowledge (Tool 1985, 293).

But cultures may be perfectly aware and familiar with instrumental valuational processes and still choose not to employ existing tools to solve important social problems. Moreover, they may employ alternative valuational criteria in that decision and consider such a decision *as* progress. Advances in technology gives us the opportunity to do more things and to make more instrumental decisions, and oddly, it also allows us to knowingly make more non-instrumental decisions as well.

Thus technology in institutional thought is many things. It is tools and the skill to use them, it is the technological aspects of cultural behavior that generates the tools and it is the instrumental valuation that is part of that process of inquiry. It is not the source of objective knowledge, nor is it the cause of progress or even a pancultural measure of progress. It is a construct that describes and categorizes cultural behavior with certain characteristics and is often associated with increased potential for application of material means and human intelligence to human activity. The next issue of moment is to see why institutionalism is well situated for theorizing about technology and gender.

Propitious (or Fortuitous?) Roots for Institutional Theorizing About Technology

This exploration will not really attempt to discover whether institutionalists were very smart or very lucky in their construction of the concept of technology. Instead I will examine an issue raised by Ann Jennings and I elsewhere — specifically why institutionalism is capable of becoming feminist (Waller and Jennings 1990). Specifically I will explore those aspects of institutionalists' understanding of technology that coincide with necessary aspects of a feminist understanding of technology.

Thorstein Veblen and Technology

In our earlier discussion of Veblen's notion of matter-of-fact behavior, I noted that this behavior, the knowledge that resulted from the behavior, and the valuational processes that were part of the behavior were cultural. This cultural character of theorizing is of crucial importance in both institutional and feminist theorizing about technology.

Of even more importance is that Veblen paid particular attention to the role of women in cultural processes. This is well known with regard to the discussions of the role of women in maintaining family status, but it extends to his other work as well.

Interestingly Veblen's attempt to define technology in *The Instinct of Workmanship* illustrates two important elements of a feminist understanding of technology. When Veblen discusses the domestication of plants and animals, he speculates on the basis of the existing anthropological evidence that this technological advance was one primarily accomplished by women (Veblen 1964, 69,78). He emphasizes that husbandry and tillage are technological developments growing out of behaviors he associates with the 'parental bent', but to his credit he does not imply that the parental bent is either exclusive or natural to women, but equally present among both sexes (though his arguments elsewhere suggest the parental bent is suppressed or devalued on the basis of gender roles).

In addition to his explicit recognition of the cultural character of technology, his speculation upon the role of women in domestication, and his refusal to universalize parental concern, Veblen avoided using a common dualistic categorization scheme for production. During this period 'technology' was often the term used to describe productive processes developed and employed by men and 'crafts' was used to describe productive processes developed and employed by women. Veblen's cultural approach and refusal to accept traditional gender roles as normal and natural certainly provided a propitious start for institutional economics with regard to theorizing about technology.

Fortuitous Choice — Mumford and White

Most institutionalists who write on technology cite the work of Lewis Mumford frequently and approvingly. The prominent feminist historian of technology, Joan Rothschild, argues that Mumford in his work *The Myth of the Machine* is a pre-feminist of sorts. The elements of Mumford's analysis that qualifies him in Rothschild's view are:
1. Mumford recognized the central role that women played in early domestication and associated technology.
2. He argued that so-called female qualities which are undervalued had an important role in technological development.
3. He assigned equal weight to subjective impulses and fantasies as formative influences in creating and transforming culture.
Thus Rothschild concludes that Mumford is an early and 'principle challenger of the persistent notion that man is the central provider and social organizer in early cultures'. Rothschild also discusses and recognizes the limitations of Mumford's analysis. (Rothschild 1983, xix–xxii).

Rothschild similarly notes that Lynn White (whose work has also influenced institutionalism) made some very interesting observations regarding women in western society. Specifically, White recognized the tendency to treat men and women differently in the context of his discussion of the tendency in western thought to categorize phenomena within 'platonic–cartesian' dualistic relationships that value one aspect of the dualism over the other (White 1968, 17). Criticism of this tendency is a prominent theme in feminist scholarship (White 1968, 14). Rothschild notes that White did not follow up on the significance of this observation in his work on the history of science and technology (Rothschild 1983, x–xii).

Before discussing further aspects of development of feminist perspectives on technology I would like to note that Veblen, Mumford, and White all adopt a cultural approach to their analyses, rather than an epochal or invention by invention approach typical of the history of science and technology literature. I believe this is inherently significant. Ann Jennings and I argue elsewhere that the cultural approach of institutionalism, especially Karl Polanyi's work, lends itself to feminist theorizing on the grounds that his substantive approach, with its emphasis on cultural continuity, leads to questions of how the construction of social relationships and shared understandings affects behavior (Waller and Jennings 1990; 1991). Therefore it is really not a matter of fortuitous choices but a result of their cultural approach that causes institutionalists to find Mumford and White's views congenial.

Many other scholars have contributed to institutional views on technology. Space does not allow for a discussion of the views of John Dewey, Jacob Bronowski, Erich Zimmerman, V. Gordon Childe or Karl Polanyi all of whom made substantial contributions. However, taken together they seem to focus on cultural continuity, technology as a cultural process, and the unity of technology and technological processes with valuational and creative behavior generally. Put simply, institutionalist theorizing is congenial to feminist thought because it is processual, cultural and holistic.

Feminist Approaches to Institutionalism and Technology

This section of the paper explores feminist approaches to institutionalism and feminist approaches to technology can be usefully combined to enhance our overall understanding of technology.

Jennings' Feminist Institutionalism

Ann Jennings' work on a feminist institutionalism provides the theoretical framework of this exploration of technology and gender (Jennings 1993a, 1993b). Of particular importance is Jennings' discussion of dualism and her reformulation of Sandra Harding's categorization of research in androcentric science into a research program for reconstructing institutionalism along feminist lines (Harding 1986).

Dualism

Jennings and Waller, building on the work of Susan Bordo (Bordo 1987), have argued that feminism and institutionalism both reject dualistic constructions of reality (Waller and Jennings 1990). Both feminism and institutionalism treat dualisms as a distortion of real relationships and lead to thinking about aspects of the same connected reality as separate and distinct, fixed and unchanging, and necessarily in a hierarchical relationship (Jennings 1993b; Jennings and Waller 1990b).

But in addition to recognizing that dualistic understandings underlie hierarchical relationships (often with a gendered aspect to the hierarchy) and present disjointed and faulty understandings of culture and social relationships, an additional consideration is raised by Jennings. Specifically she notes that dualistic intellectual schemata are used to construct our understanding of the world and society, but it is through that understanding that human beings construct society. This means that dualisms are not only constructs or conceptual schemata — through their role in the construction of our shared understandings, and the maintenance and reproduction of those shared understandings — these dualistic constructions are lived.

This means if we accept a dualistic construct that argues that the economy and the household are in separate spheres — the economy in the public and the home in the private — and if the public sphere is the realm of men and the private sphere is the realm of women, this constructs a series of dualistic relationships:

men	/	women
public	/	private
economy	/	household

Everything on the left-hand side of the dualism is socially valued over the right-hand side. The two sides of the dualism are mutually exclusive, but both sides taken together are intended to be universally inclusive. Things are public or private — not both. But when we conceptualize the world this way we begin to act and to organize our behavior as if these things are separate. This occurs in spite of the fact that most people recognize that in the real world of human lives and livelihood, the household and the economy are not separate and distinct, but part of the same matrix of social relationships. Problems arise when we construct social policy and live this artificial dualism as if reality really were separated in this way.

Thus it is not sufficient to recognize dualistic constructs and eliminate them from our discourse. These dualisms must be recognized and eliminated from our shared understanding, often an unspoken, tacit, part of our common culture, and from our lives as we live them. Thus a feminist institutionalism is not an intellectual exercise, but a form of everyday activism.

Feminist Institutionalism and Technology

Jennings has reconceptualized Sandra Harding's categorization of research programs exploring gender in science, as a framework for inquiry about gender in institutionalism (Jennings 1993b, Harding 1986, 20–24). Jennings' framework uses the following five steps as adapted for this paper: equity studies, the use and abuse of technology, the selection of problematics, reading technology as a text, and epistemological concerns.

Equity Studies

The first question is: Have the contributions of women to the history and development of technology been overlooked? The simple answer is yes. V. Gordon Childe's work is typical in that it ignores gender and follows the convention of applying male pronouns when speaking of all humankind. While this convention was long thought to be benign, in fact it devalues the contribution of women by making it invisible. This tendency is not universal, Carlo Cipolla in his history of preindustrial Europe carefully documents the employment of women in what were thought to be exclusively male occupations and precisely those industries that experienced tremendous technological change during the period of industrialization (Cipolla 1980, 72–6). If as Fernand Braudel argues, technological change from the fifteenth to eighteenth centuries progressed through the slow accumulation and development of tricks of the trade, drawn from the experience of craftpersons (Braudel 1979, 431), and women were a significant presence among these craftpersons, then the predominant tendency to ascribe the influence of women on technology to the domestic sphere is unsustainable.

Progress is being made in correcting this tendency to exclude women from the history of technology (Trescott 1979; Stanley 1993, forthcoming). Within institutionalist literature, excepting Veblen, the conventions followed by Childe (i.e., neglect) seem to be the dominant mode in discussions of technology. As Jennings and Waller note institutionalists have not followed up on the potential for feminization of their approach present in their intellectual history or their epistemological and methodological foundations (Waller and Jennings 1990).

The second aspect of equity studies is the critical analysis of women's participation in the disciplinary discourse. While the prospects for feminist reconsideration of the history of technology are improving in terms of the number of women involved in the discipline and the improved character of the content of the discourse, economics presents the other extreme. Economics is a male discipline in that the overwhelming majority of academic practitioners are men. But in addition to being a male discipline, the dominant approach in economics, with its focus on individual choice and its disregard for culture, is hostile to feminism. Feminist theory has had a transformative influence on anthropology and sociology. Feminism is also making significant in-roads in political science. Economics is uniquely untouched by feminism among the social sciences. Orthodox economics has until recently had a studied disinterest in feminist theory. Heterodox schools of economic thought are more open to feminist theorizing, but their track record is not good with regard to integrating feminist insights into the main body of theorizing within the heterodox traditions — it remains women's work (Hartmann 1981; Waller and Jennings 1990, Greenwood 1984, 1988).

It appears that in both the history of technology and in institutionalist thought there is considerable room for more work in recovering the contributions of women and in opening both areas of discourse to women.

The Use and Abuse of Technology

This is an odd topic for this chapter. If we refer to simply the use and abuse of technology in general, it is a topic of ongoing concern within the institutionalist literature. At an epistemological level the pragmatic and instrumentalist roots of institutionalism focus on the unity of inquiry, the life process, and valuation. Thus debates have raged within institutionalism about the theoretical role of technology in institutionalism (Bush 1987; Junker 1982, 1983).

But if we focus on the gendered character of the use and abuse of technology the literature is sparse. Among the specific issues that require more attention are: the gendered character of technology policy in a development context; the introduction of production techniques that have differential impacts on women; the introduction of reproduction technology and population policies; and environmental consequences of technology of particular concern to women.

Another way the social impact of technology is raised within institutionalism is in the exploration of the relationship of technology to progress. To get the gist of what I am referring to I want us to adopt a deconstructive stance regarding a prominent institutionalist text on technology. By this I mean I want you to consider this text, but you need to disregard both the author's intent and the hermeneutic discourse community within which the text was generated. Put simply, (re)consider this text as if you were a neoclassical economist completely unfamiliar with institutionalism. The text I want to (re)consider is *The Theory of Economic Progress* by C. E. Ayres.

For the casual, uninitiated reader the question of whether institutionalists associate improved technology with progress is settled in the affirmative by the end of the third sentence of the forward of the 1962 edition of Ayres' book. Ayres writes:

> The theme of this book is a very simple one. It is that human progress consists in finding out how to do things, finding out how to do more things, and finding out how to do all things better. If the question is asked whether some things are not better left unlearned, the answer is No...(Ayres 1978, xiii).

Ayres immediately begins clarifying his notion of technology as a process of human behavior rather than the growth of tools and tool skills, and tends to maintains this stance throughout the text, *but* a processual view of human behavior is an alien concept to the naive reader. Unless you have a sophisticated understanding of cultural processes, Ayres seems to equate technological change with progress.

Later, in the chapter entitled 'Technology and Progress', Ayres makes the instrumentalist argument that progress is not the attainment of a final end, but instead should be conceived of as a process (Ayres 1978, 122). Then as an example he immediately puts forth this analysis of the technological process:

> But the analysis of technological process by students of mechanical invention and of the history of science and the arts is already sufficient to indicate the existence in all culture of a dynamic force, a phase of culture which is in itself and of its own character innovational, one in which change is continuous and cumulative and always in the same direction, that of more numerous and more complex technological devises (Ayres 1978, 123).

This analysis is preceded by comments like: 'For the tool-combination principle is indeed a law of progress' (Ayres 1978, 119).

The consequences of these observations are two-fold. First, a reasonable reader could conclude that Ayres is arguing that technological advance (understood in a static sense of the growth of tools and techniques) is progress. And second, but equally as important, that the source of progress is science, mechanical invention and industrial evolution — all, as feminist historians of technology and philosophers of science have argued, are androcentric concepts (Rothschild 1988, passim).

Ayres contributes to, through his failure to dispute and by employing language and usage that reinforces gendered understandings of science and technology, an important gendered cultural perception or understanding that essentially attributes human progress to male contributions to humankind. In this sense institutionalists abuse the concept of technology, at least to those who encounter their discourse from outside the institutionalist hermeneutic discourse community — which is the vast majority of humanity.

The Selection of Problematics

The selection of problematics involves the decision as to what aspects or parts of reality warrant attention. What is of sufficient importance or interest to be regarded as worthy of inquiry? The question we will address is: Are the activities or areas of inquiry chosen by scholars, where inquiry is funded by external sources or reviewed by peer committees, or simply chosen on the basis of accepted (but unexplored) disciplinary norms or boundaries, significantly affected by gender?

This question, while generally ignored by institutionalists (Waller and Jennings 1990; Greenwood 1984, 1988), has been addressed rather thoroughly by feminist historians of technology and science (Harding 1986, 1991; Tuana 1989). Since it is impossible within the context of this chapter to actually explore the empirical incidence of such problems in institutional economics, we will focus on the analyses of feminist historians to shed light on the problem. Certain categories of phenomena are socially considered important, others are considered less important. The form this sorting often takes is, not surprisingly, a categorization schema employing a series of dualisms such as:

masculine	/	feminine
technology	/	crafts
mechanical	/	domestic
economic	/	household
public	/	private

Those categories on the left are socially important, those on the right represent the mundane. The equating of the household with the private and feminine serves to keep women's work, and their contributions to technological development invisible. The terms domestic and crafts are used to describe the same activity; technology (tools and skills), technological aspects of behavior, and valuational processes that characterize the male-technological-mechanical activity — though the mechanical innovations of domestic-craft activity are often ignored. The cultural significance of the images these terms evoke is important. Technology and mechanic bring to mind sweat, oil, and the production of truly important stuff such as steel, electricity, and buildings (never mind lemon-scented trash bags, multicolored cellophane wrap, etc.). Domestic and crafts evoke cute embroidered pillows, doilies and holiday centerpieces (never mind food production and storage, budgeting, transportation, child rearing, and endless household maintenance).

Autumn Stanley has addressed the selection of problematics in the history of technology. She argues that the very definition of technology would change from what men do to what people do. And that the definition of what constituted significant technology would change in a feminist history of technology. She argues there would be two interim changes as part of this process. First, she notes that the classification of women's inventions would change. She notes that the digging stick, most likely a women's invention, is overlooked as an early use of the lever — a mechanical device. She notes that the potter's wheel, the spindle whorl, and the rotary quern are overlooked as early developments of mechanized continuous rotary motion. The quern (grain mill) is among the earliest known developments of the mechanical crank. Early cosmetics are overlooked as chemical inventions. Women's contributions to the development of furniture, storage space, and room dividers are ignored as major architectural innovations. These miscategorizations and the resulting devaluation of these contributions would be corrected. Second, she argues that a feminist history of technology would correct the historical record to include the omitted contributions (or contributions erroneously assigned to men — usually a husband or brother) of women to many inventions (Stanley 1983, 5–6).

Reading Technology As a Text

In the section on the use and abuse of technology we read Ayres to see what he might communicate to an audience that viewed his arguments through a lens significantly different than that of an institutionalist trained in the Veblen-Ayres tradition. The purpose of this was to give us a different perspective on a familiar work. Reading technology as a text requires a similar exercise, but the lens we choose is one that focuses on the presence or absence of gender preconceptions, language, and conceptual apparatus in the text.

It is impractical to do such an analysis in this chapter. However I think there are four questions to focus upon when reading institutionalists' writing on technology:

1. Is the treatment of technology gender-conscious? Do we make an effort to address gender in technology as Veblen did? Or do we ignore gender?

2. Are the metaphors employed in our description of technology, technological processes, scientific inquiry and instrumental valuation gendered, importing unconscious gender meanings into our analysis?

3. Do we implicitly or explicitly accept and use dualistic constructions, particularly those with important gender consequences, such as: public/private, masculine/feminine, technology/craft, economy/household?

4. Do we overlook questions either because they *are* of interest or importance to women or, because they *are not* of interest to men?

In many ways what is absent from institutional texts is as important as what is in them, because to overlook something is to ignore and devalue it.

But of more importance is what may be theoretically overlooked. In institutional theory technological processes are seen as the source of the solutions to problems. It is often argued that ceremonial aspects of behavior, rationalized by tradition, inhibit the adoption of newly developed solutions. Moreover, it is ceremonial aspects of behavior, and their underlying structure of myth and legend, that legitimizes invidious distinctions in status systems. It would seem within this framework that the adoption of a new technological solution that made a person more productive, relieved a considerable burden, and made a commercial enterprise more profitable and efficient in both the cost and technical sense, would not lead to a diminution of status of the person adopting it. Though it would be likely for a technological advance that would bring these benefits and a reduction in status to be resisted.

In a delightfully titled paper 'The Barn is His, The House is Mine: Agricultural Technology and Sex Roles' Corlann G. Bush shows that the mechanization of agriculture, especially the order of mechanization, reduced the significance and status of women's work in the Palouse region (northern Idaho and eastern Washington). The introduction of mechanized farm equipment prior to the introduction of electricity and household appliances into the farmhouse, eliminated the need for large numbers of farm laborers requiring room and board, and the resulting management of large-scale budgeting, cooking, cleaning, and household services on these farms. The women still provided these services on a smaller scale, but the survival and profitability of the enterprise was no longer dependent upon these services. Bush argues that the reduction in scale and complexity reduced the crucialness of the women's work to the enterprise, thereby lowering their status (Bush 1982). Thus technological innovation was not the unmixed blessing for rural women that conventional accounts have portrayed.

Bush's analysis doesn't contradict the theoretical schema of institutional analysis, but it certainly presents a more complex view of the interaction of technology and status than most institutionalists would think of at first blush. Moreover, conventional accounts of the introduction of mechanized farm implements and electrical appliances overlooked the impact on women because they were not looking for it. Whether the good old days really were awful, as some institutionalists are fond of pointing out, is really an open question — it depends on who you are. It is just conceivable that some women in the Palouse preferred the highly valued work with the recognition of their contribution to the economic and social wellbeing of their family and community, to being relegated to a lifetime of chauffeuring their children to after-school activities.

Reading technology as a text requires acknowledgement that all inquiry is value-driven as institutionalists have always argued. The constituent preanalytic assumptions of institutionalism systematically brings some aspects of reality into the foreground of the analysis, while ignoring or deemphasizing other aspects. This could lead to systematic oversight. When the preanalytic 'lens' is changed something may still be overlooked, but possibly some aspects of reality, previously overlooked, would become apparent. Of course, some of the previously suppressed aspects or some other aspects will be omitted with the new 'lens' — every 'lens' has its flaws. The reason for changing 'lenses' or perspective is simple: you don't find what you're not looking for, and you don't answer questions you aren't asking. I would suggest that many theoretical questions need to be re-asked and explored through the lens of gender in institutionalism.

Epistemological Concerns

The final aspect of Jennings' framework addresses the epistemological concerns raised by reconsidering technology from a feminist perspective. I think there are (at least) two related epistemological concerns that arise from a feminist reconsideration of technology in institutionalism. Possibly most important is understanding that the technological process is part of a cultural life process that is both lived and indistinguishable as a separate part of the reality by the individuals involved. People neither identify nor live a life where they can differentiate between behavior warranted by matter-of-fact knowledge or traditionally warranted behavior. We do not distinguish part of our behavior as governed by 'facts' and the other part as governed by silly superstition. The concept of technology is an *artificial* cut in reality to make it tractable for inquiry.

But to only consider concepts as simplifications of reality is to naively ignore the fact that intellectual constructs, like technology, once employed take on social significance beyond their role as a simplifying construct. Technology is an important cultural symbol. If technology does not cause progress, it certainly is an important and gendered symbolic representation of progress. This has important consequences for institutionalists because technology is a central concept in institutional theory. Institutionalists must take care to describe and differentiate the behavior and activities that we identify as the technological process. Our criteria for labelling aspects of behavior as technological or instrumental must be explicit, as must the criteria employed for labelling other aspects of behavior or activity as ceremonial or traditional in particular and as non-technology in general.

Moreover the images that technology evokes are profoundly male social images. These male social images are part of the symbolic meaning of technology in this culture. The continued use of this construct in inquiry and scholarly discourse will require that we be more careful about our use of the term. Note that the evocation of cultural symbols (even when unintentional) by affecting the understanding of the audience alters the meaning of the inquiry and discourse or limits it to a very small, select, and ultimately insignificant audience. Either you communicate with the larger population or you limit your discourse to being comprehensible only to other institutionalists (who are likely to agree with you anyway) thereby limiting the impact of your discourse. Preaching to the choir may be self-satisfying and confidence building for a short period of time, but ultimately it wins no converts.

Once the ontological ambiguity of the technological process is realized, feminist insights raise new questions. Consider the following conjunction of three elements of our feminist reconsideration of technology taken together: 1) If we expand our current understanding of technology and technological processes to include those domestic and craft behaviors that have been excluded in androcentric accounts: 2) And if as feminist epistemologies suggest current understandings of the nature of science are androcentric and require expansion to include so-called feminine modes of knowledge seeking and inquiry — including recognizing the role and legitimacy of intuition and fantasy in invention and discovery: 3) And if institutionalists' concept of technology intends to include the process of inquiry that generates the tools and skills, and the valuation processes which are part of that process of inquiry: Then an expanded feminist category of technology should include the feminist's understandings of epistemology, including the so-called (using the gendered pejorative term) irrational aspects of alternative feminist epistemological approaches. This argument suggests that these three alterations in our understanding of technology would result in a conception of the technological process that is either all-inclusive, literally becoming undifferentiated from the life process, or confounded with the non-technological aspects of behavior it is supposed to differentiate among.   Put simply, if the technological process is really the application of all human intelligence to provisioning, then isn't the technological process identical to the life process itself?

I would suggest that the technological process is not the life process. I would argue that the life process is richer and more complex. But to make this argument convincingly, the technological process must be demarcated much more carefully than it has been so far.

Conclusions

If institutionalism is to become a feminist economics — and I believe it must — we will reconsider our theory and concepts with special attention to gender and we must be willing to change our theory and concepts as a result of that reconsideration. This brief exploration of the concept of technology suggests two major tasks that will both involve significant changes. First a more thorough reconsideration and redefinition (literally a reconstruction) of the technological process is necessary. It must address the following questions: What aspects of behavior are included and what aspects of behavior are excluded from the category 'the technological process'? What are the criteria for inclusion and exclusion of aspects of behavior from the category? What is the rationale for these criteria? To not answer these questions is to arbitrarily divide human understanding dualistically into categories of white magic (good) and black magic (bad).

The second change will be that the meaning of the Veblenian dichotomy must be reconsidered. Since the dichotomy is made up of categories that are themselves social constructions and include the social meanings and symbols they evoke in *our* culture, the use of the Veblenian dichotomy as either a starting point of analysis, or as the central analytic tool of the Veblen-Ayres branch of institutionalism is unsustainable.

The starting point of institutional analysis will be with a careful description and analysis of the cultural processes that organize human provisioning activity. Like Veblen, we must construct categories that assist in organizing what we have learned and described into understandable and comprehensible form. Having constructed categories for the particular society or activity under scrutiny, then generalized schemata like the Veblenian dichotomy may be useful in extending our understanding or drawing generalizations. But to assume so is to limit ourselves to one set of 'lenses' that may incorporate the unconscious preanalytic preconceptions that include and project the status system of our society. This is unsustainable in institutionalism, and certainly contrary to the intent of a radical institutionalism.

References

Ayres, C.E. (1978), *The Theory of Economic Progress*, 3rd edn, Kalamazoo, MI: New Issues Press.

Bordo, Susan (1987), *The Flight to Objectivity*, Albany: State University of New York Press.

Braudel, Fernand (1979), *The Structure of Everyday Life*, v.1, (trans. S. Reynolds) New York: Harper and Row.

Bush, Corlann (1982), 'The Barn is His, The House is Mine: Agricultural Technology and Sex Roles' in G. Daniels and M. Rose, eds. *Energy and Transport*, Beverly Hills: Sage Publications.

Bush, Paul (1987), 'Theory of Institutional Change', *Journal of Economic Issues*, 21(3).

Childe, V. Gordon (1951), *Man Make Himself*, New York: New American Library.

Cipolla, Carlo (1980), *Before the Industrial Revolution: European Society and Economy*, 1000–1700, 2nd edn, New York: Norton.

Greenwood, Daphne (1984), 'The Economic Significance of "Women's Place" in Society', *Journal of Economic Issues*, 18 (3).

Greenwood, Daphne (1988) 'A Comment on *Evolutionary Economics I*: Foundations of Institutionalist Thought', *Journal of Economic Issues*, 22 (1).

Hamilton, David (1986), 'Technology and Institutions are Neither', *Journal of Economic Issues*, 20 (2).

Harding, Sandra (1986), *The Science Question in Feminism*, Ithaca: Cornell University Press.

Harding, Sandra (1991), *Whose Science? Whose Knowledge?* Ithaca: Cornell University Press.

Hartmann, Heidi (1981), 'The Unhappy Marriage of Marxism and Feminism: Towards a More Progressive Union' in Lydia Sargent, ed. *Women and Revolution*, Boston: South End Press.

Jennings, Ann (1992), 'Not the Economy' in W. Dugger and W. Waller, eds. *The Stratified State*, Armonk, NY: M.E. Sharpe.

Jennings, Ann (1993a), 'Feminism' in G. Hodgson, W. Samuels and M. Tool, eds. *Handbook of Institutional and Evolutionary Economics*, Aldershot: Edward Elgar Publishing Ltd.

Jennings, Ann (1993b), 'Public or Private? Institutional Economics and Feminism', in Marianne A. Ferber and Julia A. Nelson, eds. *Beyond 'Economic Man': Feminist Theory and Economics*, Chicago: University of Chicago Press.

Jennings, Ann and William Waller (1990a), 'Constructions of Social Hierarchy', *Journal of Economic Issues*, 24 (2).

Jennings, Ann and William Waller (1990b), 'Rethinking Class and Social Stratification' paper presented at the 1990 annual meeting of the Southern Economics Association.

Junker, Louis (1982), 'The Ceremonial–Instrumental Dichotomy in Institutional Analysis', *The American Journal of Economics and Sociology*, 41(2).

Junker, Louis (1983), 'The Conflict Between the Scientific-Technological Process and Malignant Ceremonialism', *The American Journal of Economics and Sociology*, 42 (3).

Mayhew, Anne (1987), 'Culture: Core Concept Under Attack', *Journal of Economic Issues*, 21 (2).

Mumford, Lewis (1966), *The Myth of the Machine*, New York: Harcourt, Brace and World.

Rothschild, Joan (1983), 'Introduction: Why *Machina Ex Dea*?' in J. Rothschild, ed. *Machina Ex Dea*, New York: Pergamon Press.

Rothschild, Joan (1988), *Teaching Technology From A Feminist Perspective*, New York: Pergamon Press.

Samuels, Warren (1990), 'The Self-Referentiality of Thorstein Veblen's Theory of the Preconception of Economic Science', *Journal of Economic Issues*, 24 (3).

Stanley, Autumn (1983), 'Women Hold Up Two-Thirds of the Sky' in J. Rothschild, ed. *Machina Ex Dea*, New York: Pergamon Press.

Stanley, Autumn (forthcoming), *Mothers of Invention*, Metuchen, NJ: Scarecrow Press.

Swaney, James (1989), 'Our Obsolete Technology Mentality', *Journal of Economic Issues*, 23 (2).

Tool, Marc R. (1979), *The Discretionary Economy: A Normative Theory of Political Economy*, Santa Monica, CA: Goodyear Publishing Co.

Trescott, Martha Moore (1979), *Dynamos and Virgins Revisited: Women and Technological Change in History*, Metuchen, NJ: Scarecrow Press.

Tuana, Nancy (1989), *Feminism and Science*, Bloomington, IN: Indiana University Press.

Veblen, Thorstein (1964), *The Instinct of Workmanship*, New York: Augustus M. Kelley.

Veblen, Thorstein (1990), *The Place of Science in Modern Civilization*, New Brunswick, New Jersey: Transactions Publishers.

Waller, William (1982) 'The Evolution of the Veblenian Dichotomy', *Journal of Economic Issues*, 16 (3).

Waller, William (1993), 'The Veblenian Dichotomy and Its Critics' in G. Hodgson, W. Samuels and M. Tool, eds. *Handbook of Institutional and Evolutionary Economics*, Aldershot: Edward Elgar Publishing Ltd.

Waller, William and Ann Jennings (1990), 'On the Possibility of a Feminist Economics', *Journal of Economic Issues*, 24 (2).

Waller, William and Ann Jennings (1991), 'A Feminist Institutionalist Reconsideration of Karl Polanyi', *Journal of Economic Issues*, 25 (2).

Waller, William and Linda Robertson (1991), 'Valuation as Discourse and Process', *Journal of Economic Issues*, 25 (4).

White, Lynn, Jr. (1968), *Machina Ex Deo*, Cambridge: MIT Press.

5. Feminism and Science Reconsidered: Insights from the Margins

Paulette Olson

Institutionalists have taken a strong position in their writings against the ahistorical, reductionistic and universalizing approach of orthodox economics. They have been less concerned with addressing the racist, sexist and classist biases inherent in mainstream theory and methodology. A notable exception, however, is the work of those who identify themselves as radical institutionalists. These writers have begun to address the social constructions of race, class and gender and how these constructions have been used to legitimate various forms of inequality. Much of this work builds upon the methodological insights of feminist theorists whose stated political agenda is the elimination of all systems of domination and oppression.

This essay extends the boundaries of radical institutionalism by examining the *insights from the margins*; namely, the postcolonial critique of western humanism. The most profound contribution of this critique is the exposition of a constituted *otherness* embedded in western scholarship. Through a process of othering, nonwestern peoples and their cultures are represented as inferior, backwards and deviant in relation to a superior, progressive and civilized West. Such a representation has had serious material consequences, for instance, the annihilation of indigenous Indian groups in Brazil in the name of progress and development. By exposing the relationship between power, representation and science, the postcolonial critique forces us to confront our own privileged position as social theorists.

The discussion will originate with a review of some crucial insights offered by the feminist critique of science. In the next section, this critique will be reconsidered and reconceptualized in order to account for the role of power in the production of social knowledge. The framework for this discussion draws from the postcolonial critique of western humanist thought. This literature builds upon the work of Edward Said. In his book, *Orientalism*, Said traces the origins, development and material/political effects of the intellectual construction he calls Orientalism. The cultural and ideological legacy of Orientalism will be examined in the following sections. The context will be a discussion of development economics and feminist scholarship on Third World women. A review of this literature allows us to reconstruct our understanding of the social and historical processes that continue to privilege the monolithic, authoritative voice of western science at the expense of nonwestern peoples and their cultures. Our primary purpose is to synthesize this literature and to demonstrate that it is consistent with and contributes to the stated academic and political agenda of radical institutionalism.

The Feminist Critique of Science

In this section, the feminist and science debate will be critically reviewed.[1] We argue that although the prevailing myths of objectivity and value-neutrality in the sciences have been seriously challenged, many western feminists reveal an inability to eliminate these assumptions from their own scientific practice. This failure and its political implications will be emphasized later in the chapter in our discussion of feminist scholarship on Third World women.

One of the most significant contributions of the feminist critique of science is the importance of using gender as an analytical category in order to expose the deeply androcentric biases in the practice of science. This focus on gender has resulted in the reinscription of women into history, theoretical deconstructions of mainstream science revealing the various manifestations of the androcentrism inherent in scientific theory and practice and the reconstruction of science along feminist lines. The feminist reconstructive effort has included an articulation of various feminist epistemologies, hyphenated identities and associated frameworks and feminist philosophical works, among others.[2]

The primary theme which emerges from these writings is that science is socially constructed and as such embodies a history and a political agenda. In brief, these scholars document how science emerged in Western Europe as a central institution replacing the authority of the Catholic church in matters of social truths; this corresponded to the rise of capitalism, rapid technological change and European imperialism. Western science provided the foundation for western humanist thought legitimizing knowledge which systematically privileged elite white males of European descent, particular ways of knowing such as rational and mechanistic thought, and western values and practices (Harding 1986).

By documenting the political and historical context of science, these writers challenge the possibility of a pure objective knowledge. Indeed, the claim to scientific objectivity has been exposed as masking the relationship between science and political power through the creation of a fictional subjective/objective dualism which has served to justify various forms of oppression and the destruction of the natural world (Merchant 1980).

Feminist discourse on science has also attacked the pervasive use of hierarchical dualisms which serve to construct reality along gender lines. This feminist critique identifies the set of gendered dualisms employed in the practice of science; these include reason versus emotion, culture versus nature, universal versus particular, objective versus subjective. Within western culture, we understand these dualisms as fundamentally hierarchical whereby the former, associated with science, rationality and the masculine is consistently privileged over the latter, corresponding to the nonscientific, the irrational and the feminine. This assignment of gender metaphors to social reality results in a partial, dichotomized and decontextualized vision of the world whereby deviations from the male norm are considered inferior (Harding and Hintikka 1983).

Another related concern expressed in the feminist literature is the importance of accounting for race, class, ethnicity, and culture as well as gender within social inquiry (Moraga and Anazaldua 1983; hooks 1990). Gender as a conceptual category clearly does not fully capture the complex web of oppression and inequality defined by an individual's location in social reality. Consequently, some feminists offer an alternative definition of objectivity whereby they specify that, regardless of whether or not the research follows the scientific method, if the research is explicitly antiracist, anticlassist and antisexist, this is an objectivity increasing move. In other words, it is possible to reduce the distortions of vision caused by racism, sexism and classism and thereby come closer to a more correct vision. As Sandra Harding has argued:

> ...it is only coercive values — racism, classism, sexism — that deteriorate objectivity; it is participatory values — antiracism, anticlassism, and antisexism — that decrease the distortions and mystifications in our culture's explanations and understandings. One can think of these participatory values as preconditions, constituents, or a reconception of objectivity (Harding 1986, 249).

Clearly, the values embodied in this manifesto are progressive and the contributions of these feminists are substantial. However, there are two major limitations which exist by virtue of the way in which the parameters of the debates have been framed. First, these arguments are constructed at an extremely abstract level; and secondly, they remain within the confines of western humanist discourse. Because of these limitations, the historical and political context of the relations of power and the role of the intellectual in this scheme are denied. In order to illustrate how we might transcend these limitations while retaining the valuable insights and crucial moral commitment of western feminists, we will reframe the relevant debates using the *insights from the margins*.

Insights From the Margins

The most fundamental attack on the methodology and implications of science has been launched by the postcolonial critique of western humanism. These oppositional voices come from a variety of disciplines — from physics to the culturally-marginalized sciences of sociology, literary criticism, anthropology, cultural history, Near Eastern studies and all those contributing to the *Bulletin of Concerned Asian Scholars*.[3] These oppositional voices highlight the eurocentricism and ethnocentricism of scientific theory and practice by questioning the metaprinciples foundational to western science and the political projects they support. Common to all of these oppositional strategies is a critique of the centered consciousness of western humanism. Specifically, these writers problematize the discourse of western humanism which universalizes what is particular to Western Europe and the United States. According to these scholars, humanism as a western ideological and political project has repeatedly defined western culture and history as the *human* civilization against which all *non-human* societies are judged. Symptomatic of this discourse is the representation of nonwestern peoples and cultures as different and consequently, inferior, thus legitimizing western superiority and centeredness. Rejecting this centered discourse, these oppositional voices offer us detailed insights into the complex realities of nonwestern peoples and their cultures through contextualized comparative analysis.

A first encounter with this literature has a destabilizing effect for those of us immersed in the western humanist tradition. These writers are consciously and admittedly political and therefore, by definition, their writings make us uncomfortable and shake the very foundations of our thinking which is mired in neutrality and objectivity. Instead of appealing to some central authority (e.g., science), methodological consistency or scientific objectivity to gain legitimacy, these writers find commonality in their politically motivated discourse against the master narratives of western humanism. Where they find commonality is not at some abstract level, but in their united political strategy against dominating, coercive systems of knowledge. Their work is grounded in the concrete daily struggles of dominated peoples. Whether writing about the civil rights movement in the United States or the Chipko movement in India, these writers give dignity and voice to those whose interests have been previously marginalized, silenced or ignored. Their common political agenda is to create a space for *others* to speak on their own terms and to challenge all hegemonic frameworks that insist on privileging western humanism (and all other *centered* discourses) and on the secondariness of nonwestern traditions. Among the most fundamental challenges emerging from this scholarship is a critique of the discourse of Orientalism and its political and ideological legacy — the project of development.

The Postcolonial Critique of Orientalism

Those critical of the concept of development take as their starting point the historical relationship between western (i.e., Europe and North America) and nonwestern societies — a relationship based on the control and domination of the latter by the former. Between the seventeenth and nineteenth centuries, the so-called underdeveloped and developing countries were brought into a world system of European-dominated financial, political and economic relationships via colonial conquest. As discussed in more detail below, one important aspect of this world system was the establishment of Orientalism — a set of ideological and intellectual constructions justifying European imperialism. The legacy of Orientalism inherent in late twentieth century scientific and policy approaches to development constitutes the heart of the postcolonial critique.

Much of the postcolonial critique of western humanism in general and the project of development in particular builds upon the insights of Edward Said in his classic book *Orientalism*. According to Said, during the nineteenth century, the Orient was rediscovered by Europe in the sense that European imperialism expanded into the Orient providing the basis for a shift in Europeans' perceptions of non-European societies. This shift was the result of both internal and external forces. European society was, itself, experiencing rapid technological, economic and political change. The introduction of new technologies, mass production enterprises and new financial organizations translated into European *success* abroad in the form of political and military intervention, economic exploitation and territorial expansion. Indeed, between 1815 and 1914, European colonial domination had expanded to approximately 85 percent of the earth's surface (Said 1979, 41). This *success* was presented as empirical proof of European superiority and Oriental inferiority.

This distinction gained greater authority with the emerging scientific disciplines of Indo-European philology, comparative anatomy, ethnology, anthropology, history and of course, economics. By 1850, every major university in Europe had a fully developed curriculum of oriental studies in at least one of these disciplines. Many asiatic societies and western governments began funding the travel and research of orientalist scholars (Said 1979, 191). Orientalist periodicals proliferated which, in turn, expanded *knowledge* about the Orient. Indeed, orientalist scholarship became science. Together the practitioners of science generated a new view of non-European societies that increasingly differentiated Europeans from non-European *others*. A whole system of ideas, definitions, explanations and representations was developed to legitimate the intellectual and cultural authority and superiority of the Occident (West) over the Orient (East).

This process of othering was ideologically expressed in nineteenth-century orientalist literature and social theory through a set of hierarchical dualisms. For instance, European examples of *profitable, dynamic* and *efficient* economic institutions were contrasted with the *static, unorganized* and *unproductive* economic lives of Asian cultivators and African pastoralists. European religion and theology was contrasted with *primitive superstitions*. Likewise, *rational* forms of constitutional government and the *progressive* nature of social institutions of Western Europe were the standard by which non-European laws, customs and social/familial structures were judged *backward, traditional* or *stagnant*. Across the political spectrum, from John Stewart Mill to Karl Marx, European *experts* engaged in an intellectual discourse of difference and superiority as part of the centered consciousness of western humanism. Through this discourse, Europeans learned that the Orient was *frozen in antiquity*; with scientific development, Europe would march on leaving the Orient behind. The implication was that the burden of progress rested on the West to *assist* the East.

These intellectual constructions were further corroborated by works of fiction and by eye-witness accounts of colonial administrators, journalists, military personnel, explorers, missionaries and travelers of their encounters in the Orient (Said 1979, 192). Images of exotic peoples, primitive customs, savage behavior and decadence were interwoven with *expert* accounts to construct social knowledge which defined and controlled the representation of the Orient. This curious combination of images and scholarship reflected the power relations between the Orient and the Occident within the context of nineteenth-century imperialism. Indeed, the Orient was made the *silent other* because the West was far more powerful militarily and culturally than the Orient. As Said explains: the cultural strength of the West was '...its will to power over the Orient' and the simultaneous inability of the Orient '...to resist the projects, images, or mere descriptions devised for it' (Said 1979, 94). Since it was perceived that intellectual and cultural authority resided in the West, western expertise about orientals — their cultures, histories, traditions, languages, race, character and potential — became a truism. The Orient was considered incapable of representing itself. As Marx once said: 'They cannot represent themselves; they must be represented'.[4] Only the oriental scholar had the authority and power to rescue nonwestern peoples from their '...obscurity, alienation, and strangeness which he himself had properly distinguished' (Said 1979, 121).

Central to this nineteenth-century construction of otherness was the representation of non-European women. If non-European societies were considered backward, primitive or decadent, then women in these societies were considered disadvantaged relative to their European counterparts. Legal, social and religious practices such as polygamy in Africa, foot-binding in China, harems in the Middle-East or widow-burning in India were not systematically analyzed by the *experts*. Rather, these practices were judged on the basis of appearances only and depicted as primitive customs and traditions which contributed to their oppressed status and restricted them from being like western women. Serious investigations into the material circumstances or specific context of women in particular societies were nonexistent in nineteenth-century scholarship. The lives and roles of non-European women were simply considered inferior relative to the lives and roles of European women because of their location in societies designated as inferior. To reinforce the European sense of superiority, anthropological theory, fictional writings and visual images all contributed to a set of stereotypes characterizing non-European women as different from and inferior to white, middle-class, Christian, European women. The depiction of sexually-charged slave girls and black mammies under slavery repeatedly appeared in the abolitionist literature. Cartoons and drawings of semi-nude black women, Middle-Eastern dancers and sexually available Polynesian women coupled with literary descriptions of African witch-women, ignorant village midwives and mysterious harems combined to create stereotypical images and fantasies for western male consumption (de

Groot 1991a, 113–15; de Groot 1991b, 89–128).

One important consequence of this stereotyping was that it precluded a contextualized comparative analysis of European and non-European women and thereby, served the strategies of domination. By creating a set of cultural and ideological images, scholars, journalists, artists and missionaries kept the realities of non-European women's experiences under colonialism hidden from their European audience. By emphasizing hierarchical differences between European and non-European women based on white, Christian, middle-class values, the stereotypical images of non-European women as exotic specimens, sexual objects and helpless victims denied the positive aspects of women's position in non-European societies. For instance, the fact that Egyptian women had the ability to defend their property and inheritance rights in a court of law was not discussed because it would have challenged the European sense of superiority, in general, and the gender relations of power in Victorian Europe, in particular (de Groot 1991a, 116). Thus, from a political perspective, the ideological power of portraying non-European women as oppressed victims was significant; European paternalistic control of the colonies was perceived as an improvement in the lives of non-European women.

Only the West understood and accepted these social truths about the Orient. As Said explains:

> That Orientalism makes sense at all depends more on the West than on the Orient...(T)hese representations rely upon institutions, traditions, conventions, agreed-upon codes of understanding for their effects, not upon a distant and amorphous Orient (Said 1979, 22).

Those designated as orientals understood themselves as something different from what the West said about them. However, given the nineteenth-century mindset, any response by orientals to Orientalism would have been interpreted as absurd. Those who resisted the dominant ideological, political and cultural constructions of the Orient were muted; their histories were denied in the West. What was taken as social truth was the representation of the Orient by the colonizers:

> Truth, in short, becomes a function of learned judgment, not of the material itself, which in time seems to owe even its existence to the Orientalist...His Orient is not the Orient as it is, but the Orient as it has been Orientalized (Said 1979, 67, 104).

The Legacy of Orientalism

Building upon Said's critique of Orientalism, the *insights from the margins* deconstruct postcolonial scholarship and reveal its complicity with post-war neocolonialism. Among the most fundamental challenges emerging from this scholarship is the postcolonial critique of development. What remains problematic in development discourse is the uncritical acceptance of western progress and superiority and the unquestioned belief that the West is somehow *helping* those less fortunate than ourselves to *develop*. In the next section, an example of the hegemonic discourse of development and its political implications will be presented. And in the following section, several examples of western feminist scholarship will be reviewed to elucidate the analytical and methodological traps involved in making Third World women *visible* in the development process.[5]

The Postcolonial Critique of Development

The concept of development is widely understood to signify a teleological process which embodies progress, economic growth and material betterment. The field of development economics has contributed to this understanding. It was a post-World War II innovation associated with decolonization of much of Africa, the newly won political independence of many Arab and Asian countries and the emerging Cold War which, in turn, triggered both United States hegemonic aspirations and paternalistic interests in those regions (Hunt 1989, 51, 96). Regardless of their theoretical perspective, development economists shared a vision of what constituted a model society to which nonwestern societies aspired. That universal model was, of course, the industrialized West.[6] The underlying assumption was that *developing* or *underdeveloped* countries deserved these labels because they were far behind on the same growth path taken by the more *developed* economies of the West. That is, developed countries were superior, advanced and mature examples to these less fortunate countries by virtue of the very definition of the field of development economics. It followed, therefore, that only the West possessed the economic and technical advances necessary for *take-off* into self-sustained economic growth. As the theoretical categories of *pioneers* and *latecomers* made clear, science and expertise resided in the West: nonwestern societies had the problems, western science had the answers.

Central to the construction of otherness in development discourse is the representation of Third World people as *social* deviants. Indeed, economists and other development experts have devoted much research to identifying the cultural and social *obstacles to development*. As Lisa Peattie observes:

> The economists worried about how to develop entrepreneurship, a disciplined labor force, a pattern of economically productive investment, in nations whose existing cultural and social patterns seemed inappropriate to maximizing the pursuit of material prosperity (Peattie 1981, 38).

This concern received support from anthropologists, sociologists, plant geneticists, psychologists and other development experts (George 1988, 259–60). Together the shared claims and policies of western science reinforced the unquestioned belief that nonwestern peoples and cultures were backward and inferior relative to the modern and technologically superior West (Joseph et al. 1988; Verhelst 1990).

The discourse on overpopulation serves as one example of this relationship between power and the production of knowledge. As part of the hegemonic discourse of development, demographers have identified overpopulation as the main cause for widespread poverty and starvation in the Third World (George 1988, 259). This universal social truth, in turn, legitimized contraceptive experimentation and the forced sterilization of Third World women. This targeting of Third World women and their reproductive roles elucidates the relationship between power, representation and science in two fundamental ways. First, birth *control* imported from the West targeted those with the least power to resist nationally-mandated policies, reinforcing western superiority. Second, the reductionistic focus on reproductive technologies as *the* solution to widespread starvation and poverty masks both the complexity of the problem and the failure of science to solve similar problems in the West. What can not be over-emphasized, and constitutes a crucial insight of the postcolonial critique, is that development issues are circumscribed by practical geopolitical interests of the post-industrialized West. In this case, the politics of overpopulation, obscured by an *objective* and *value-neutral* development discourse, exonerates the consumption behavior and investment patterns of the industrialized West that lead to ecological, cultural and social destruction in the non-West.

The Postcolonial Critique of Western Feminist Scholarship

Another field of research that elucidates the cultural and ideological legacy of Orientalism is western feminist scholarship on Third World women.[7] Through the dedicated work of feminist scholars, women have been *added to* the international development agenda. This agenda embodies a variety of approaches and ongoing debates about theoretical frameworks, policy directions and political strategies. The stated objective is global sisterhood. However, these good intentions and moral commitments are often undermined by the process of othering. The main analytical trap is initiated when *women* are incorrectly posited as a universally constructed category. That is, women constitute an oppressed group by virtue of their gender. Then to produce what Chandra Mohanty calls the *Third World difference*, they add on homogeneous images of Third World women (e.g., poor, uneducated, victimized, etc.). Finally, to complete the colonizing move of western humanism, this representation of Third World women is contrasted with the self-presentation of western women as modern, educated and having freedom to make their own decisions. That is, western feminists, in constructing the composite *other* simultaneously construct themselves as the norm or referent (Mohanty 1991, 55). Admittedly, contemporary feminist discourse does not possess the same authority as nineteenth-century Orientalism or the discourse of development, but it remains an important part of the ideological and cultural framework that participates in the colonization of nonwestern peoples under the guise of *objective* scientific research.

Following the publication of Ester Boserup's seminal work, *Women's Role in Economic Development*, development specialists became concerned with making Third World women *visible* in development theory and practice (Tinker 1990). The *women in development* (WID) literature sought to expose the androcentric biases in assumptions, theories and methodologies in the field of development. It was particularly critical of the gender-biased use of government statistics, the differential effects on women and men in the development process and how this process had relatively disadvantaged women, and the use of the concept *worker* to obscure the enormous work-load of Third World women (Waring 1988). These scholarly concerns coincided with the demands for equal opportunity by the 1960s women's movement in the West, the associated political agenda of liberal feminism in the United States and state-sponsored feminism associated with national independence abroad. Together these concerns influenced the policy agenda of the United Nations Decade for Women (1975–1985), which in turn, provided financial support and legitimacy for the WID agenda. The main goal of this international conference was to *integrate* women into the development process by recognizing their problems, needs and concerns.

Not unlike development economics, the basic premise of the WID discourse is development = economic progress. From this premise, western feminists make reductionistic, cross-cultural comparisons of the effects of development policies on Third World women. Based on western standards and criteria, feminist scholars evaluate whether development policies have positively or negatively affected women in Africa, Latin America, India or Asia. What is problematical is that the criteria by which these policies are evaluated are based on formula solutions predetermined by western standards. For example, can we necessarily conclude that Third World women will be *better off* with a factory job in an export processing zone? Clearly, this determination can not be made without a careful, contextual analysis of the complex lives of women in the Third World.

Chandra Mohanty's critique of Perdita Huston highlights the result of applying western standards (Mohanty 1991, 63). In Huston's investigation of Egypt, Kenya, Sudan, Tunisia, Sri Lanka and Mexico, she identifies a universal set of problems and needs expressed by women in these countries. To reinforce this universality, Huston asserts a cross-cultural, cross-class commonality among these women based on an observed value system in '...the importance they assign to family, dignity, and service to others' (Mohanty 1991, 64). And to complete the *colonizing move*, Huston claims that few, if any, women in these countries have *choices* or the *freedom to act*. Consequently, they require development assistance from the West. In Huston's analysis, the universality of gender is methodologically proven through the identification of a set of similar problems, needs and a shared value system applicable to a constructed homogeneous group — Third World women. The solution is, therefore, to incorporate women into the development process by giving them access to education, training, positions of authority, etc. The demands of liberal feminism in the West automatically become the goals of Third World women; a sort of global affirmative action.

What is problematical about this characterization of women in the Third World? First, the analytical strategy of universalizing women in the Third World denies the complex interaction between class, cultures, historical processes and ideological institutions. As Mohanty observes, it is highly unlikely that the problems and needs and, therefore, the interests and goals among African, Mexican and Indian women will be identical. Nor can a homogeneous set of problems, needs, interests or goals be assumed among urban versus rural, upper-class versus working-class in any one country or culture. Moreover, the prescription — western development — can not be expected to affect different groups of women in the same way (Mohanty 1991, 63).

Second, the use of universal categories such as African, Mexican or Indian women to describe their physical or geographical location is not inappropriate for certain purposes. However, what is inappropriate and what constitutes a colonizing move is the representation of Third World women as a homogeneous sociological group characterized by a common powerlessness. Once their helplessness (e.g., lack of choice and freedom) and the power of western feminists to assist them (e.g., in the form of western-style development) is established, the colonizing move is complete. It is here that the political and moral commitment by liberal feminists in the West to improve the lives of women in nonwestern societies falls short of its political agenda. Here they join with western scientific, literary and other scholarly discourse to construct images of a composite other — Third World women — as powerless victims in the global economy. The political effect of this colonizing move is to preclude the possibility of forging political alliances among women globally.

The stereotypical representations, explanations and definitions of Third World women as powerless victims are reinforced through various methodological strategies. Mohanty identifies three: the arithmetic method, the use of universal concepts and the use of universal dualisms. The arithmetic method is a simple exercise in quantitative technique. Data is gathered to support an 'agreed-upon code of understanding' in the West about the subordinate status of Third World women. For example, it has been observed that most muslim women in Saudi Arabia, Iran, Pakistan, India and Egypt wear veils. This empirical observation *adds up* to the universal fact that the sexuality of women in these countries is controlled by men (Mohanty 1991, 66). The mathematical skills of the scholar are not in question here. What is problematical is the analytical leap from the cultural practice of veiling — a quantifiable Third World difference — to an assertion of its universal significance in controlling women's sexuality. The conclusion, although consistent with other hegemonic discourse about muslim countries, is often at odds with social reality. As a strategy for studying women's oppression, the arithmetic method is inappropriate because it totally bypasses the concrete, historical meaning of the veil within various ideological, cultural and political contexts. Consequently, it distorts our understanding of the experiences of women different from ourselves. As Mohanty points out:

> Iranian middle-class women veiled themselves during the 1979 revolution to indicate solidarity with their veiled working-class sisters, while in contemporary Iran mandatory Islamic laws dictate that all Iranian women wear veils (Mohanty 1991, 67).

In the first historical context, wearing the veil was a symbol of resistance. In the second, it represented a coercive mandate from above. As this case makes clear, it is only on the basis of contextual and historically-specif ic analyses that we can develop a genuine understanding and respect for difference. Universalizing the oppression of muslim women by constructing a Third World difference (i.e., the veil) robs middle-class muslim women of their historic and political agency and thereby undermines any hope of global sisterhood. Indeed, the representation of muslim women by western feminists as universally oppressed by some *backward tradition* constitutes a colonizing move. This is clearly not grounds for global political unity.

The second methodological strategy employed by western feminists is to use concepts like the sexual division of labor, reproduction, marriage, the family, etc. to explain the universal exploitation of women without reference to cultural and historical context (Mohanty 1991, 67–8). For example, the sexual division of labor, at its most abstract level, implies that men and women are assigned different tasks. From empirical observation it can also be asserted that women are concentrated in the service sector in the economies of most countries. From this empirical proof of the sexual division of labor, it is often concluded that women's work is devalued relative to men's. Although a strong case for the latter can be made, the mere existence of the sexual division of labor does not constitute adequate proof. This method of argumentation fails because there is a confusion between description and explanation which occurs when the content and contextual meaning of work is not analyzed. Careful analysis will show that there is not always a simple causation from the sexual division of labor to the devaluation of women's work. Moreover, the devaluation of women's work is not synonymous with the devaluation of women. But only cultural and historical analysis at the level of everyday life can highlight this distinction. From a political perspective, it is important to understand that reducing various forms of oppression to a single, universal notion of patriarchy or male dominance through the use of abstractions creates a false sense of unity among women globally. For as Mohanty correctly argues: 'Beyond sisterhood there is still racism, colonialism and imperialism'! (Mohanty 1991, 68).

The third methodological strategy identified by Mohanty is the use of universal dualisms. The dualisms male/female and nature/culture and other gendered dualisms derived from these pairs are universally applied as organizational categories for understanding different cultures. Their *truth* is then substantiated through case studies. In this case, western dualistic constructions based on gender difference become generalizable to Third World women without specif ic contextual and historical consideration. As a result, the complex material realities, specific oppressions and political choices of Third World women are systematically ignored. The use of universal dualisms by western feminists constitutes another colonizing move. It obscures the distinction between those who are represented and those who are self-presented and thereby undermines a respect for genuine and important differences. The possibility of forming effective political strategies across women globally is, therefore, lost.

In sum, regardless of the methodological strategy employed by western feminist scholars, most assume women in the Third World as a homogeneous category of analysis. In particular, Third World women assume a victimized status prior to their entry into social relations.[8] Some form of patriarchy is presupposed whereby men and women are preconstituted in binary, oppositional terms. Regardless of racial, ethnic or class location, women are preconstituted as powerless and oppressed before they are placed within legal, religious, educational, familial and economic structures. Likewise, Third World men are preconstituted as possessing power and exercising that power through various structures and systems of male domination. That is, sexual difference is the main analytic category used to discuss social relations in the Third World. Once patriarchy is assumed as a universal category, the next analytical step is to create a Third World difference. Accordingly, legal, religious, educational, familial and economic structures are judged by western standards as either developing or underdeveloped. And not unlike nineteenth-century western discourse, contemporary feminist scholars create images of Third World women by characterizing them as religious, family-oriented, legal minors or illiterate. These ahistorical, stereotypical images, in turn, reinforce the assumption that Third World people are backward and uncivilized in contrast with the progressive and civilized West. It is in this colonizing move that power is exercised in western feminist discourse (Mohanty 1991, 55).

So what is problematical about these analytical and methodological strategies? Certainly, we are not questioning the humanitarian or moral commitment of western feminists. Rather we see the problem stemming from the unquestioned acceptance of western standards and values as superior and the associated paternalistic attitudes towards Third World peoples. By privileging the West over all *other* societies and cultures and characterizing all *others* as backward and ignorant, western feminists perpetuate and maintain authoritative and coercive systems of knowledge and thereby, uphold exploitative relations between peoples.

Conclusion

This essay has shown that not unlike nineteenth-century Orientalism, postcolonial scholarship has produced a body of knowledge that codifies nonwestern people as *others*. A cursory examination of the basic tenets and concepts central to development theory and feminist scholarship on Third World women underscores the pervasiveness of the imperialistic legacy in current academic discourse. Reductionistic labels such as *underdeveloped* or *traditional* are ideologically-loaded designations that are understood by a well-prepared western audience unlikely to question scientific *truth*. By muting the voices of nonwestern people, homogenizing their experiences and defining their differences as inferior, academic discourse legitimizes the cultural authority of the West.

Radical institutionalists interested in eliminating all systems of domination must join the *insights from the margins* and challenge the hegemonic discourse of western humanism by giving voice to those whose interests have been previously marginalized or ignored. Rather than defining the experience of *others* as abstract deviations from essentialized western norms, the starting point of economic inquiry must be the concrete, daily experiences, ideas and needs of marginalized people. Simply put, the current *view from above* must be replaced with a *view from below*. In the spirit of self-reflection and a concern with gaining a genuine understanding of people different from ourselves, we must relinquish the attitude of expert and adopt an attitude of student. Marginalized people must be allowed to become subjects of their own knowledge; interpreters of their own social reality. This is not to suggest that the insights of the researcher are without value. Indeed, any individual or society can be known by *outsiders* in different ways than they can know themselves. And this different perspective may indeed generate valuable insights. Instead, what is advocated here is an exchange of views based on mutual recognition and equal respect. By relinquishing our authority, we directly challenge the claims of scientific objectivity and expertise that insist on the subject's incapacity for self-representation and self-understanding — the main themes of both Orientalism and postcolonial scholarship.

Since we cannot deny our privileged role in the production of knowledge, we have a responsibility to seek a *better* understanding of marginalized peoples through contextual and comparative analysis at the level of everyday life. This understanding is *better* in the sense that it forces us to become aware of our own sexist, racist, classist and ethnocentric understanding of people different from ourselves, to recognize that their lives are as comprehensible, meaningful and valid as we believe our lives to be, and thus opens up the possibility of forging political alliances across race, class, gender and national boundaries. Thus the *radical* in institutionalism suggests a radical altering of the terms of economic discourse and the way research is currently conducted.

Notes

1. For an in depth review of the feminism and science debate see Perlich (1990).
2. For instance, see Harding (1986) for a discussion of standpoint, empiricist, and postmodern epistemologies; Jaggar and Rothenberg (1984) for a discussion of liberal, marxist, radical, and socialist feminist frameworks; and Diamond and Orenstein (1990) for a discussion of ecofeminism.
3. For instance, see Said (1979; Shiva (1989); Spivak (1989); Mohanty, Russo, and Torres (1991); also see Said (1985, 13–14) for an additional list of authors.
4. Quoted in Said (1979, xiii). For a discussion of the centeredness of Marxist thought see Solomon Namala, unpublished paper, 'A Deconstruction of Marxism and the Asiatic Mode of Production,' University of Utah, Department of Economics, 1991.
5. Here the term *Third World women* refers to women residing in the neocolonized or decolonized countries of Asia, Africa, and Latin America whose economic and political institutions have been changed by western colonization and domination.
6. The practice of development has not been without its critics during the post-war period. For example, dependency theorists, the world systems theorists, feminists and ecologists, have all criticized the particular forms of development. However, their analysis remains closely tied to the western humanist tradition. For example, Samir Amin claims that problems currently plaguing underdeveloped countries is the result of colonialism and argues for a delinking strategy. Again, both the problem and the solution lies in the West — external to the countries in question.
7. *Western feminism* refers to those who assume middle-class, urban culture as the norm and not merely those who identify themselves as culturally or geographically from the West (Mohanty 1991, 52). In short, the term is used here to denote a feminist whose work falls within the western humanist tradition.
8. As Mohanty (1991, 57) points out, Third World women have been defined as victims of male violence, the colonial process, the Arab familial system, the economic development process, and the economic basis of the Islamic code.

References

de Groot, Joanna (1991a), 'Conceptions and Misconceptions: The Historical and Cultural Context of Discussion on Women and Development' in Afshar, H., ed. *Women, Development and Survival in the Third World*, New York: Longman Group.
de Groot, Joanna. (1991b), '"Sex" and "Race": The Construction of Language and Image in the Nineteenth Century', in Mendus, S. and J. Rendall, eds. *Sexuality and Subordination: Interdisciplinary Studies of Gender in the Nineteenth Century*, New York: Routledge.

Diamond, Irene and Gloria Feman Orenstein (1990), *Reweaving the World: The Emergence of Ecofeminism*, San Francisco: Sierra Club Books.

George, Susan (1988), *A Fate Worse Than Debt*, New York: Grove Press.

Harding, Sandra (1986), *The Science Question in Feminism*, Ithaca, New York: Cornell University Press.

Harding, Sandra, and Merrill Hintikka, (1983), *Discovering Reality: Feminist Perspectives on Epistemology, Metaphysics, Methodology, and Philosophy of Science* Dordrecht: Reidel.

hooks, bell (1990), *Yearning: Race, Gender and Cultural Politics*, Boston: South End Press.

Hunt, Diana (1989), *Economic Theories of Development: An Analysis of Competing Paradigms*, Savage, Maryland: Barnes and Noble Books.

Jaggar, Allison M. and Paula S. Rothenberg, eds. (1984), *Feminist Frameworks: Alternative Theoretical Accounts of the Relations Between Women and Men*, 2nd edn, New York: McGraw-Hill Book Company.

Joseph, George, Vasu Reddy, and Mary Searle-Chatterjee (1988), 'Eurocentrism in the Social Sciences', *Race and Class*, 31, Spring.

Merchant, Carol (1980), *The Death of Nature: Women, Ecology, and the Scientific Revolution*, San Francisco: Harper and Row Publishers.

Mohanty, Chandra (1991), 'Under Western Eyes: Feminist Scholarship and Colonial Discourses', in Mohanty, C., A. Russo, and L. Torres, eds. *Third World Women and the Politics of Feminism*, Indianapolis: Indiana University Press.

Mohanty, Chandra, Ann Russo, and Lourdes Torres, eds. (1991), *Third World Women and the Politics of Feminism*, Indianapolis: Indiana University Press.

Moraga, Cherrie and Gloria Anazaldua (1983), *This Bridge Called My Back: Writings by Radical Women of Color*, New York: Kitchen Table: Women of Color Press.

Peattie, Lisa (1981), *Thinking About Development*, New York: Plenum Press.

Perlich, Pam (1990), 'The Relation of Science to the Feminist Project', *Review of Radical Political Economics*, 21, Summer/Fall.

Said, Edward (1979), *Orientalism*, New York: Vintage Press.

Said, Edward (1985), 'Orientalism Reconsidered', *Race and Class*, 27, Autumn.

Shiva, Vandana (1989), *Staying Alive: Women, Ecology and Development*, London: Zed Books Ltd.

Spivac, Gayatri Chakravorty (1989) *The Post Colonial Critic: Interviews, Strategies, Dialogues*, New York: Routledge.

Tinker, Irene (1990), *Persistent Inequalities: Women and World Development*, New York: Oxford University Press.

Verhelst, Thierry G. (1990), *No Life Without Roots: Culture and Development*, London: Zed Books Ltd.

Waring, Marilyn. (1988), *If Women Counted*, San Francisco: Harper and Row.

6. Cultural Contours of Race, Gender, and Class Distinctions: A Critique of Moynihan and Other Functionalist Views

Ann Jennings and Dell Champlin

In 'The Negro Family: The Case for National Action' (1965), Daniel Patrick Moynihan argued that racism was no longer a major determinant of the social position of black Americans. In *Family and Nation* (1986) he restated the position which remains influential in policy circles despite a generation of scholarly critique. The denial of racism as a problem, and hence the rejection of any need for a theory of American race relations, has been regarded as racist by many who do see racism as a serious social issue. Moynihan, himself, need not harbor animosity toward minorities for him to have complicity in the perpetuation of racial advantage or disadvantage. Moynihan was concerned with the problems confronting black Americans, but his accounts explain away racism rather than addressing it. Behaviors and arguments that unconsciously sustain racist processes and categories are a form of racism even if overt and intentional behavior is lacking.

The notion that racism may be unintentional means that a better understanding of the social channels of racism is needed. Some of the theoretical preconceptions that led Moynihan to deny the incidence of racism are very common. These preconceptions, identified here as 'functionalism', reflect the dominant views of white society and cannot provide the basis for an adequate theory of race. Functionalism refers to the conflation of social function with structure in the norms or 'animating myths' of society (Jones 1983, 23). If a function is seen as universally necessary, then so is its associated structure. Functionalist conceptions have dominated American life since the nineteenth century and have produced theories of class and gender. Class is seen as determined by economic/market relationships and gender by reproductive/familial relationships. Race is a different matter, however. Functionalist social theories have had to restrict the social significance of racial distinctions either by making race exogenous or by reducing it to a consequence of either class or gender. For example, Moynihan's perspective reduced race to gender and has been called 'not so much racist as sexist' (Giddings 1984, 329).

The purpose of this essay is to explore the functionalism of Moynihan and several other types of social theory that have obstructed adequate understandings of race distinctions in American society. In particular, functionalism has precluded a satisfactory account of the articulation of race with other modes of invidious distinction such as gender and class. The essay concludes with insights from black feminist scholars as well as the nonfunctionalist aspects of Thorstein Veblen's work that can serve as a foundation for future theories.

The Moynihan Report

In 1965, Assistant Secretary of Labor, Moynihan, wrote an internal report comparing trends in unemployment, illegitimacy, marital separations and receipt of AFDC benefits among blacks and whites. One finding of the Moynihan Report was that new AFDC cases had begun to rise as unemployment went down, particularly for black Americans. This reversal of earlier trends led Moynihan to favor policies to repair the decay he believed he observed in black families. 'What, after all, was the AFDC program but a family allowance for *broken families*?' he has recently asked (Moynihan 1986, 8).

The Moynihan Report elicited a storm of controversy, and civil rights leaders who had once approved its position distanced themselves one by one (Giddings 1984). It was labeled racist, its data and conclusions challenged, and its arguments attacked as narrow and shortsighted (Rainwater and Yancey 1967, Omi and Winant 1986). Ironically Moynihan attributed black family deterioration to slavery and generations of discrimination and drew on accounts by influential black scholars. He was also part of the first administration since Reconstruction to make a serious commitment to civil rights.

'The Negro Family: the Case for National Action' was not mainly about race; it was about the structure of gender roles in American families. Race was only the frame, a 'marker' for an epidemic of familial aberration. The black community's problem, Moynihan suggested, was that it could not transmit the values necessary for economic success from generation to generation. The root problem was neither economic disadvantage nor continuing racial discrimination. The *core* problem was a pathological black family (Moynihan 1965).

Moynihan's reasoning that race and economic disadvantage were no longer the root of black poverty was based on two observations. First, about half of black families were stable, middle-class and 'patriarchal', meaning that the husband was both dominant and the main breadwinner. If racial discrimination were the problem, middle-class black families would presumably be rare. Second, since AFDC dependency was rising independently of unemployment among black males, something else must be causing family break-up and poverty. Moynihan fingered black 'matriarchy', described as 'the often reversed roles of husband and wife'. (1965, 76, page numbers from 1967 reprint). Moynihan saw black matriarchy as the toll exacted on the black male psyche by generations of slavery, Jim Crow and discrimination. 'Segregation and the submissiveness it exacts is surely more destructive to the male than the female personality'. (Moynihan 1965, 62).

Moynihan documented black matriarchy with statistics on the educational and labor market achievements of black women. He also cited studies of wife-dominance in black families, which he saw as a devaluation of black men and a prelude to family break-up. Once households were broken, matriarchal family pathology continued in female-headed households, which Moynihan believed favored daughters over sons, reduced educational achievement, deprived sons of discipline and perpetuated the disadvantages for black men that would threaten stable families in the next generation. Moynihan even recommended military service for young black men seeking escape to '...a world away from women, a world run by strong men of unquestioned authority...' (1965, 88–9).

Moynihan's conclusion that matriarchy, not discrimination, caused black poverty is seriously flawed by the fact that his evidence for matriarchy could not be disaggregated by socioeconomic status. Moreover, his concern with rising AFDC claims in the face of falling unemployment rates ignored the relaxation of AFDC eligibility requirements instituted just when this 'problem' was being observed (Carper 1967). Almost all that remains of Moynihan's case after a generation of scholarly critique is that poor black communities have different familial patterns than middle-class whites. Moynihan now believes that poor blacks share those patterns with poor whites, though he does not see this as damaging his initial position. Nor does it, insofar as his argument concerned not race but improper gender roles. The main objective of this essay is not to refute Moynihan's conclusions, done long ago, but to expose theoretical preconceptions that he shares with other social theorists and with some of his critics.

Moynihan reveals in *Family and Nation* (1986) that his goal has always been the restoration of 'normal' families among the poor. His mission stems from a reductionist view of social inequalities and from the functionalist view of the family on which it rests. In 1965 Moynihan reduced racial disadvantages to gender role reversals. By later including poor whites he attributed class disadvantage to family malformation as well. Broken families cause both class and race immobilities:

> (T)he Bureau of the Census had reported...a momentous event (in 1971): 'There was no apparent difference in 1970 between the incomes of white and Negro husband–wife families outside the south where the head was under 35 years'.

In three centuries as a society this was the first moment of income equality between black and white. True, it characterized only a limited group, but it was coming into a great legacy: the long-withheld fruits of true equality. Caste (race?), as an impermeable barrier, was behind us. Problems of class were shown to be surmountable. 'Poverty is now inextricably associated with family structure'. (quoting himself):

> ...It was a perception that would free the subject of family from the subject of race. Or ought to (Moynihan 1986, 45–7, emphasis in original).

Moynihan's reduction of social disadvantages to gender abnormalities implies that the restoration of normal familial roles can eradicate virtually all undeserved social inequality. This argument implicitly denies that any form of invidious distinction is a normal part of American society. Race is merely an attribute of a social group where pathological families reproduce poverty. Where normal families predominate, 'the long withheld fruits of true equality' are being realized. The fact that this applies to 'only a limited group' is also consistent with his basic position. Some are still afflicted by the 'abnormal family structure' that past discrimination produced.

Moynihan does not see normal gender relations within families as a mode of social inequality. This reflects some shift in his thought between 1965 and 1986, from support for patriarchal inequality toward a view of gender as an irreducible familial complementarity. Where 'male leadership' (Moynihan 1965, 29) was his ideal in 1965, by 1986 he had adopted descriptions of broken families as incomplete and illegitimate, suggesting gender complementarity as the basis of social equality rather than of inequality.

Moynihan's reconception of gender roles as a necessary unity rests on a universalized conflation of gender roles and the family itself. He quotes Bronislav Malinowski for support: '(T)he father is indispensable for the full sociological status of the child as well as of its mother,...the group consisting of a woman and her offspring is sociologically incomplete and illegitimate'. (Malinowski 1930, quoted in Moynihan 1986, 170).

Now it is the violation of a 'universal sociological law' that produces invidious social distinctions. We can 'free the subject of the family from the subject of race' or class and, implicitly, from the subject of gender as well. Blacks, the poor or women are stigmatized mainly by 'incomplete and illegitimate' family forms. Gender hierarchy, like class and race, is real only if women disregard the precondition (complete families) for full social equality. The social order is vindicated when normal social relations are seen as equitable, and normal socialization places the fruits of true equality within the reach of all. Discussions of race, class or gender problems are supplanted by paeans to the universal family, and social policies to reduce inequality should focus on the repair of families as normal gender units.

Moynihan's complacent and traditional conception of social relationships accounts for his continuing popularity among policy makers. Moynihan's argument resonates with our most cherished social images because nineteenth-century functionalism still dominates twentieth-century cultural beliefs.

Functionalist Prescriptions

Malinowski's description of the universal family, reproduced in the *Family and Nation*, was originally published in 1913. The universal family consisted of a bounded group (parents and children), possessing a definite place (home and hearth), and sharing emotions of familial love (no different from the emotions shared within English families). Anthropologists Collier, Rosaldo and Yanagisako offer the following assessment:

> The flaw in Malinowski's argument is the flaw common to all functionalist arguments: Because a social institution is observed to perform a necessary function does not mean either that the function would not be performed if that institution did not exist or that the function is responsible for the existence of the institution (Collier et al. 1982, 27).

Malinowski's 'discovery' that Australian Aborigines recognized conjugal relations in addition to coitus appeared to settle debates over the universality of the family. Whether the recognition of legitimate paternity had similar significance across cultures was not questioned, although Malinowski's assertion that fathers were always integral to family units passed into obscurity (Collier et al. 1982) until Moynihan's revival of it.

Rosaldo (1980) has noted the eurocentric, androcentric inadequacy and the inaccuracy of 'functionally grounded universals'. Her analysis views nineteenth-century functionalism as a dualistic compartmentalization of society into separate spheres for men and women. Men were 'public' persons engaged in the economic struggle to wrest a living from the production of goods, while women were 'private' persons busy instilling proper values in the next generation of ruggedly masculine individuals and ensuring the moral survival of society within families. The notion of separate spheres and the 'cult of domesticity' for women has been associated by feminist historians with American and British industrialization (Matthei 1982, Kessler-Harris 1982). Prior to industrialization economic production had not escaped household and familial control enough to make clear distinctions between 'economic' and 'familial' functions of 'production' and 'reproduction' (Nicholson 1986, Jennings 1992). Women's *exclusive* responsibility for nurturing and childrearing became the social norm when wage earning became the norm for men. The new cultural standards of family life ushered in by this separation of spheres acquired a prescriptive force which they largely retain today, as evidenced by Moynihan and by continuing undervaluation of women's productive abilities (Jennings and Waller 1990a).

Rosaldo points out that the norms of *exclusive* roles and domains for men and women never reflected the actual experience of many nineteenth-century women (see also Matthaei 1982, Kessler-Harris 1982). Many men's wages did not permit the maintenance of wives and children in proper domesticity, and significant numbers of married women were engaged in paid labor or in family enterprises throughout the nineteenth-century.[1] The misrepresentation of actual social arrangements in separate spheres doctrines illustrates their prescriptive nature as animating myths. Proper gender norms were inseparable from social class and status as evidenced by feminist debates over the importance of family wage struggles (Jennings and Waller 1990b). Veblen also emphasized that women's productive efforts were concealed by the canons of nineteenth-century social reputability and social stratification (Veblen 1989).

Functionalism, Cultural Dualism and Social Hierarchy

Functionalism rests on the compartmentalization of social spheres. Mutually exclusive domains or structures allow structure and function to be conflated and universalized in prescriptive social habits of thought. Compartmentalization is associated with dualisms that figure prominently in western traditions of social hierarchy. Dualistic habits of thought first bifurcate, then rank social domains, functions, groups and values. They establish categories of irreducible difference that can be violated only at social peril.

Cartesian dualisms are not simple pairs of opposed terms such as mind/body, objective/subjective and so on. They are combined in networks of opposed things, activities, persons and values that augment and reinforce one another, mapping out the cultural terrain. Thus, since the nineteenth-century rational economic man has been seen as objective, competitive, progressive, productive and amoral in contrast to emotional, familial woman, who is subjective, nurturing, unchanging, reproductive and the guardian of morality (Jennings 1993).

Rosaldo's critique of 'functionally grounded universals' is consistent with institutionalist challenges to dualism that are based on the anthropological concept of culture (Jennings 1993). Cultural formations are wholes with intricately interwoven connections between all aspects of our lives. Dualisms are cultural fictions in the sense that irreducible differences do not exist between these opposing pairs; they nevertheless shape our understanding of cultural linkages and social processes. Dualisms act as animating myths that prescribe hierarchical social distinctions. Challenging social hierarchy thus requires challenging dualistic functionalist compartmentalizations.

In conventional cultural beliefs dualistic preconceptions confer higher status on rational, masculine, economic pursuits and devalue emotional, feminine and familial activities. This is the basic attitude of neoclassical economics which exalts rational, objective competition over emotional, subjective cooperation. It is possible to criticize the ordering of dualisms, however, without criticizing the premises that support them or the social hierarchies that result. This is what Moynihan has done. He has inverted the usual economy/family ordering by arguing that the family, as the most basic unit of society, is more important to social wellbeing than the economy. His position revalues the family but not women, since it is divergence from normal gender roles (broken families) that causes economic disability. By reinforcing women's functionalist association with the family and denying consequent social disadvantages, Moynihan validates existing gender hierarchies. He also fails to explain invidious distinctions of race.

Unfortunately, Moynihan's work is only one variety of functionalist social theory. Due to similar functionalist preconceptions, some of Moynihan's would-be critics share his limitations in adequately understanding social hierarchy. This is especially true when race is considered, since reductionisms similar to Moynihan's reduction of race to gender generally result.

Four Varieties of Functionalism

To better understand the relationship of Moynihan's functionalism to other functionalist social accounts, it is useful to examine some conceptions of the relationship between social class and gender. It has been common in functionalism to associate class relationships with the productive, economic, market relationships of men and to associate gender with the reproductive familial relationships thought to govern women's lives. In this sense, it is possible to see class/gender as a further dualism within nineteenth-century functionalist understandings. At least four interpretations of this construction are possible depending on whether priority is assigned to the economy or to the family and on whether class and gender are seen as equitable complementarities or inequitable hierarchies. All four interpretations, neoclassical economics, Moynihan, traditional Marxist economics and radical feminism, tend to reductionism and consequently sustain aspects of social hierarchy. Moreover none can adequately address race issues.

Table 1: Varieties of Functionalism

Economy given Priority	*Family given Priority*
Neoclassical Economics:	Moynihan:
Class as complementary	Gender as complementary
Gender reduced to class	Class reduced to gender
Traditional Marxism:	Radical Feminism:
Class as hierarchy	Gender as hierarchy
Gender reduced to class	Class reduced to gender

The basic orientation of the four varieties of functionalism is summarized in Table 1 according to their focus on class or gender and their equity assessments. The Moynihan account sees the family as basic and as a unit of gender complementarity. All types of social inequality whether economic, racial or gender, are traced to gender malformations. Normal social relationships are equitable, however, and 'the fruits of true equality' are within reach of all with sound family relationships.

Neoclassical economics similarly conceives of social relationships as normally equitable. The basic complementarity here, however, is the relationship between capital and labor. It may be labeled 'class' (and was in classical economics), so long as it is understood as a relationship between neutral 'factors of production'. No social hierarchy or power relationships are recognized, especially since labor can choose to acquire its own capital and raise its earning power through self-investment in personal, 'human capital' (Becker 1975). Human capital theorists and 'New Home Economists' also reduce gender to complementarities in the skill acquisitions of men and women. The family is seen as an economic unit that facilitates efficient specializations in the production of market goods or of children who are treated as consumer durables (Becker 1981, Jennings and Waller 1990a). Some neoclassical economists concede that discrimination can disadvantage women but often see it as an inefficient allocation of capital and labor that competitive forces should eliminate. Race inequities are similarly treated as capital and labor misallocations (Becker 1971). Neoclassical economists, like Moynihan, view inequity as abnormal. Neither of these functionalist orientations challenges social hierarchy.

The critique of social hierarchy found in traditional Marxist economics focuses on class inequities in productive relationships. It views gender distinctions mainly as props for class inequalities, particularly insofar as reproduction has not been commodified (Engels 1884, Zaretsky 1976). Class links men to wage-earning and women to reproductive roles. It is the autonomous cause of gender inequalities, though the prioritizing of men's class concerns over women's gender concerns has prompted many feminists to see traditional Marxist economics as sexist (Hartmann 1976, Jaggar 1983, Jennings 1992). Race, meanwhile, is treated as a division within the working-class by, and for the benefit of, capitalists (Cox 1948). It parallels the construction of gender as a consequence of class relationships.

Radical feminists, finally, argue that gender oppression within patriarchal families predated, and was the original model for, class oppression in economic production (Firestone 1970, MacKinnon 1982). The argument highlights the social struggles of women that other functionalist accounts obscure, but it still does not challenge the basic functionalist compartmentalization of class and gender (itself a gender construction) (Jennings 1992). Radical feminism has also tended to gloss over class differences among women in gender struggle, just as traditional Marxism has often neglected gender differences among workers in class struggle (Jaggar 1983). Both views, by 'essentializing' either gender or class as the autonomous category, have ignored the mutuality of class and gender stemming from their joint construction in the compartmentalization of spheres (Jennings and Waller 1990b). Nor can radical feminism improve on reductionist accounts of race (Spelman 1988, 114–19).

Reductionism is characteristic of each of the varieties of functionalism noted above; all reduce 'additional' social distinctions to a more basic distinction. Race is consistently obscured and is never 'basic'.

Functionalism and Race

It is difficult to produce a nonreductionist account of race from a functionalist perspective. With no functional locus, no 'institution of race', it forfeits equal standing with gender or class. It might be suggested that slavery once supplied the missing institution or that Jim Crow gave race a 'political' foundation, but the question of what universalized function slavery or Jim Crow served quickly arises. Reductionism reemerges as the most likely course of thought. Nor is it possible to turn race 'on its head' to examine the experiences of those disadvantaged by it, as is often done for class or gender. Reductionism prevents this, since race is seen as a secondary form of the class or gender oppressions that whites also suffer. Functionalism roots social distinctions in compartmentalized structures which are then ranked in importance. Disputes across various theories become a 'competition' between structures and their associated oppressions in which race almost inevitably loses out.[2]

Race, gender and class could be viewed alternatively as 'parallel' or 'additive' oppressions. The problem with this is that no person has a race (or class or gender) standing without some simultaneous standing — privileged or disadvantaged — with respect to other important social distinctions. The 'pure forms' required for additivity do not exist. The case of working-class black women illustrates the failure of additive notions of oppression. Their situation is sometimes described as the sum of race, class and gender oppressions, but if race is the oppression also suffered by black men, class the oppression of working-class men and gender the oppression of white women, the experiences of black women themselves need nowhere appear. Parallel notions of oppression must ignore, or somehow 'hold constant', other privileges and result in the erasure of some experiences.

The lesson of these exercises is that class, gender and race cannot be treated independently; functionalism promotes a reductionism that sustains some forms of privilege and discounts other disadvantages. This has occurred with race in particular. Nineteenth-century functionalist categories exclude race. They are eurocentric, relying on principles of class and gender that have been reserved for whites. The historical record gives important clues to the evolution of these exclusions which have resulted in the effective denial of legitimate black experiences.

The first century of American race relationships may be seen as a fluid period of social experimentation leading to the systematic exclusion of blacks from white norms. Blacks were not uniformly denied property rights when they first arrived in 1619, were not subject to permanent servitude (though whites sometimes were) and were originally assigned higher status than white servants and workers (Giddings 1984). By 1640 slavery was more certain for arriving Africans, but Breen's accounts of seventeenth-century labor rebellions indicate that landless blacks and whites often made common cause (Breen 1987). Free and bond labor distinctions were not yet systematized in racial terms; however, race was a key element in the way that class relations were eventually established.

The system of race that emerged was grounded in an inversion of traditional European gender beliefs, and race has since figured in white gender relations (e.g. in white women's virtue) especially in the South. An example of the gender content of early colonial attempts to define race and slavery is found in laws concerning interracial marriages. Virginia ruled in 1661 that the status of children of interracial marriages would depend on the mother rather than the father as in English law. The measure provided economic incentives in the form of more slaves to voluntary or forced white male–black female unions while punishing black male–white female unions with exile. By contrast Maryland's initial attempt to end interracial marriage by giving white women who married slaves their husband's status ended perversely as masters were motivated to marry white female indentured servants to slaves in order to enslave them (Giddings 1984). Exclusion from white norms became a tenet of racial slavery. The race, class and gender dimensions of these cases are not separable; the social terms of race, class and gender evolved together in new circumstances.

Whites eventually mandated matrifocal elements in slave life that have since been viewed as black aberration when contrasted with white norms. Nevertheless black feminists and some black nationalists have been adamant that black communities possess their own cultural values that derive from their African heritage and not just from centuries of white oppression. Black feminists commonly describe this heritage as more egalitarian than white norms and tend to reject white compartmentalizations of productive and reproductive roles for men and women. White functionalist accounts of class and gender begin with, rather than explain, categories that have been racially exclusive and which emerged historically with race distinctions; they also obscure the integrity of traditional African American social practices.

Black feminists have written extensively on these issues, but their work has often been ignored just as the real experiences of black women have often been invisible. Validating black women's experiences is threatening not just to racist practices but to the functionalist categories that have pitted class and gender concerns against one another and against race in social theory and in the real struggles of black women. Functionalist, compartmentalized views of oppression have forced black women to carry on their own resistance efforts on multiple fronts. Such fragmentation is the real consequence of functionalist habits of thought in American society.

Tools for New Theory

Theories that fully explore the articulation of race, gender and class in America must draw on nonfunctionalist conceptions. Two major resources are black feminism and the cultural theories of Veblen. The work of black feminists, so often silenced or ignored, affords a necessary antidote to functionalism and offers a holistic vision of the multiple social disconnections of race, class and gender in our society.[3] Veblen's analyses of the interrelationships between cultural compartmentalizations, gender and pecuniary hierarchy (class) are insightful and, in combination with the arguments of black feminists, have informed the critiques of functionalism in this essay.

Black feminists have argued that race, gender and class are simultaneous oppressions which mutually structure one another. While race is a starting point in black feminist analyses, their noncompartmentalized views of oppression indicate far more than a 'racial' perspective. Black feminist accounts reconceptualize common understandings of class and gender and contain a holistic view of social distinctions. The view that class or gender can be separated from the experience of race among African Americans is regularly rejected.

Black feminists also describe social values and norms in black communities that are less compartmentalized than the dominant norms of American society. Hill Collins argues that African American cultural thought does not typically make public/private distinctions such as paid vs. unpaid work, productive vs. unproductive work, and individual goals and activities vs. those of the family or community (Hill Collins 1990). Such aspects are neither seen as conflicting nor differentially valued (see also

King 1988, Brown 1988). However, Hill Collins notes that black communities do see themselves as compartmentalized from white society both as a consequence of racism and as a mode of resistance to white values. The distinction is partly an assertion of an afrocentric world view (see also Caulfield 1974, Harley 1988).

Black feminist writings avoid sharp distinctions between experiential description and theoretical analysis. Noncompartmentalized cultural understandings seem to be linked to noncompartmentalized methodologies. Hill Collins argues that afrocentric epistemologies dismiss common white fact/value distinctions, abstract and universalized claims to 'objective' knowledge, and the view that reliable knowledge is incompatible with disagreement (Hill Collins 1988). Instead, subjective knowledge is valued as a means of ensuring that the multiple aspects of social problems are adequately explored before group decisions are taken. The value assigned to knowledge is neither individualistic nor relativistic, however; it is community-based emphasizing engaged debate and responsibility for others. Hill Collins sees these afrocentric knowledge processes as empowering for those subordinated and erased through domination. They are also forms of knowledge discounted by functionalism.

Black feminists frequently contrast the fragmentation of life and struggle imposed by functionalist norms with the integrity of noncompartmentalized African American norms. An exquisite tension exists in these accounts between the imagery of 'wholeness' and of 'dismemberment'. Joseph and Lewis (1981) describe black women as 'Siamese twins', possessed of both joined and conflicting race and gender interests. The lives of black Americans are both whole and fragmented as a consequence of a multicultural society and dominant social distinctions that disconnect spheres, groups and values. The notion that such contradictions should not exist in social theory must itself be rejected as dualistic and as a product of the either/or thinking that itself promotes contradictions. One other social theorist concerned with multiple, culturally complex and nonfunctionalist understandings of 'invidious distinction' is Thorstein Veblen. Two aspects of Veblen's work are especially valuable: his holistic concept of culture; and his recognition that functionalist habits of thoughts are the servants of social hierarchy.[4]

Veblen's cultural nonfunctionalism is illustrated by his view of the economy. 'There is no...neatly isolable range of cultural phenomena that can be rigorously set apart...(as) economic' (Veblen 1919, 77). We have culturally isolated 'the economy' and defined it as 'the market', but most behavior is complex having simultaneous economic, reproductive and political aspects. The conflation of 'economy' and 'market' serves to legitimate undeserved wealth. In rejecting such compartmentalization, Veblen was challenging a system of status which rewarded those who 'cultivated the main chance', rather than productive activity.

Veblen combined this analysis of pecuniary culture with explanations of the 'barbarian status of women', who were assigned roles as idle consumers to demonstrate the pecuniary prowess of their husbands or fathers (Veblen 1899). Women's productive efforts remain under-recognized today, given the continuing sway of pecuniary values. Veblen's work remains useful, both for its analyses of cultural beliefs and for his explanations of the staying-power of old habits of thought.

The task of progressive social theory is, in part, to remove the blinders of old habits of thought. Tools are available in both black feminism and Veblen for new, nonfunctionalist social theories. What has been lacking is a recognition of the importance of nonfunctionalist theoretical tools. One-dimensional views of social hierarchy, rooted in either class or gender, but never in race, effectively dismiss whole social groups, their experiences, their voices and their values. Functionalism cancels precisely those holistic, noncompartmentalized understandings that are capable of identifying the privileges sustained by functionalist social beliefs.

Notes

1. Official statistics show only about 5 percent of married white women in the labor force in 1900, but undercount or exclude farm wives, women who ran boarding houses, married women working at piecework or in family businesses, and often count those who worked for wages only if they earned the majority of family income (Peterson 1990).

2. Commenting on a Central Park rape, bell hooks (1990) asks, 'Why must people decide whether this crime is more sexist than racist, as if these are competing oppressions?'

3. Black feminists have not specifically described their work as 'nonfunctionalist', but they challenge 'parallelist' (compartmentalized) and 'monistic' (reductionist) models of social hierarchy and 'either/or' modes of thought. They question notions of 'competing oppressions' and claim they are 'multiplicative, not additive' and 'simultaneous'. They note the exclusionary consequences of 'gender-first' social critiques, 'class-first' approaches and even 'race-first' movements. See Giddings (1984), Terborg-Penn (1983), Lorde (1984), Joseph (1981), Hill Collins (1990), Dill (1979), and the essays in Malson et al. (1988).

4. Veblen's theories of cultural evolution are tainted by his racist anthropological sources. His work (1899, 1919) does not address American race relations, however, dealing with the racial character of 'national stocks' in discussions of 'barbarian' and 'savage' stages of social development. His nonfunctionalist method remains noteworthy and does not depend on these outdated concepts.

References

Becker, G. (1971), *The Economics of Discrimination*, 2nd edn, Chicago: University of Chicago Press.

Becker, G. (1975), *Human Capital*, 2nd edn, New York: NBER.

Becker, G. (1981), *A Treatise on the Family*, Cambridge, MA: Harvard University Press.

Breen, T.H. (1987), 'The Giddy Multitude: Race and Class in Early Virginia' in R. Takaki, ed. *From Different Shores*, New York: Oxford University Press.

Brown, E.B. (1988), 'Womanist Consciousness' in M. Malson, et al., eds. *Black Women in America*, Chicago: University of Chicago Press.

Carper, L. (1967), 'The Negro Family and the Moynihan Report' in L. Rainwater and W. Yancey, eds. *The Moynihan Report and the Politics of Controversy*, Cambridge, MA: MIT Press.

Caulfield, M.D. (1974), 'Imperialism, the Family, and Cultures of Resistance', *Socialist Review*, 4 (2): 67–85.

Collier, J., M. Rosaldo and S. Yanagisako (1982), 'Is There a Family? New Anthropological Views' in B. Thorne and M. Yalom, eds. *Rethinking the Family*, New York: Longman.

Cox, O. (1948), *Caste, Class and Race*, Garden City, NY: Doubleday and Co.

Dill, B. (1979), 'The Dialectics of Black Womanhood', *Signs*, 4 (3).

Engels, F. (1884), *The Origin of the Family, Private Property, and the State*, New York: International Publ., 1972 reprint.

Firestone, S. (1970), *The Dialectic of Sex*, New York: Wm. Morrow.

Giddings, P. (1984), *When and Where I Enter*, New York: Bantam.

Harley, S. (1988), 'For the Good of Family and Race' in M. Malson et al., eds. *Black Women in America*, Chicago: University of Chicago Press.

Hartmann, H. (1976), 'Capitalism, Patriarchy, and Job Segregation by Sex', *Signs*, 1 (3) pt. 2: 137–69.

Hill Collins, P. (1988), 'The Social Construction of Black Feminist Thought' in M. Malson et al., eds. *Black Women in America*, Chicago: University of Chicago Press.

Hill Collins, P. (1990), *Black Feminist Thought*, Boston: Unwin Hyman.

hooks, bell (1990), 'Reflections on Race and Sex' in *Yearning: Race, Gender, and Cultural Politics*, Boston: South End Press.

Jaggar, A. (1983), *Feminist Politics and Human Nature*, Towota, NJ: Rowman and Allenheld.

Jennings, A. (1993), 'Public or Private? Institutional Economics and Feminism' in J. Nelson and M. Ferber (eds), *Beyond 'Economic Man': Feminist Theory and Economics*, Chicago: University of Chicago Press.

Jennings, A. (1992) 'Not the Economy' in W. Dugger and W. Waller, eds. *The Stratified State*, Armonk, NY: M.E. Sharpe.

Jennings, A. and W. Waller (1990a), 'Constructions of Social Hierarchy', *Journal of Economic Issues*, 24: 623–32.

Jennings, A. and W. Waller (1990b), 'Rethinking Class and Social Stratification', paper presented at the annual meeting of the Southern Economics Association.

Jones, G.S. (1983), *Languages of Class*, Cambridge, England: Cambridge University Press.

Joseph, G. (1981), 'Incompatible Menage A Trois: Marxism, Feminism, and Racism' in L. Sargent, ed. *Women and Revolution*, Boston: South End Press.

Joseph, G. and J. Lewis (1981), *Common Differences: Conflicts in Black and White Feminist Perspectives*, New York: Avon.

Kessler-Harris, A. (1982), *Out to Work*, New York: Oxford University Press.

King, D. (1988), 'Multiple Jeopardy, Multiple Consciousness' in M. Malson et al., eds. *Black Women in America*, Chicago: University of Chicago Press.

Lorde, A. (1984), 'An Open Letter to Mary Daly', in *Sister Outsider*, Freedom, CA: The Crossing Press.

MacKinnon, C. (1982), 'Feminism, Marxism, Method, and the State', *Signs*, 7 (3): 533–44.

Malson, M. et al., eds. (1988), *Black Women in America*, Chicago: University of Chicago Press.

Matthaei, J. (1982), *An Economic History of Women in America*, New York: Schocken.

Moynihan, D. P. (1965), *The Negro Family: The Case for National Action*, Office of Policy Planning, US Department of Labor, Washington, DC: US Government Printing Office, reprinted in L. Rainwater and W. Yancey, eds. *The Moynihan Report and the Politics of Controversy*, Cambridge, MA: MIT Press, 1967.

Moynihan, D. P. (1986), *Family and Nation*, New York: Harcourt Brace Jovanovich.

Nicholson, L. (1986), *Gender and History*, New York: Columbia University Press.

Omi, M. and H. Winant (1986), *Racial Formation in the United States*, New York: Routledge.

Peterson, J. (1990), 'What's in a Number: Ideology and Gender Bias in Economic Statistics' presented to the annual meeting of the Association for Evolutionary Economics.

Rainwater, L. and W. Yancey, eds. (1967), *The Moynihan Report and the Politics of Controversy*, Cambridge, MA: MIT Press.

Rosaldo, M. (1980), 'The Use and Abuse of Anthropology', *Signs*, 5: 391–417.

Spelman, E. (1988), *Inessential Woman: Problems of Exclusion in Feminist Thought*, Boston: Beacon Press.

Terborg-Penn, R. (1983), 'Discontented Black Feminists: Prelude and Postscript to the Passage of the Nineteenth Amendment' in L. Scharf and J. Jensen, eds. *Decades of Discontent*, Wesport, CT: Greenwood.

Veblen, T. (1899), *The Theory of the Leisure Class*, New York: Mentor.

Veblen, T. (1919), 'Why is Economics Not an Evolutionary Science', in *The Place of Science in Modern Civilization*, New York: B.W. Huebsch.

Zaretsky, E. (1976), *Capitalism, the Family and Personal Life*, New York: Harper and Row.

PART III

Examining the Issues of Gender

7. Traditional Economic Theories and Issues of Gender:
The Status of Women in the United States and the Former Soviet Union

Janice Peterson

Earlier chapters have discussed the limits of traditional economic theories in considering issues of gender and the status of women in capitalist systems. In neoclassical economics, women's status is studied from the perspective of individual characteristics and choice. Market outcomes are seen to reflect the preferences and abilities of the individual decision-makers involved. Neoclassical models of the labor market, for example, ignore the role of social norms and institutions in shaping and constraining individual labor supply decisions. In addition, many neoclassical models completely ignore the discriminatory behavior of employers on the demand-side of the labor market. When labor market discrimination is considered, it is generally dismissed as a temporary phenomenon that can not withstand the forces of competition over the long run.[1]

The public–private dualism is reflected in neoclassical economics in the conceptual separation of the economy from the family. The family is seen as private, separate and distinct from the public sphere of the market economy. The free enterprise market economy is defined as the only legitimate sphere of economic activity. The social provisioning activities that take place within the home are defined as private, and therefore noneconomic (Waller and Jennings 1990, 619).

The association of women with the family has defined them as noneconomic. This has allowed neoclassical economists to ignore many issues of importance in understanding the economic status of women. To the extent that issues such as the domestic division of labor have been addressed, neoclassical discussions have generally provided further 'justification' for women's secondary position in the economy.

113

Neoclassical models of the household, for example, view the domestic division of labor in terms of the principle of 'comparative advantage', ignoring the distribution of power implied in the structure of social institutions such as the family and the labor market.

The inability of traditional capitalist economics to consider gender inequality as an important concern has prompted many feminist scholars to examine noncapitalist economic theories and systems. The oppression of women under capitalism was given explicit attention in the works of the founding socialist writers. In addition, many socialist and communist nations made gender equality part of their official doctrine.

The former Soviet Union has been of particular interest to feminist scholars. Throughout the history of the Soviet Union, the state was officially committed to the equality of the sexes and actively promoted women workers. Female labor played a critical role in the development of the Soviet economy. However, while many observers agree that women progressed economically and socially after the Bolshevik revolution, women never achieved full economic and social equality with men.

The purpose of this chapter is to examine the status of women in the United States and the former Soviet Union, two systems guided by very different economic ideologies. It will examine some of the traditional indicators of economic status — labor-force participation, occupational segregation, relative earnings — and review some of the policy discussions that have taken place in each nation. It seeks to find points of commonality and difference that can inform us in the development of new approaches and policies to guide us into the next century.

The Economic Status of Women in the United States

The increased participation of women in the paid labor force is one of the most important economic trends of the last half century. Since 1940, women's share of the total paid labor force increased from 25 percent to over 40 percent, and the female labor force participation rate increased from 30 percent to over 50 percent. The greatest increase in female labor force participation has been among married women with children. By the mid-1980s, 50 percent of all married women with young children (under 3 years old) were in the labor force, up from 26 percent in 1970 (Bergmann 1986, 20–21, 25).

Many economists interpret this trend as a sign that women's opportunities outside the home have increased and that traditional roles and attitudes are changing (Bergmann 1986, 3). One explanation focuses on the cost–benefit analysis performed by women in their labor supply decisions. It is argued that increasing wages have increased the opportunity cost of allocating time to the home. In addition, declining birthrates and increases in household technology have reduced the amount of time necessary for housework, thus reducing the opportunity cost of allocating time to the market (Bergmann 1986, 27, 41–9).

Alternatively, the increased labor-force participation of women is viewed in terms of declining living standards and economic need, not increased economic opportunities. It is argued that since the early 1970s, inflation and changes in the structure of employment have reduced real incomes and living standards for many segments of the population. In the face of declining real incomes, families have required two incomes to maintain a standard of living previously achieved by one (male) breadwinner. In addition, the increase in the number of families headed by single women has increased the number of women who enter the labor force as the sole providers for their families (Spitz 1988, 45).

Increased female labor-force participation rates must be interpreted carefully. Different groups of women have had very different experiences vis-a-vis the formal labor market. Many women — working-class women, women of color, and immigrant women — have always had relatively high labor-force participation rates. For some women increased labor-force participation reflects increased opportunity and achievement, for others, it reflects a continuing struggle to make ends meet.

The extent to which increased labor-force participation improves the status and wellbeing of women depends on the way they are treated in the workplace and the types of jobs they perform. The degree of occupational segregation provides some insight into the access women have to different types of employment. Women workers are said to be occupationally segregated because the majority are found in a small group of occupations, most notably retail sales, light assembly, clerical and other service work. These occupations are often viewed as 'suitable' for women, conforming to stereotypical views of women's nature and abilities. These occupations generally offer low wages and benefits and few opportunities for advancement (Blau and Ferber 1986, chapter 6; Bergmann 1986, chapters 4, 5).

When occupational categories are broken down in detail, the extent of male–female job segregation actually increases. Women are found to be concentrated in the lower-paid, lower-status jobs within as well as across occupations. In addition, studies have found that even at the firm level, women and men seldom work together in the same occupation in the same location. Often when men and women are found doing the same kind of work within a firm, women are given different job titles with lower pay (Spitz 1988, 52).

There have been some occupational gains by women, particularly in professional–managerial jobs, where their share of employment has increased rapidly over the last decade. However, women continue to account for a relatively small share of the workers in these high-paying and prestigious jobs and they are seriously underrepresented in the top positions within these occupations. The conditions of employment and types of work performed by the majority of women workers have shown little improvement (Pennar and Mervosh 1985, 84–5; Bernstein 1988, 48; Wagman and Folbre 1988, 59).

Women's continued inferior position in the labor market is reflected in the statistics on relative earnings. Despite the increases in women's attachment to the paid labor market over the 1950–1980 time period, their earnings (full time, year round) as a percentage of men's changed little, hovering around 60 percent. In fact, for a while women's earnings actually declined relative to those of male workers, falling from 64 percent in 1955 to 59 percent in the mid–1970s (Spitz 1988, 54).

During the 1980s, women's wages began to grow relative to men's. By the end of the decade, women's earnings (full time, year round) were 68 percent of their male counterparts, however, over the course of the 1980s the female earnings distribution became more unequal (Wagman and Folbre 1988). This suggests that the improvement in women's average earnings reflects the successes of a relatively small group of women. In addition, the narrowing of the earnings gap reflects the deterioration of the economic conditions of men. It has been estimated that roughly one-half of the decrease in the earnings gap is due to the decline in men's real wages (Bernstein 1988, 48; Mishel and Frankel 1991, 81–2).

Another critical factor in determining whether increased participation in the paid workforce improves women's wellbeing is the extent to which it is matched by a decline in their responsibilities at home. Studies indicate that the increased participation of women in work outside the home has not resulted in a significant redistribution of work within the home. Women still perform the majority of domestic tasks, regardless of their employment outside the home. This results in what sociologist Arlie Hochschild has called the 'second shift' for women — one shift in the workplace and one shift at home. The majority of women interviewed on this issue report that they find their second shift exhausting and a source of stress. In many cases, it is a constraint on both their ability to progress in their jobs and enjoy family life (Hochschild 1989).

In addition, social institutions have been slow to change in ways that accommodate new types of workers and family structures. The nuclear family with the male breadwinner and female homemaker is still assumed to be the norm in many places, increasing the stress on families that do not fit this model. The woman's second shift has not been viewed as a legitimate social problem, resulting from institutional rigidity, but is treated as a strictly private matter.

As US women have increased their participation in wage labor they have increasingly borne the pressure of the second shift and have encountered an often hostile work environment. Under these pressures women have increasingly demanded that the government and employers recognize these issues as legitimate problems and actively pursue policies to promote progressive institutional change. Women workers have called for the provision of parental leave, affordable day-care, and more flexible work schedules, as well as an end to discriminatory behavior in the work place.

To the extent that these problems are recognized in neoclassical economics, it is argued the market system is capable of dealing with such issues without expensive and economically distorting intervention from the government. It is argued that the economy has responded well to the changing preferences and needs of women, supplying them with ample opportunities to participate in the economy in appropriate ways. In fact, the changing status of women is often used as an example of the progressivity and flexibility of US capitalism (Pennar and Mervosh 1985; Council of Economic Advisers 1987, chapter 7).

Many economists, for example, have argued that the growth of the service sector has facilitated women's entry into the workforce by providing them with 'suitable' jobs. In addition, the growth in part-time work and other forms of contingent labor is often presented as a positive trend for women workers. It is argued that this trend is a reflection of the responsiveness of the private enterprise system to the needs and preferences of women workers, providing them with the increased flexibility they need to mix market work with home responsibilities (Blank 1990; Christensen 1987).

As currently constructed, however, this increased flexibility comes at a very high price for many workers. On average, part-time jobs offer lower wages than comparable full-time jobs, in addition to providing fewer benefits such as pensions and health insurance. Part-time workers are often more vulnerable in times of recession and may not be covered by unemployment insurance or other worker protection laws. Part-time jobs often do not offer the same types of opportunities for advancement offered by full-time jobs. Even in professional jobs, workers who take part-time schedules often find that they are tracked differently (US General Accounting Office 1991; Blank 1990; Ehrlich 1989, 132).

Much of the economics literature dismisses these concerns, arguing that part-time work is voluntarily chosen. However, studies indicate that over the last decade the growth in part-time work has come largely from increases in involuntary part-time employment (Mishel and Frankel 1991, 137). The growth in part time work is as much a reflection of the changing structure of the economy and cost–cutting employment practices of US corporations as it is a response to the needs of women. In addition, inadequate child-care, an inequitable division of labor in the home, and institutions that continue to assume the traditional family as the norm, vastly increase the need for flexibility on the part of women.

An examination of the economic progress of women in the United States raises important concerns about the economic status of women under capitalism. On one hand, the past half century has been characterized by important and positive changes for some women; at the same time, women as a group remain in a secondary position and the economic conditions faced by many women have not improved. As the next section indicates, the status of women in the former Soviet Union raised some very similar concerns in the context of the Soviet economy.

Classical Marxist Theory and the Economic Status of Women in the Former Soviet Union

While the cultural and material circumstances faced by the Soviet state had a large impact on the status of Soviet women, economic ideology was important in shaping the responses to these circumstances. Soviet writings on the status of women drew heavily on classical Marxist theory, which argues that the oppression of women reflects the inherent inequality and injustice of capitalism and class society, arising from the institution of private property. Women's liberation requires the abolition of class society, through the abolition of private property and capitalism.

A central concern of classical Marxist analysis is the exploitation of the working class. An individual's class status is determined by his or her relationship to the means of production. Women's interests are viewed as a subset of class interests and, 'what is good for the working class is thought to be good for women' (Kruks, Rapp and Young 1989, 11; Acker 1988, 18–19). In this context, women's interests that are not subsumed to class are often ignored.

The assumption in classical Marxism that class interests are primary diminishes the possibility of conflicts between individuals within the same class.[2] Members of families are assumed to have the same class interests and membership as their male wage earner. By confining exploitation to the capitalist firm, the possibility of exploitation in the home is ignored. The rhetoric of class interest obscures issues of inequality between men and women (Folbre and Hartmann 1988, 190–93).

The public–private dualism, which devalues women's domestic labor in neoclassical theory, is present in classical Marxism as well. In classical Marxist analysis, power and exploitation have their roots in commodity production. Activities that take place in the home fall outside the sphere of commodity production. Thus, the domestic labor performed primarily by women is outside the focus of Marxist analysis. Domestic labor is viewed as private; it is defined as non-social and unproductive (Acker 1988, 18–19).

Friedrich Engels does examine the family and women's place within it in *The Origin of the Family, Private Property and the State*, where he attempts to link changes in the mode of production with the organization of familial relationships. He argues that the institution of 'monogamous marriage' arose with capitalism to serve the needs of property owning males — to insure a man's ability to leave his wealth to his children. With the rise of monogamous marriage the patriarchal family became the basic economic unit in society and women and children became dependent on an individual man (Engels 1972, 138; Jaggar 1983, 65).

According to Engels, female dependence on a male is the source of his power, giving him 'a position of supremacy without any need for special titles or privileges' (Engels 1972, 138). To achieve equality with men, women must become economically independent. What is required for the liberation of women, according to Engels, is to 'bring the whole female sex back into public industry' (Engels 1972, 138).

Thus, in the classical Marxist view, the subordination of women is rooted in economic arrangements. It is the housewife's exclusion from wage labor and economic dependence on her husband that is the source of her special oppression under capitalism. With her entry into wage labor, this form of oppression disappears, and she experiences the same oppression as all other members of the working class. There is little recognition that women and men may have different experiences as workers (Jaggar 1983, 215).

Engels recognized that it is not possible for women to fully participate in social production if they are also held fully responsible for all domestic work. He argued that the solution to this problem was the socialization of housework. Under socialism, many of the functions performed by the patriarchal family would be collectivized, thus liberating women from the double burden of housework and wage work. Thus, the time that women would have to spend on domestic work would be reduced by making it part of social production, not a reallocation of work within the home. Women would lose their domestic responsibilities to social agencies while men took on no new domestic roles (Buckley 1989, 48).

The importance placed on moving women into social production in the Marxist theory of female emancipation is clearly reflected in Soviet policy. Throughout its history, the Soviet state pursued a variety of measures to facilitate and encourage women's labor-force participation, including child-care, maternity leave and other provisions for working mothers that exceeded those in many capitalist nations (Lapidus 1978, chapter 4; Lapidus 1985, 21-3). The former Soviet Union achieved the highest female labor force participation rate of any industrial society. Beginning in the early 1970s, over 90 percent of the able-bodied adult women were employed or engaged in study, and over 50 percent of the Soviet labor force was female (Peers 1985, 117; Lapidus 1985, 16).

Marxist ideology on female emancipation was not, however, the only impetus for encouraging high rates of female labor-force participation. Economic and demographic factors were important as well. The economic expansion initiated by the First Five-Year Plan in 1928, and the commitment to rapid industrialization that followed, required an enormous increase in the size of the labor force (Lapidus 1978, 166; Peers 1985, 117-18). In addition, the casualties of two world wars, civil war and internal violence created a severe imbalance in the structure of the Soviet population. Large sex-ratio imbalances also made high rates of female labor force participation a necessity (Lapidus 1985, 15-16; Peers 1985, 117-18).

Women workers were widely distributed across sectors and occupations in the Soviet economy, from the manual labor of the agricultural sector to the highly skilled work of the scientific and technical occupations. However, despite the presence of women in occupations often viewed as traditionally male, a substantial amount of occupational segregation continued to exist. Women workers were heavily concentrated in service, public health and social welfare, education and cultural occupations. In industry, women were heavily concentrated among food, textile and garment workers (Lapidus 1978, 171-5; Lapidus 1985, 18-20).

In addition, Soviet women were badly underrepresented in top-level and managerial jobs throughout the economy. While women comprised half of the industrial labor force, they were employed as supervisors far less frequently than men. Despite their heavy concentration in agriculture, few women occupied high administrative positions there. And while men moved into the more highly paid and mechanized work, women were often left to perform much of the heavy manual labor (Lapidus 1978, 175–85; Lapidus 1985, 18–20; Allot 1985, 188).

In the professions, women were well represented among the workers with higher education. This did not, however, necessarily translate into higher incomes for them. Teachers constituted the largest group of professionals with higher education, followed by physicians and engineers. Engineers were paid relatively well; teachers and physicians were not. In the professions, as in agriculture and industry, the proportion of women declined as the level of responsibility, status and earnings increased (Lapidus 1978, 185; Peers 1985, 121).

Although Soviet law required 'equal pay for equal work', the difference in the types of jobs held by male and female workers meant that women earned less on average than men. The Soviet wage structure reflected the priorities of Soviet development, and consequently work in the basic industrial sectors was rewarded more highly than work in other sectors. Women were underrepresented in or excluded from many of these high-priority sectors, and were concentrated in occupations that were much less well-paid. By western estimates Soviet women's earnings were 68 to 75 percent of men's, an earnings gap similar to that in the United States (Peers 1985, 122; Lapidus 1985, 20; *The Economist*, 1986, 45).

Despite the Soviet state's support of women workers, Engels' socialization of housework was never fully realized. The fact that domestic work was viewed as essentially noneconomic gave investments in such services a relatively low priority. Although the provision of public child-care was an exception to the low investment in services that characterized Soviet economic growth, the commitment to child-care was far from sufficient given the high labor-force participation rates of women. In addition, the low priority placed on consumer goods in the Soviet Union exacerbated women's burden, increasing the amount of time and energy that had to be devoted to shopping, meal preparation and housework.

With housework far from socialized, Soviet women were faced with a heavy 'double burden' of work in and outside the home. In addition to a 41-hour work-week, Soviet women spent an average of 40 hours per week on domestic chores (Peers 1985, 123). The Soviet woman's double burden reflected more than the lack of consumer goods and services. A series of time-budget studies illustrated that although Soviet women devoted roughly as much time as men to employment outside the home, the division of household chores remained very uneven (Gray 1989, 37; Buckley 1981, 93).

For many years the high levels of female labor-force participation were viewed by Soviet officials and many Western observers as evidence that Soviet women had achieved full economic and social equality. From 1930 to the mid-1960s, the official view on the 'woman problem' was that it had been solved (Buckley 1985, 25; Lapidus 1978, 4). Beginning in the 1960s, however, the declining birthrate and corresponding labor shortages prompted a reassessment of this view and a renewed emphasis on policies directed at women. Particular attention was paid to the relationship between women's work lives and their fertility, raising concerns over the effect of women's double burden on their health, child-bearing, and family stability (Buckley 1981, 93–8; Lapidus 1985, 15; Peers 1985, 116).

Discussions on how to improve the economic status of women focused on ways to help women balance their dual roles in the work place and the home. One response was to increase the opportunities for part-time work for women. The vast majority of Soviet women worked full time, and until the 1970s part-time work was seldom an option. Beginning in the 1960s, many Soviet economists and policy makers saw part-time work as a way to increase the effective use of female labor and reduce women's double burden (Moses 1983; Buckley 1981, 97–8; Buckley 1989, 169–71).

There was considerable discussion of the desirability of part-time work as a solution to the problems faced by women workers.   Many of the concerns raised were similar to those discussed in the United States. Those opposed to increasing part-time employment among women argued that it would reduce their access to leadership positions within the economy and the political system. In addition, critics were concerned that in times of rapid technological change those working part-time would fall behind the new technology and lack the skills to participate in the production process. Many Soviet women expressed concerns that reductions in their work shift would actually reduce the sharing of domestic work. Surveys of women who transferred to reduced shifts in the early 1970s indicated that they actually increased the amount of time they spent on housework (Moses 1983, 19–20; Buckley 1981, 97; Buckley 1989, 170).

During the decade of the 1980s, the views and policies of Mikhail Gorbachev became very important to the status of Soviet women. Gorbachev was credited by the western press with taking a very active interest in women's issues (*Time*, 1988, 30; *The Economist*, 1986, 45). The economic changes proposed under Gorbachev's economic reform program — 'perestroika' — were seen by many to have the potential to improve the economic wellbeing of Soviet women in a variety of ways.

Gorbachev repeatedly expressed concern over the problems faced by working women and called attention to their lack of representation in the upper levels of the economy and government (Gray 1989, 191). He shared this concern, however, with a fairly traditional view of women's role in society. In 1987, for example, he argued that one element of perestroika entailed debating how women's 'truly female destiny' could be 'fully returned to her since socialist development had not left her with sufficient time for housework, child rearing and family life' (Buckley 1989, 194).

To help remedy the problems of women's double burden, Gorbachev pledged to expand on the types of policies for women that had existed in the past, such as extending pre-school child-care and increasing the number of day-care centers, extending the opportunity for part-time employment, and extending maternity benefits (*Time*, 1988, 30; *The Economist*, 1986, 45; Buckley 1989, 15, 191). In addition, some of the changes called for under perestroika promised to help reduce women's double burden through the increased provision of consumer goods and services. There was, however, little official discussion of pursuing a more equitable division of labor in the home.

Some of the structural changes proposed under perestroika also had the potential to help women as workers. Expanding the service sector, improving health care and education, developing agriculture and light industry, and reducing the amount of heavy manual labor through increased automation and mechanization were all proposed changes with the potential to improve the situation of Soviet women. Many of the areas targeted for expansion were primarily female fields, offering the possibility of improved wages and status. Reducing the amount of heavy manual labor also offered the possibility of improved working conditions for women, who traditionally performed much of this work (Peterson 1989, 14–15).

At the same time, these types of changes could introduce a great deal of vulnerability and uncertainty for women workers. Past efforts in the Soviet Union to improve the status and earnings of certain professions were accompanied by a reduction in the number of women in them. In the past, men replaced women in jobs which became mechanized. It cannot simply be assumed that as occupations and jobs are upgraded they will continue to be performed by women (Peterson 1989, pp. 14–15). This concern is confirmed by the experiences of women in Eastern Europe. As many Eastern European economies experience serious unemployment, women are losing their jobs at a disproportionately high rate (Johnson 1990; Simpson 1991).

While Soviet women achieved a great deal, their increased labor-force participation did not have the liberating results predicted by Engels. Although the Soviet state recognized women as workers and promoted their participation in social production, it did so within the context of fairly rigid gender expectations. This is reflected in both the nature of their participation in the economy and the division of labor at home.

An examination of the status of women in the Soviet Union bears out some of the fears raised by feminist critics of classical Marxism — the fear that the secondary treatment of gender subordination in Marxist analysis would result in the secondary treatment of women in socialist economies. Soviet ideology stressed that socialism would solve the 'woman problem' along with all other social problems. The lack of recognition of gender as a force of its own, which may overlap with but is certainly not contained in class, has meant that many of the unequal relationships identified by Marx and Engels in capitalist systems were perpetuated in the Soviet Union.

Conclusion

An examination of the traditional indicators of economic status in the United States and former Soviet Union reveals some interesting similarities and differences in the situations of women in these two very different economic systems. Labor-force participation has been the focus of much of the discussion of the economic status of women in both nations. High female labor-force participation rates were one of the distinguishing features of Soviet economic growth. The significant increase in female labor-force participation rates in the United States has been one of the more notable economic trends of the last half century. As more women work for pay they challenge men's monopoly over income and reduce their economic dependence. Yet, gender ideology has been slow to change in the face of these changing material conditions. This is illustrated by the fact that the division of labor in the home has shown little significant change, in either the United States or the former Soviet Union.

In the United States, public provision of child-care and other services to facilitate increased female labor-force participation remains highly controversial. While there was more public support for these programs in the former Soviet Union, the entrance of women into the work place was not accompanied by the socialization of housework. Because of both the lack of supportive social institutions and an inequitable distribution of work within the home, women were as likely to bear a double burden of housework and work outside the home in the Soviet Union as in the United States.

The challenge to traditional gender ideology posed by women's participation in the paid labor force is limited by the types of jobs they have. Although women in the United States and the former Soviet Union have very different histories with respect to paid labor, there are many similarities in their status as workers. Although Soviet women were found in occupations that are predominantly male in the United States, these were often low-status occupations in the Soviet Union. There was a high degree of occupational segregation in the Soviet economy that was not unlike that found in the United States. Like their counterparts in the United States, Soviet women received lower average wages and held fewer positions of power than Soviet males.

As in the United States, many Soviet policy-makers viewed solutions to women's double burden in terms of helping women balance *their* roles in and out of the home. The experiences of women in both the United States and the former Soviet Union suggest that policies will not promote equality between men and women without a change in the underlying gender assumptions. Policies that do not challenge these assumptions will merely reformulate existing structures of inequality. Even policies that have the potential to generate progressive change, such as the institution of flexible work schedules, must be formulated carefully with these issues in mind.

The traditional indicators of economic status show that women have remained in secondary positions in both the United States and the former Soviet Union. This must draw our attention to issues of power that cut across economic ideologies and economic systems. It challenges us to carefully consider the assumptions and categories used in our own analysis. The experiences of US and Soviet women indicate the importance of evaluating theory and policy in terms of its potential to challenge all of the systems of power perpetuating the subordination of women. This challenges us to evaluate the ideologies that have guided our thinking in the past, to assess their strengths and weaknesses, and to try to move forward in a reasonable way.

Notes

1. Feminist economists working within the neoclassical tradition have been critical of many elements of neoclassical theory. See, for example, Bergmann (1986), and Blau and Ferber (1986).
2. Later Marxist theorists have given explicit attention to divisions within classes. Feminists working within the Marxist tradition have been particularly critical of elements of classical Marxism. See Jaggar (1983).

References

Acker, Joan (1988), 'Women and Work in the Social Sciences' in Ann Stromberg and Shirley Harkess, eds. *Women Working: Theories and Facts in Perspective*, 2nd edn, Mountain View: Mayfield, CA: 10–42.

Allot, Susan (1985), 'Soviet Rural Women: Employment and Family Life' in Barbara Holland, ed. *Soviet Sisterhood*, Bloomington: Indiana University Press: 177–206.

Bergmann, Barbara (1986), *The Economic Emergence of Women*, New York: Basic Books.

Bernstein, Aaron (1988), 'So You Think You've Come a Long Way, Baby?', *Business Week*, 29 February: 48–52.

Blank, Rebecca (1990), 'Are Part-Time Jobs Bad Jobs?' in Gary Burtless, ed. *A Future of Lousy Jobs?*, Washington, DC: Brookings: 123–64.

Blau, Francine and Marianne Ferber (1986), *The Economics of Women, Men, and Work*, Englewood Cliffs, NJ: Prentice Hall.

Buckley, Mary (1981), 'Women in the Soviet Union', *Feminist Studies*, 8, Summer: 79–106.

Buckley, Mary (1985), 'Soviet Interpretations of the Woman Question' in Barbara Holland, ed. *Soviet Sisterhood*, Bloomington: Indiana University Press: 24–53.

Buckley, Mary (1989), *Women and Ideology in the Soviet Union*, Ann Arbor: University of Michigan Press.

Christensen, Kathleen (1987), 'Women and Contingent Work', *Social Policy*, 17 Spring: 15–18.

Council of Economic Advisers, (1987), *Economic Report of the President, 1987*, Washington, DC: US Government Printing Office.

The Economist, (1986), 'A Ladies' Man', 298 March 15: 45.

Ehrlich, Elizabeth (1989), 'The Mommy Track', *Business Week*, 20 March: 126–34.

Engels, Friedrich (1972), *The Origin of the Family, Private Property, and the State*, New York: International Publications.

Folbre, Nancy and Heidi Hartmann (1988), 'The Rhetoric of Self-Interest: Ideology, Gender and Economic Theory' in Arjo Klammer, Donald McCloskey and Robert Solow, eds. *The Consequences of Economic Rhetoric*, Cambridge: Cambridge University Press: 184–203.

Gray, Francine Du Plessix (1989), *Soviet Women: Walking the Tightrope*, New York: Doubleday.

Hochschild, Arlie (1989), *The Second Shift: Working Parents and the Revolution at Home*, New York: Viking.

Jaggar, Alison (1983), *Feminist Politics and Human Nature*, Totowa, N.J.: Rowman and Allenheld.

Johnson, Ian (1990), 'East German Women Bear the Brunt of Hardships Under Unification', *Buffalo News*, August 13: A3.

Kruks, Sonia, Rayna Rapp and Marilyn Young, eds. (1989), *Promissory Notes: Women in the Transition to Socialism*, New York: Monthly Review Press.

Lapidus, Gail Warshofsky (1978), *Women in Soviet Society*, Berkeley: University of California Press.

Lapidus, Gail (1985), 'The Soviet Union' in Jennie Farley, ed. *Women Workers in Fifteen Countries*, Cornell International Industrial and Labor Relations Report #11. Ithaca, NY: Cornell University, ILR Press: 13–32.

Mishel, Lawrence and David Frankel (1991), *The State of Working America, 1990–1991*, Armonk, NY: M.E. Sharpe.

Moses, Joel (1983), *The Politics of Women and Work in the Soviet Union and the United States*, Berkeley: University of California Press.

Peers, Jo (1985), 'Workers by Hand and Womb: Soviet Women and the Demographic Crisis' in Barbara Holland, ed. *Soviet Sisterhood*, Bloomington: Indiana University Press: 116–44.

Pennar, Karen and Edward Mervosh (1985), 'Women at Work', *Business Week*, January 28: 80–85.

Peterson, Janice (1989), 'Perestroika — What Does it Mean for Soviet Women?' paper presented at the annual meeting of the Association for Institutional Thought, Albuquerque, New Mexico, April 1989.

Simpson, Peggy (1991), 'No Liberation for Women', *The Progressive*, 55, February: 20–24.

Spitz, Glenna (1988), 'The Data on Women's Labor Force Participation', in Ann Stromberg and Shirley Harkess, eds., *Women Working: Theories and Facts in Perspective*, 2nd edn, Mountain View: Mayfield: 42–60.

Time (1988), 'Heroines of Soviet Labor', 6 June: 28–37.

US General Accounting Office (1991), *Workers at Risk*, Washington, DC: US General Accounting Office (Human Resources Division).

Wagman, Barnett and Nancy Folbre (1988), 'The Feminization of Inequality', *Challenge*, 31 November/December: 56–9.

Waller, William and Ann Jennings (1990), 'On the Possibility of a Feminist Economics: The Convergence of Institutional and Feminist Methodology', *Journal of Economic Issues*, 24 June: 613–22.

8. Equality and the Women's Movement: What's Missing?

Gladys Parker Foster

Economic equality for women remains elusive more than a generation after the relaunching of the women's movement in the 1960s. The pay gap has scarcely improved, while increasing numbers of women have fallen into poverty. Worse yet, poverty is the fate of more and more children. The poverty of women and the poverty of children are related.

The modern women's movement, in its laudable desire to achieve equality for women and its consequent focus on similarities between the sexes more than on differences, has concentrated on trying to extend equality of opportunity to women. The idea is that if barriers to equal opportunity for women are removed women will contribute equally and will thus be assured of equal rewards. The focus of equality has been mostly legalistic and mostly negative, emphasizing the removal of restraints (see Chafe 1978, 149, 151).

The concept of equality, however, needs help if it is to serve the cause of women well. One problem is that it leaves out children, at least in a society where contribution and reward are held to be equated by competition under the doctrine of laissez-faire. Children cannot contribute to the Gross Domestic Product, and the contributions of the bearers and the nurturers of children are not counted. Thus there seems to be no acceptable way within the market system to allocate income to children and to childbearers and nurturers.

Feminism is the belief that all persons, regardless of sex, should have the opportunity to realize their full potential and to participate fully in the social process. It is evident that the human race must be reproduced. Whoever performs the tasks associated with reproduction should not be penalized for it by being denied full development and participation in society.

Institutional economics provides fundamental principles that can guide us in moving forward on this issue. First, institutional adjustment is what institutional economics is about, and some institutional adjustment will be required. Second, institutional economics has an explicit criterion of judgment for choosing among alternative ways of solving problems. Third, it is multidisciplinary. Fourth, it recognizes the importance of culture; it is social rather than individualistic. Fifth, it sees the market structure as only one of an indefinite variety of institutional structures. Sixth, it has an historical rather than an instantaneous view of time. Seventh, it views the provision of goods and services as output or production, whether it takes place in the business world or elsewhere, and whether or not it is accounted in the Gross Domestic Product. Finally, it reconciles theory with practice.

But institutional economics has done little to help the women's movement to realize its goals. Radical institutional economics, however, shows promise in that it explicitly focuses on issues of the 1960s, including the women's movement, and because it urges a more systemic and revolutionary and activist approach. Radical institutionalism can provide the needed vigor and direction (see Waller 1988, 667; Waller and Jennings 1990; Jennings and Waller 1990; also the chapter by Whalen and Whalen in this volume).

Some Notions About Equality

Thomas Jefferson in the Declaration of Independence declared that all men are created equal. To what extent he meant to include women is not clear. What is clear is that Jefferson meant by equality not sameness but the right to life, liberty and the pursuit of happiness.

Thorstein Veblen wrote that the contribution of women in early society was greater than that of men: women did the productive work while men carried out the mostly unproductive but more honorific tasks (Veblen 1964, 42–6, 50–61). He, almost alone among economists, viewed childbearing and 'women's work' as productive. He supported the New-Woman movement for equality (see Veblen 1953, 229–34; see also Dugger's chapter in this volume).

Joan Robinson observed, 'Equal without saying in what respects is just a noise', and went on to suggest that the idea that all men are equal expresses a protest against privilege by birth. It expresses a moral standard for private life and a program for political life (Robinson 1962, 2–3).

But the concept of equality has not always been applied so nobly. J. Fagg Foster found fault with what he called the equational theory of justice, that is, that justice is done when something is brought into equality or balance with something else (Foster 1991). Neoclassical price theory, he argued, is an application of the equational theory of justice in the economic process. If price equals cost, if reward equals contribution, if utility equals disutility, then justice is done. The efficacy of the market process, which brings these things into equality with each other, is unquestionable. Equilibrium is attained. 'Man gets what he is worth'. 'You get what you pay for'.

The reproduction of the human race, however, which arguably is the most productive occupation in society, is a prime example of the inapplicability of the so-called equational theory. Our preoccupation with that theory makes the solution of problems of income distribution much more intractable. It has contributed to the notion that marriage should be thought of as an egalitarian arrangement, the termination of which will impact both partners equally. It has led to the expectation that women can go into the workforce and compete with men and have children too without missing a beat. Expecting them to do this is akin to expecting military personnel to provide their own weapons and sustenance and to pay for their own medical care, something we would consider ridiculous.

The fact is that equality of opportunity in the work place does not exist for those who have the major responsibility for the reproduction of the human race.

As William H. Chafe points out, it has become clear that the possibility of equal opportunity requires positive intervention of a substantive kind instead of the old laissez-faire premises. A political as well as a personal response is required, posing a fundamental challenge to the traditional values of individualism and laissez-faire liberalism (Chafe 1978, 150–51).

Alison M. Jaggar argues that equality as a fundamental liberal value fails to provide criteria for the distinction between genuine choices and those coerced or manipulated. The liberal tradition conceives of freedom as the absence of external obstacles to individual action and assumes individuals are autonomous agents. Equality of opportunity is not necessarily compatible with individual liberty, for example in an environment of children (Jaggar 1983, 193–5).

Zillah R. Eisenstein urges the articulation of a theory of sexual egalitarianism that denies neither women's sexual particularity (childbearing) nor their shared human qualities with men. In a sexually egalitarian society a woman should be both equal and free to say that her capacity for childbearing should not determine her social, political and economic options. Sexual equality would mean that men and women would share in the power relations of society with no regard to their (biological) sex or sexual preference. We are far from there yet, she goes on. Now woman is to be both mother and wage-earner, while her options in the labor force are seriously limited by the patriarchal organization of society, the family and the market. Dismantling the institution of motherhood while retaining biological motherhood would require an entire reorganization of the sexual, economic, political and cultural arrangements of society. This is revolutionary, but we are taking some steps in that direction (Eisenstein 1984, 207, 236–44).

When the concept of equality is examined in the light of institutional economic theory, it becomes clear that it is a worthy goal when applied instrumentally, or non-invidiously, as Jefferson and Veblen and Robinson seemed to conceive of it. But it can be destructive when applied in the market sense of equation between contribution and reward. It is important to get beyond this.

The instrumental criterion of institutional economics can provide a way to do this. It asks not what will equate utility and disutility but what will be the effect on the progress of society if a certain choice is made.

Institutional Economics and the Women's Movement

Institutional economics studies the entire culture and conceives of solutions to social problems in terms of changes in institutions rather than as adjustments of individuals to a given institutional structure. It looks not to ideologies but to open-ended searches for coherent theory informed by observation and testing. It does not accept values uncritically, imposed on society from outside the process of problem-solving; it arrives at values through the same process as it arrives at solutions in general, that is, by using reason and looking at consequences.

Some kind of value theory is used in all societies. All societies must make choices; this requires a criterion of judgement. Says Marc Tool: 'Since all social choices require the application of criteria, and since choices produce consequences, one may reflect upon the *character* of consequences emerging from the use of a criterion and thus upon the propriety of the criterion itself. Value judgements are brought within social inquiry' (Tool 1977, 829).

Steven R. Hickerson says the instrumental value principle is:

a trial and error process through which inquiry and experience lead to the formation of value judgments and to courses of action (institutional adjustments) designed to correct problems that are subject to continuous assessment. This...is the route to problem solving, not only of waste disposal problems but also problems of stability, equity, and the production and distribution of real income (Hickerson 1987, 1138).

According to instrumental value theory, the function of the economic process is the provision of goods and services serviceable to humanity. What does this mean? It means that the character of goods and services, as well as the quantity and the distribution, should be determined in such a way as to improve the optimum development of the potential of all human beings and the maximum participation of all in the social process. This is the best way to assure the progress of civilization. Economic value is located in the productive process. All useful work, that is, work that contributes to the progress of civilization, whether it earns a profit or not, is productive, that is, valuable.

Providing useful goods and services includes investing in human beings. Human beings, says Carolyn Shaw Bell, constitute the chief source of a nation's wealth, and the care and attention given by parents is paramount to developing the human potential. This is the most neglected area of human capital development. Bell notes that much government activity is not regarded as investment, but economists could well reveal that many so-called 'social programs' constitute investment opportunities for enormous wealth (Bell 1984, 434, 437; see also Hayes et al. 1990, 5).

Ultimately there is probably no more effective way to change society for the better, says Ann Dally, than to improve the quality of life for infants and young children. This means improving the lives of their mothers. The benefits would be enormous. The material benefits alone might far outweigh the costs. The mental health of a nation depends on the environment in the earliest years. In order to save money in the present we ensure that vast numbers of people will drain public resources in the future. Yet society needs and wants children and wants them to be healthy in body and mind (Dally 1983, 322–4).

Contrast the logic of institutional economics with that of neoclassical laissez-faire economics, which says that the market is the model for organizing the economy and that problems are to be solved within that structure. The market determines the worth of an activity. Women's problems are personal; the individual should adjust. Child-care is a private family matter. Note how the public/private dichotomy, the idea of the economic world of the market and the noneconomic world of home life, rationalizes the exploitation of women. The idea that the family should be exempt from government regulation denies protection to women and children (see Jaggar 1983, 144).

What is the Problem?

The problem is that women work very long hours but cannot gain enough income to provide for themselves and their children.

The problem is global. While women represent half the world's population and one-third of the paid labor force, they receive only one-tenth of world income and own less than 1 percent of world property. They are also responsible for two-thirds of all working hours (Jaggar 1983, 138).

Although the problem of inadequate income for women and children is worldwide and seemingly more or less independent of ideology, the focus in this chapter is on the problem in the United States. Chapters in this volume by Bernadette Lanciaux and Janice Peterson describe the status of women in Japan and the former Soviet Union, respectively.

In the US the number of persons living in poverty remains intractably high and is increasing, and the vast majority of the poor are women and their children. According to official government figures, 35.7 million persons were in poverty in 1992 (less than $13,924 annual income for a family of four or $6,932 for an individual) — 14.2 percent of the population.

The median income of female householders in 1990 was $18,069, while the median income of male householders was $31,552. Thirteen percent of female householders had income under $5,000, and 16.2 percent had between $5,000 and $9,999. Twenty-three percent of children under the age of six, and sixty-one per cent under that age living with the mother only, were living below the poverty level (US Bureau of the Census 1992, 446, 457).

Despite the increasing participation of women in the labor market, study after study reports that women continue to do the great bulk of the housework (see Bergmann 1986, 261–5; Berch 1982, 92; England and Farkas 1986, 94; Fuchs 1988, 78; see chapters 7 and 9).

In trying to cope with their new roles, women have had to assume an increasingly disproportionate share of society's burdens. Mother has had to become 'supermom'. As William M. Dugger says so well, the liberated woman has fallen victim to the old speed-up.

Women have entered and are continuing to enter the workforce in increasing numbers, and the likelihood is that this trend will continue. In 1988 more than 10.5 million children under age six, including nearly 6.6 million infants and toddlers under age three, had mothers in the labor force. Another 18 million children between the ages of six and thirteen had working mothers (Hayes et al. 1990, 3).

The major program in the US for sustenance for mothers and children is

Aid to Families with Dependent Children (AFDC). How adequate is it? Suzanne Helburn and John Morris did a study of costs of living for low-income single-parent families in Boulder, Colorado in March and April 1988 (Helburn and Morris 1989). They went into the community and meticulously noted actual costs of necessary goods and services for a mother and two children aged six and four. They thus identified what they called a subsistence budget, which came to $9,800. This included food, housing, clothing, transportation, child-care and taxes. Only used clothing was purchased. The diet they included would be insufficiently nutritious for long-term consumption. No entertainment was included, no candy, no gifts, no alcohol, no cigarettes, no finance charges. Unfortunately, however, AFDC and food stamps combined would generate no more than $4,900, only half the subsistence budget of $9,800. Only if this family could get subsidized housing and substantial help from family and/or friends could it survive. What if the mother were to get a job? Her total living expenses would rise from $9,800 to $18,600, mostly because of the addition of child-care costs and taxes. This would require an hourly wage of $8.94. Very few women, even if they could find a job, could find one that pays that much. A minimum wage of $4.25 an hour would provide only $8,840, less than half the $18,600 needed.

In the US in 1990 there were 4.2 million families receiving AFDC. The total number of recipients was 12.2 million; of this number, 8.2 million were children. The average monthly cash payment per family was $392 (US Bureau of the Census 1992, 370). This comes to $4,704 per year per family. It is very sobering to think of 8.2 million children living at such a low level.

Sheila B. Kamerman and Alfred J. Kahn studied the programs of six countries — France, the Federal Republic of Germany, the German Democratic Republic, Hungary, Sweden and the US — with respect to child-care programs, maternity and child-care leaves, children's allowances, flexible work schedules and shorter work hours, male–female pay levels, extent of labor-force participation of women, birthrates, announced public policies and so on (Kamerman and Kahn 1981).

They found that France had the most extensive and generous program, with a policy of supporting a neutral position, that is, providing neither incentives nor disincentives for mothers to go to work or to stay home, but rather offering support for both options, permitting women to choose. The French birthrate has fallen steadily for the past thirty years except for a brief post-World War II baby boom, similar to that of other countries. France is close to zero population growth. France is unusual in that the main considerations seem not to be labor-market issues or population concerns but rather the provision of income for low-income families and the development of good care for children (Kamerman and Kahn 1981, 11, 19–21).

The US is the only country in the study to have no announced policy on these matters. The US, it should be noted, does have a number of programs or policies in addition to AFDC that aid families with children. Some are employment related: the dependent care tax credit (DCTC) and employer-based dependent care assistance plans (DCAPs). Other programs include voucher plans, welfare-related income disregard programs, parental leave policies, and education and training programs. Tied to the federal income tax are the personal income tax exemption and the earned income tax credit. In addition there are provider subsidies and education-related programs (Hayes et al. 1990, 201–23).

What do we know about the effects of outside-the-home day care on children? Kamerman and Kahn provide information to the effect that children develop at least adequately, and perhaps better, when their mothers work (Kamerman and Kahn 1981, 249–50). Hayes, et al. also provide some evidence, while at the same time pointing out that the relationship between child-care and child development is complex, and that there are no perfect studies and few that are conclusive. The cumulative weight of evidence, they say, from empirical studies, clinical work and professional practice, suggests that child-care participation is not a form of maternal deprivation; that child-care is not inevitably or pervasively harmful to children's development, indeed there are aspects of development for which child-care is beneficial; and that the quality of child-care is important to children's development (Hayes 1990, 45–83).

There is more concern and more controversy, however, about the effects of outside child-care on newborns. Selma Fraiberg argues persuasively that the formation of the love bond that takes place between mother, or other care-giver, and baby during infancy is of paramount importance. The child loves because s/he is loved. The absence of human bonds in infancy or the rupture of human bonds in early life can have permanent effects upon the later capacity for human attachments and for the regulation of aggression. Maternal deprivation is a territory in which the diseases of non-attachment originate. We are pushing mothers into the workforce because of poverty, but the children are not faring well (Fraiberg 1977, 61–4, 132–4).

Recommendations and Conclusions

For the most part the women's movement bought into the values of the market, male-dominated society. It accepted the prevailing American view that progress lies in competition in the marketplace, and that if women have a problem, it is their problem.

The situation is not only deleterious for women and children but for employers as well. The parent with heavy child-care responsibilities cannot always give as much in the work place as the job demands. Thus ammunition is provided to conservatives who argue that women workers really are not equal and should not be paid as well. The market, they contend, says as much. But making women do all of the adjusting is no solution; this does not improve productivity. Perhaps a more appropriate response to such critics is that employers may well benefit from offering services and arrangements to help parents in the work place, because workers become more productive. But again, individuals, whether mothers or employers, should not always be expected to do all of the adjusting on their own. The larger society must help.

The entire society, says Dally, needs to become more aware. Innumerable things could be done, many of which would cost nothing. Needed are safe places for mothers to meet and children to play, gadgets to hold elevator doors open while prams and toddlers go through, courtesy from bus conductors, shop planning, facilities for children in laundries, different park and playground equipment (Dally 1983, 324–5).

As just noted, not all changes must be governmental. Custom can be enormously important in regulating behavior. Some changes occur simply through changes in societal outlook. We should strive for a greater and better-informed awareness of the problems of children and their care-givers and of society's responsibilities. Schools should inform students about the 24 hours a day, 365 days a year job of parenthood. A much-neglected area is in the attitudes of boys; the view continues to be widespread that it is the responsibility of girls and women to regulate sexual behavior. The responsibility of fathers as well as mothers for making babies should be pointed out. Education and the media are two vehicles for effecting change.

In a market-oriented society children have often been thought of either as 'consumer goods' or as 'products'. It is tempting to try to fit them into the capitalistic ideology. The perception of children as consumer goods or as products trivializes reproduction. To say, however, that children are not products is not the same as saying that procreation is not productive. The fact is that bearing and nurturing children is productive and those who provide this service must be recompensed for it in order that they may live (see Greenwood 1984, 674–5; Berch 1982, 20–21).

The idea of getting income to childbearers carries with it another concern. It is the notion that the anticipation of such income may encourage a higher birthrate and irresponsible reproduction. It is no doubt true that some persons, with or without subsidies, have children for the wrong reasons, or at least with little or no thought of the seriousness of the undertaking and of the commitment demanded of parents. Some may indeed do it for the money. Some teenagers, as well as others who have little hope of participation in the economic process, may feel that having children is their only meaningful option in society. They can produce someone who will love them. The tragic problem of 'children having children' in our society exists and must be addressed.

The concern linking reproduction to income subsidies, however, seems unwarranted. Fertility decisions are based on more complicated factors. If there is any correlation at all, increasing income seems to have a negative effect on the birthrate. Most modern industrialized countries have children's allowances. Countries that have affluent and highly advantaged women, along with adequate child-care options and children's allowances, appear to be those that also have lower birthrates (see Kamerman and Kahn 1981, 12–27, 246, 249). Clearly, withholding income from prospective parents does not stop irresponsible procreation. Providing meaningful options seems more effective.

Can society trust women to make responsible decisions about fertility? Anyone in a position to make mistakes will make some. Women, however, are more likely than anyone else to make responsible decisions about how many children to have and how long to stay home and care for a newborn. And the greater their control over their lives, the greater their stake in the system, the more likely they are to make responsible decisions.

What, then, are the solutions? Some are obvious. We must find ways to get needed income to childbearers and to care-givers. We must adopt programs to keep mothers in school; shorter and more flexible work hours, perhaps with government subsidies; maternity/paternity leaves with job security guarantees; an end to sex discrimination and occupational segregation; an effort to take comparable worth seriously; greater participation of husbands in household tasks; an increase in AFDC payments; child support from absent parents; a universal health care program.

We must revive the economy. Much of the problem of poverty for women and children is attributable to general economic stagnation. The low level of economic activity that we have come to think of as acceptable has its greatest effect on those at the lower end of the scale. We made great progress in reducing poverty in the 1960s but subsequently abandoned most of the programs. A list of desirable economic policies should include a realistic industrial policy to restructure industry and to retrain workers; it also should include measures to redistribute income so as to stimulate purchasing power and thereby help business.[1]

A solution most strongly to be advocated is a generous children's allowance for all children. This could take the form of a large increase in the amount of each exemption for children in the federal income tax. In the 1940s when it was adopted the exemption bore some reasonable resemblance to the cost of supporting a child. In 1948 three-quarters of the median family income of $3,486 was exempt from federal tax because of the personal exemption and the standard deduction. By the mid-1980s, the median family income had increased from $3,486 to $29,184, and less than one-third of median family income was exempt from taxation (Hayes et al. 1990, 211). Those who owe no income tax could get a payment, in the form of a negative income tax.

What about the question of cost? A children's allowance of $2,000 annually for all children under age twelve would cost about $83 billion. Providing $4,000 for every child aged newborn to five and $2,000 for every child aged six to twelve would come to about $126 billion (Hayes et al. 1990, 244, 246).

Is the cost excessive? First of all, one should ask the cost to society of not providing better for children. Further, much revenue could be recouped if those who are affluent enough not to need a children's allowance were required to pay more through a progressive income tax structure. The mechanism is already there. Collecting an income tax is very cost-effective. It would get rid of the need for means-testing, something that is degrading, inefficient, productive of cheating and simply not necessary. Additionally, one could compare the costs of children's allowances with the costs of weapons systems and other things society bears without objection. Finally, note the likely positive financial effect of children's allowances: increases in productivity could be expected, and this would increase output and lessen the deficit.[2] A children's allowance should be highest for newborns, when the time and energy requirements are highest, tapering off as the child gets older.

The question of who is the care-giver should be left up to the parents. There are strong arguments for more sharing of tasks associated with childrearing. Help from society must go to mothers for pregnancy and nursing; beyond this, it should go to the predominant care-giver regardless of sex.

In addition to children's allowances, an extensive day care program should be provided by the government, broad enough to include all children and incorporating the Head Start program. This could be paid for by users according to ability to pay, along with a subsidy as needed.

Still other possibilities include the kibbutzim that Israel pioneered, the 'family hotel' or 'collective house' of Sweden (see Bergmann 1986, 296), the 'service mall' proposal for America (Bergmann, 297), and other redesigns of communities to make them 'mother and children friendly', as urged by Dally and as described by Dugger.

Any society must reproduce itself. Those who do the work of reproduction should have the options, the control over their lives, the status, and the perquisites that everyone else has. This means that society must accommodate itself to this reality. Whether it be organized capitalistically, socialistically, or according to some other ideological prescription, or whether it be so mixed as not to be identifiable along ideological lines, society must adjust its institutions to solve the income problems of women and children. The problem is social, not personal.

Notes

1. In 1960, 22.2 percent of Americans were living below the poverty level; by 1969 that figure had been reduced to 12.1 percent (US Bureau of the Census 1989, 452). Unemployment fell from 6.7 percent in 1961 to 3.5 percent in 1969 (*US Department of Labor*, 1987, 8).
During the 1960s the US had a program of stimulative fiscal and monetary policies aimed largely at increasing effective demand. Since then these policies have been reversed.
Policies to revive demand would reduce the deficit. The last time the federal budget was balanced was in 1969 — actually there was a surplus of $3.2 billion that year — at a time of expansionary economic policies designed to increase expenditures for consumption and investment, as well as military spending. Prosperity increases government revenues and reduces outlays, thereby reducing the deficit. Most deficits occur in times of recession or low economic performance, that is, high unemployment. Unemployment in the 1980s and 1990s so far has been historically high, and so have deficits.
2. Victor R. Fuchs also recommends children's allowances and state-provided child-care, as well as financing them through the income tax or other broad-based taxes (Fuchs 1988, 95, 118–19, 136).

References

Bell, Carolyn Shaw (1984), Human Capital Formation and the Decision Makers', *Journal of Economic Issues*, 18 (2) June.
Berch, Bettina (1982), *The Endless Day: The Political Economy of Women and Work*, New York: Harcourt Brace Jovanovich.

Bergmann, Barbara R. (1986), *The Economic Emergence of Women*, New York: Basic Books.

Chafe, William H. (1978), *Women and Equality*, Oxford: Oxford University Press.

Dally, Ann (1983), *Inventing Motherhood*, New York: Schocken Books.

Dugger, William M. (1989), *Radical Institutionalism: Contemporary Voices*, New York: Greenwood Press.

Eisenstein, Zillah R. (1984), *Feminism and Sexual Equality: Crisis in Liberal America*, New York: Monthly Review Press.

England, Paula and George Farkas (1986), *Households, Employment, and Gender: A Social, Economic, and Demographic View*, New York: Aldine.

Foster, J. Fagg (1991), 'On The Theory of Justice', *Journal of Economic Issues*, 25 (4) December.

Foster, J. Fagg (1981), 'Syllabus for Problems of Modern Society: The Theory of Institutional Adjustment', *Journal of Economic Issues*, 15 (4) December.

Fraiberg, Selma (1977), *Every Child's Birthright: In Defense of Mothering*, New York: Basic Books.

Fuchs, Victor R. (1988), *Women's Quest for Economic Equality*, Cambridge, MA: Harvard University Press.

Greenwood, Daphne (1984), 'The Economic Significance of "Women's Place" in Society: A New-Institutionalist View', *Journal of Economic Issues*, 18 (3) September.

Greenwood, Daphne (1984), 'The Institutional Inadequacy of the Market in Determining Comparable Worth: Implications for Value Theory', *Journal of Economic Issues*, 18 (2) June.

Hayes, Cheryl D., John L. Palmer and Martha J. Zaslow eds. (1990), *Who Cares for America's Children? Child Care Policy for the 1990s*, Washington, DC: National Academy Press.

Helburn, S. and J. Morris (1989), 'Can Single Mothers Afford to Raise Their Children in Boulder? The Morris and Helburn Study', 1988/89, *Research Perspectives*, 17, Winter, City of Boulder Division of Research and Evaluation, Colorado.

Hickerson, Steven R. (1987), 'Instrumental Valuation: The Normative Compass of Institutional Economics', *Journal of Economic Issues*, 21 (3) September.

Jaggar, Alison M. (1983), *Feminist Politics and Human Nature*, Sussex: The Harvard Press, Rowman and Allanheld.

Jennings, Ann and William Waller (1990), 'Constructions of Social Hierarchy: The Family, Gender, and Power', *Journal of Economic Issues*, 24 (2) June.

Kamerman, Sheila B. and Alfred J. Kahn (1981), *Child Care, Family Benefits, and Working Parents: A Study in Comparative Policy*, New York: Columbia University Press.

Miller, Edythe S. (1972), 'Veblen and Women's Lib: A Parallel', *Journal of Economic Issues*, 6 (2 and 3) June and September.

Mead, Margaret (1949), *Male and Female*, New York: William Morrow.

Montagu, Ashley (1973), *The Natural Superiority of Women*, New York: Collier Books.

Morris, J. and S. Helburn (1989), 'Can Single Mothers Afford to Raise Their Children in Boulder? The Morris and Helburn Study', 1988/89, *Research Perspectives*, 17, Winter, City of Boulder Division of Research and Evaluation, Colorado.

Olson, Paulette I. (1990), 'Mature Women and the Rewards of Domestic Ideology', *Journal of Economic Issues*, 24 (2) June.

Peterson, Janice (1990), 'The Challenge of Comparable Worth: An Institutionalist View', *Journal of Economic Issues*, 24 (2) June.

Peterson, Janice (1987), 'The Feminization of Poverty', *Journal of Economic Issues*, 21 (1) March.

Robinson, Joan (1962), *Economic Philosophy*, Chicago: Aldine.

Sidel, Ruth (1987), *Women and Children Last: The Plight of Poor Women in Affluent America*, New York: Penguin Books.

Tilly, Louise A. and Joan W. Scott (1978), *Women, Work, and Family*, New York: Holt, Rinehart and Winston.

Tool, Marc R. (1977), 'A Social Value Theory in Neoinstitutional Economics', *Journal of Economic Issues*, 11 (4) December.

US Bureau of the Census (1992), *Statistical Abstract of the United States: 1992*, Washington, DC.

US Department of Labor (1987), *Employment and Earnings*, Bureau of Labor Statistics 34, November.

Veblen, Thorstein (1964), *Essays in Our Changing Order*, Leon Ardzrooni, ed. New York: Augustus M. Kelley.

Veblen, Thorstein (1953), *The Theory of the Leisure Class*, New York: Mentor Books.

Waller, William and Ann Jennings (1990), 'On the Possibility of a Feminist Economics: The Convergence of Institutional and Feminist Methodology', *Journal of Economic Issues*, 24 (2) June.

Waller, William T., Jr. (1988), 'Radical Institutionalism: Methodological Aspects of the Radical Tradition', *Journal of Economic Issues*, 22 (3), September.

Waring, Marilyn (1988), *If Women Counted: A New Feminist Economics*, San Francisco: Harper and Row.

9. Radical Institutionalism, Sociology, and the Dual Career Couple

Jacqueline Bloom Stanfield

Introduction

Thorstein Veblen is one of those nineteenth-century social theorists who is claimed as a 'founding father' by more than one discipline. A 'founding father' of a discipline is one whose works have been fundamental to the development of the discipline and the profession and one whose theories and ideas have stood the test of time. Two disciplines that claim Veblen are sociology, even though he did not classify himself as a sociologist, and institutionalist economics (Dugger 1989a, Ashley and Orenstein 1990).

Veblen first studied sociology and then went on to study economics. He concluded that classical mainstream economic thought did not coincide with his beliefs about human economic and social behavior. Veblen argued that society could not persist if the average person had the characteristics of the members of the predatory class as mainstream economic thought at that time assumed. In contrast to that, he argued that the average person was characterized by the instinct of workmanship, of parenting, and of idle curiosity which were social behaviors that allowed individuals to survive in economic society. These ideas of Veblen's make him a classical sociological theorist as well as the founder of institutionalist economics.

Institutionalism and sociology have been linked since Veblen's time. Ayres discussed the inevitable division of the social whole into distinct parts which are the evolving or changing social institutions (Ayres 1962). Dugger argued that radical institutionalism is a processual and cultural paradigm that focuses on social and cultural change (Dugger 1989a). Radical institutionalism is a processual paradigm because it sees the economy as an evolving set of institutions and a cultural paradigm because it focuses on cultural change. Similarly, macro-level sociological analysis also focuses on evolving institutions, while micro-level sociological analysis focuses on the individuals who make up those institutions.

Sociologically, social refers to society. Society is comprised of the interacting individuals who play the roles and occupy the statuses that are the foundation of the social structure. Culture, on the other hand, is all of the shared products of human society. These shared products include both material and nonmaterial products. Material products include the 'technology' that societies develop to survive like weapons and tools, while nonmaterial products include the language, values, and beliefs that societies also develop to ensure their survival. Sociology assumes that society and culture co-exist, and change in one, therefore, means change in the other.

One social and economic institution that has gone through many changes is the American family. Specifically, the modern American family has increasingly become detached from economic production while at the same time increasingly functioning as an agency for the management of consumption. In other words, even though the household produces domestically, it is not the virtually self-sufficient producing unit that emerged during colonial America. As American society has become more socially complex, the division of labor has become more pronounced. Much of this increased specialization has occurred because of the separation of economic production from the family. The modern American family as an economic institution consumes. The modern American family as a social institution is a major consuming unit of society and is linked directly to the other major social institutions, e.g., the economy. This is the process of social and economic process in the modern period.

This growth of production outside of the home and the growth of the paid labor force engaged in commodity production has been an important variable in the dynamic between society and economy. Many social changes are included here. For example, in the modern period the extended family has declined in importance, social life has become more impersonal, and the division of labor has increased. The most important of these changes are those associated with the structure and function of the family.

The purpose of this chapter is sociologically, and therefore institutionally, to examine the evolution of the American family. Social and cultural changes that have affected the family and allowed for the development of the family with a dual career couple are examined.

Social and Cultural Change and the Dual Career Couple

Social and Cultural Change

Over a decade ago Levitan and Belous posed and answered the question, 'What's happening to the American family?' by saying that the American family is changing, not vanishing (Levitan and Belous 1981). Change in the family is still a major topic among family theorists as the definition of family continues to broaden and include more than the traditional nuclear family (Zimmerman 1988). The empirical study of the family began in the latter part of the nineteenth century with the goal of alleviating the confusion and disorganization that the industrial revolution had caused in the family (Yorburg 1983, 8). Two specific changes in the family that resulted from the industrial revolution are the loss of family functions and changes in the role of women.

The family no longer fulfills all of the functions which it performed in the late nineteenth century. The early American frontier family was an economically independent and self-sufficient family which produced its own food, clothing, and housing; educated its children; conducted its own religious services; and practiced its own brand of medicine (McNall and McNall 1983). These functions have shifted to the social institutions, even though the family performs other functions like the brokerage, procreation, and affection functions. Even though sociologists agree about these losses of functions, they differ in their theoretical explanations and interpretations of these changes in functions.

Evolutionary theories of the nineteenth century handle this loss of family functions idea quite well (McNall and McNall 1983, 290–91). In a simple society, like America in the nineteenth century, the family is dominant. However as technological and sociocultural evolution occur, society becomes more complex and the family becomes less dominant. In other words, the evolving social institutions take over some of the family's functions.

Early in the twentieth century, emphasis in sociology shifted from the study of the evolution of the family to the study of social problems and to the advocacy of social reform (Hutter 1981, 5). This meant the study of the family in the context of such social problems as illegitimacy, prostitution, and child abuse as caused by rapid industrialization and urbanization. The major advocates of the social reform movement were the functionalists of the Chicago School. A theme for study by the Chicago School, led by William F. Ogburn, was the loss of family functions. According to the functionalist perspective, the existence of any phenomenon in a society or group is explained in terms of the function it performs for the maintenance or preservation of the group or society, and the primary focus is on the needs of the system. The system of the family did not 'need' the functions of education, protection, religion, and economics in contemporary industrial society because other systems, i.e., the social institutions, were performing them (Yorburg 1983, 17).

Ogburn's primary concern was with processes of social change and their effects on the family (Ogburn 1964). For Ogburn, family is the adaptive culture of values, ideas and attitudes; and the adaptive culture lags behind the material culture (technology) resulting in a social maladjustment between the two. The argument is that the inventions and discoveries of modern technological society have led to the decline of the family's economic, educational, recreational, religious, and protective functions. Functionalist theory views the family as a passive recipient adapting to the changes in the materialistic culture which is viewed as the active causal agent.

Conflict theory has a long history of concern about the family and emphasizes the conflict and inequality in society and the family (Yorburg 1983, 19). Conflict theory does not deal specifically with loss of functions, but Marx and Engels examined the changes which occurred in the nuclear family as a result of the rise of industrial and monopoly capital (Tucker 1978, 734–75). Veblen also examined the functions that women performed in society and noted the inequality that existed between men and women in the family and society (Veblen 1934). These theorists were examining such issues as the separation of work from home and the loss of economic independence of women. This privatization of the family, brought about by the rise of industrial and monopoly capital, was the key to understanding for Veblen, Marx, and Engels, these changes in family functions (Hutter 1981, 28).

At the individual rather than the institutional level, Burgess defined the family as a 'unity of interacting personalities' rather than as a system. Interactionist theory emphasizes various forms of family interaction patterns and studies the family as a small-scale social phenomenon (Burgess 1926). Burgess and later Burgess and Locke interpreted the loss of family functions in terms of industrialization and urbanization and the impact this industrialization and urbanization had on the individuals in families (Burgess 1926, Burgess and Locke 1945). Basically, the family changed from being a traditional institutional family to being a modern companionate family. In the companionate family, the family has lost all of its functions except the procreation and affection functions because other social institutions take care of the lost functions.

The difference between the interactionist explanation and the evolutionary, conflict, and functionalist explanations is that interactionism does not attempt to explain or interpret large-scale, grand, or macro-level questions about social change. Rather, it attempts to explain or interpret micro-level change, or change at a more readily observable level of analysis (Yorburg 1983, 28). Regardless of which sociological theoretical perspective is used for analyzing the family, the relationship between society and economy is obvious.

A second change in the American family has been the changing role of women (Levitan and Belous 1981, viii; McNall and McNall 1983, chapter 11; Yorburg 1983, 25-7; Huber 1973, 1-4; Stanfield 1985). Sociologists agree that the role of women has changed, but once again they differ in their explanations.

The traditional role of women in the frontier family of the Great Plains was very restricted to home-oriented tasks (McNall and McNall 1983). Women ran the households, kept the financial books, taught the children, cooked, cleaned, and sewed. However, in the 1900s, increases in technology and the development of agriculture as an industry encouraged families to move from the farm to the city. This greatly changed the role of women. The woman's life was no longer limited to the home, as she began attending school and working outside the home.

Conflict theory explains the changing role of women in terms of economic factors (Aldous 1981). The explanation goes like this. Women have always contributed to the family's economic resources. In frontier times they did piecework; bartered or sold butter, eggs, or produce from their gardens; and took in laundry (McNall and McNall 1983, chapter 11). Then with industrialization women began working outside the home and began acquiring their own independent incomes. As women have become less economically dependent on men, husband/wife relations have become more egalitarian allowing the wife to become even more involved with activities outside of the home (Yorburg 1983, 25). In other words, the role of women has expanded to include their participation in the paid labor force.

Likewise, functionalists are able to explain the changing role of women. These theorists explain the changing role of women in terms of changes in the economy and technology since the industrial revolution propelled women into gainful employment outside the home (Ogburn 1964). In other words, women have taken on more responsibilities outside of the home, and this has increased their responsibilities within the home.

The changing role of women is a phenomenon with which interactionist theory can also deal. This type of theory is applicable to an understanding of group interaction and individual development and change in a certain segment of the society (Yorburg 1983, 39–40). When concern is with overall societal change in regard to the family, evolutionary, conflict, or functionalist theory is most appropriate. However, when zeroing in on one specific area of change, for instance the changing role of women, interactionist theory is more applicable.

World War II can be used as an interactionist example to describe the change in the role of women. During World War II, women were recruited from the home to the paid labor-force while the men were away (Deckard 1983). As a result, women began to question their traditional role (even though they fully expected to return home after the war) because they discovered they could fulfill two roles — wife/mother and employed person — at the same time. Also at this time, colleges, universities, and trade schools opened their doors to women. This gave women the skills necessary to compete for better jobs. Reliable contraceptive devices became widely available to women in the 1960s, and this allowed women to plan their pregnancies and thus their labor-force participation or career involvement. In effect, these seemingly few changes brought about a change in American family life; the role of women changed, and this is one of the factors that was fundamental to the development of the family with a dual career couple.

The family experienced change as a result of the industrial revolution. Functions were lost to other institutions, and the role of women changed allowing them opportunities outside of the home. This allowed for the development of the family with a dual career couple. Both radical institutionalism and sociology assume, examine, and explain social and cultural change; radical institutionalism and sociology agree about the loss of family functions and the changing role of women.

The Dual Career Couple

According to the United States Bureau of the Census, in 1988 there were 51.8 million married couples, and 43.5 million of those married couples had at least one worker. Approximately 31.4 million of those married couples were couples in which both husband and wife were employed outside of the home, and only about 8 million of these were dual career couples (US Bureau of the Census 1989).

A dual career couple is a couple in which both husband and wife pursue careers and maintain a family life together which may or may not include dependents (Rapoport and Rapoport 1969; Stanfield 1991). In addition dual career couples are more likely to be in their mid-career years, to have smaller families, to be well-educated with about one-third of the couples having five or more years of college, to have earnings that far exceed those of any other type of household, to vote, and to be more mobile (Spain and Nock 1984).

Family research literature prior to 1980 documented the existence of the dual career couple using the two major concepts of role strain and coping. Current family literature continues to use the concepts of role strain and coping to explain the work/family conflicts of employed parents and continues to emphasize the individual rather than the couple. However, some additional concepts are being incorporated into the study of the dual career couple. This section examines role strain, coping, and the additional concepts currently being used to examine the dual career couple.

Role strain is the felt difficulty in fulfilling role obligations (Goode 1964). The focus of current role strain research is the wife/mother role strain in the dual career couple, work/family role strain of employed parents, and role strain in dual earner households. Regardless of the focus, the research examines determinants and consequences of role strain.

The research that focuses on the wife/mother in the family with a dual career couple argues that the wife/mother is the one adding a primary role and therefore she is the one most affected by role strain. Determinants of wife/mother role strain fall into one of two overlapping categories (Stanfield 1985). The first category deals with strains caused by the expectations of the career woman; the second with strains caused by those of the wife/mother. It is the overlap of the two sets of role expectations that cause the role strain felt by the wife/mother. The strain she feels is the consequence. This wife/mother role strain was well-documented prior to 1980 (Rapoport and Rapoport 1969, 3–30; Hall 1972, 471–86; Herman and Gyelstrom 1977, 319–33; Johnson and Johnson 1977, 391–5; Bryson, Bryson, and Johnson 1978, 67–77; St. John-Parsons 1978, 30–42; Epstein 1971, 549–64; Berman, Sacks, and Lief 1975, 242–53; Weingarten 1978, 43–52; Holahan and Gilbert 1979, 451–67).

Kelly and Voydanoff focus on the increasing problem of work/family role strain, and identify three broad categories of independent variables that are determinants of work/family role strain for employed parents (including single parents) (Kelly and Voydanoff 1985). These three categories are individual sources of work/family role strain, family related sources of work/family role strain, and work related sources of work/family role strain. Each determinant can be broken down into demands and coping resources, and the determinants are the sources of work/family role strain. Different kinds of employed parents have differing susceptibilities to work/family role strain, and Kelly and Voydanoff suggest sets of characteristics that employers, clinicians, and other service providers can identify and use with their employees and clients. In other words, they identify the determinants of work/family role strain and then address policy implications.

After documenting that the number of dual earner families in industrialized societies is growing rapidly, Galambos and Silbereisen state that the purpose of their study is to examine how each spouse's role strain and the wife's work hours are related to life outlook, marital interaction, and family conflict in an industrialized society dual earner household (Galambos and Silbereisen 1989). They achieved their purpose by distributing questionnaires that measure role strain, life outlook, marital interaction, and family conflict to a sample of dual earner couples. Conclusions about the husband's role strain differ from conclusions about the wife's role strain. Husband's role strain is isolated from any role strain felt by the wife, but wives' with husbands who have role strain have additional role strain. In other words, strained wives with strained husbands report more conflict.

In summary, the work and family lives of employed parents are still being explained with the concept of role strain. The role strain of the individual continues to be emphasized even though some family researchers indicate their unit of analysis is the household.

Coping with strain is a second major concept that has been used to explain the lives of dual career couples. Pearlin and Schooler defined coping as the things people do to avoid being harmed by life strains (Pearlin and Schooler 1978). Individuals have two kinds of resources that they can use in developing coping responses: social resources and psychological resources. Coping responses are the specific behaviors and perceptions which people use when they are actually dealing with their life problems. In other words, resources are what people have available to use in developing responses, and responses are what people actually do in relation to or in reaction to a strain or a problem. Coping functions at a number of levels, and is attained by a plethora of behaviors and perceptions related to the domains of the stress process, i.e., stressors, stress mediators, and stress outcomes (Pearlin 1989, 241).

McCubbin, et al. and Kelly and Voydanoff deal with the increased interest in coping strategies of families because of the changing view on stress and strain (McCubbin, et al. 1980, 1; and Kelly and Voydanoff 1985, 367). Traditionally, family stress was viewed as dysfunctional to the family. However, the current view is that stress and strain are not only prevalent but also normal, and that understanding the processes of adaptation or family coping styles is necessary to discover why some families are better able than other families to cope with strain.

Pearlin and Schooler examined the coping strategies families used when faced with problems in family life, and concluded that the family reaction to stress or strain is neither rigid nor random (Pearlin and Schooler 1978, 5). As the severity of hardships increase and as families experience other changes or stressors, they adapt and cope. Coping here is viewed not as a response to a single event but as an active force in shaping what will happen. A family strategy of coping is progressively modified over time, and coping becomes a process of achieving balance in the family.

Bielby and Bielby continue in the Pearlin and Schooler tradition of examining the process of achieving balance in the family by examining the process by which married men and married women in dual earner households balance the competing demands of work and family (Bielby and Bielby 1989; Pearlin and Schooler 1978). They conclude that the process of balancing work and family roles differs for married men and married women, and that even though there are trade-offs each has their own process. For example, married working women give precedence to family while married working men do not have to make trade-offs between work and family.

Gilbert and Holahan and Elman and Gilbert also examine individual coping strategies (Gilbert and Holahan 1982; and Elman and Gilbert 1984). Gilbert and Holahan compare high and low effective copers who have role conflict between their student/professional, parental, and self-development roles (Gilbert and Holahan 1982). Their strategies for coping with role conflict include depression, expressing feelings, asking others to change, and perspective taking. Elman and Gilbert investigate ways that young career women deal with possible conflicts between their parental and professional roles (Elman and Gilbert 1984). The different coping strategies that one could use include structural role redefinition (i.e., redefinition of the job), personal role redefinition, increased role behavior, cognitive restructuring, and tension reduction.

The shift from individual to family coping is identified by Olson, McCubbin, et al., as a basic theme in coping research (Olson, McCubbin, et al, 1983, 136). Family coping occurs when the family has to exert unusual effort to observe, to experience, to define, to understand, and/or to take some kind of special action so that it can return to the more orderly routines of family life (Reiss and Oliveri 1980, 431). The seminal works here are Hill's ABCX model; Koos' coping as a roller coaster process of adjustment; and McCubbin and Patterson's Double ABCX Model (Hill 1958; Koos 1946; and McCubbin and Patterson 1981). Along with this shift from individual to family coping has come the realization of the interactional nature of coping and the compromise and coordination required in the family. In effect, family coping is viewed as a set of interactions within the family and transactions between the family and the community.

Family coping literature has also focused on individuals coping with the conflicts between professional and parental roles, but not how the family as a group copes with conflict (Bielby and Bielby 1989, 776). Hall identified three individual strategies of coping with role conflict (Hall 1972, 474). Type I strategies are structural role redefinition strategies. Type II is personal role redefinition strategies, and Type III is reactive role behavior. Gilbert, Holahan, and Manning combined Hall's Type I and Type II coping into a role redefinition strategy, and their other strategy is role expansion which encompasses Hall's Type III (Gilbert, Holahan, and Manning 1981, 420). These too are strategies which the individual can use within the family to cope.

Dual career couple coping strategies have only in the past decade been researched. Skinner identifies two types of coping strategies (Skinner 1980, 478). These two types are coping strategies within the family and coping strategies involving support systems external to the family. These are identified as family coping styles, but in actuality they are dual career wife coping strategies.

However, alternate ways that dual career couples cope with role strain have been identified (Stanfield 1987). In-depth dual career couple interviews were conducted during which couples had to negotiate their responses to questions. Based on this research, Stanfield identified two dual career couple styles of coping with role strain: the Flexible style and the Rigid style (Stanfield 1987). Flexibles and Rigids were each characterized by a different level of role strain at home, role strain at work, and role strain due to the competing demands of home and work; and by different levels of role compartmentalization; flexibility of work schedule; division of household labor; and prioritizing.

In summary, coping continues to be a major explanatory concept for the dual career couple. Coping is examined as a process and in relation to individuals, to individuals in married couples, and to couples.

In addition to role strain and coping, several other concepts are currently being used to explain the dual career couple. There is recognition among family researchers that dual career couples are made up of family members other than the wife/mother, and so research is focusing directly on men (Rosin 1990; Schnittger and Bird 1990) and children (Knaub 1986) in families with a dual career couple. In addition, dual career issues are being examined (Jordan, Cobb, and McCully 1989; Falkenberg and Monachello 1990).

Rosin states that research on men in dual career couples has been limited and that most dual career couple research has focused on women's experiences in the dual career couple (Rosin 1990). What research there has been concerning men in dual career couples has focused on (1) the impact of working wives on men's job, marital, and life satisfaction and (2) the effect of wives' employment on husbands' domestic participation (Rosin 1990, 170). Therefore, Rosin examines the effects of dual career participation on men in relation to career, family, and marital satisfactions and dissatisfactions. Being part of a dual career couple appeared to contribute to men's satisfaction because they had career autonomy. The men's primary source of dissatisfaction was the sense of abandonment resulting from their wives' unavailability to fulfill traditional female roles. Rosin concludes that men in dual career couples are no longer cushioned by the presence of a traditional wife and that men, i.e., husbands, also will have to learn to balance the competing demands of work and family.

Schnittger and Bird document earlier research on dual career couple coping, but indicate that previous research pays little attention to the differences in the ways that dual career men and women cope (Schnittger and Bird 1990). There are specific gender differences in regard to coping. Men are less likely than women to use the coping strategies of delegating, using social support, cognitive restructuring, and limiting avocational activities even though men now are becoming involved in family roles to an extent not documented previously. Men are just as likely as women to cope with work and family demands by subordinating careers, compartmentalizing work and family roles, and avoiding some responsibilities altogether.

Children are another component of family life. Knaub examines children's perceptions about growing up in a dual career household (Knaub 1986). She questioned children about which was their most influential parent, what were their family strengths, their experience in the dual career household, the benefits of the dual career household, problems of the dual career household, and housework. Children's perceptions of the dual career couple lifestyle were positive. Mothers and fathers were both identified as 'most influential'; families were characterized by concern, respect, and support; children were supportive of the lifestyle and any problems (both parents working) were outweighed by the benefits of the lifestyle.

Identification of issues faced by dual career couples is also currently being found in the family research literature. Jordan, Cobb, and McCully identify and examine clinical issues faced by dual career couples (Jordan, Cobb, and McCully 1989). Clinical issues include occupational issues, household and child-care issues, and personal issues, and their focus is on how social workers can intervene and help dual career couples cope with the issues. Falkenberg and Monachello distinguish between the terms dual career family and dual income family and argue that dual earner family is a term that encompasses both (Falkenberg and Monachello 1990). They then revert back to examining the experiences and problems of the wife and to addressing the problems and issues faced by the spouses of working wives in dual earner families.

Family researchers have branched out from the major concepts of role strain and coping. Men's roles, children's perceptions, and issues in the family with a dual career couple are additional concepts being used to examine the dual career couple. However, the major concepts used for examination continue to be role strain and coping.

Conclusion

A major premise of this chapter was that both radical institutionalism and sociology assume and examine social and cultural change, and that both the sociological and the radical institutionalist paradigms are useful in analyzing the evolution of the patriarchal American family. Veblen scrutinized the way that women were removed from productive employment; Ayres said that the family was a 'typical' institution and therefore characterized by evolution; and Dugger said that women's roles now included participation in the paid labor force (Veblen 1934; Ayres 1962; and Dugger 1989b).

Therefore, due initially to the industrial revolution, the family as an institution has evolved from an economically self-sufficient and productive unit to a major consuming unit in society, and one result of this evolution is the family with a dual career couple. These are the findings of radical institutionalism in regard to the modern American family and the dual career couple, and they coincide with the findings of family sociologists.

References

Aldous, Joan (1981), 'From Dual Earner to Dual Career Families and Back Again', *Journal of Family Issues* 2: 115–25.

Ashley, David and David Orenstein (1990), *Sociological Theory: Classical Statements*, Boston: Allyn and Bacon.

Ayres, Clarence E. (1962), *The Theory of Economic Progress*, New York: Schocken Books.

Berman, E., S. Sacks and H. Lief (1975), 'The Two Professional Marriage: A New Conflict Syndrome', *Journal of Sex and Marital Therapy*, 1: 242–53.

Bielby, William T. and Denise Bielby (1989), 'Family Ties: Balancing Commitments to Work and Family in Dual Earner Households' *American Sociological Review*, 54: 776–89.

Bryson, R., J. Bryson and M. Johnson (1978), 'Family Size, Satisfaction, and Productivity in Dual-Career Couples', *Psychology of Women Quarterly*, 3: 67–77.

Burgess, Ernest (1926), 'The Family as a Unity of Interacting Personalities', *The Family*, VII: 1.

Burgess, Ernest, and Harvey J. Locke (1945), *The Family From Institution to Companionship*, New York: American Book.

Deckard, Barbara S. (1983), *The Women's Movement*, New York: Harper and Row Publishers.

Dugger, William M. (1989a), *Radical Institutionalism: Contemporary Voices*, New York: Greenwood Press.

Dugger, William M. (1989b), *Corporate Hegemony*, New York: Greenwood Press.

Elman, Margaret R., and Lucia A. Gilbert (1984), 'Coping Strategies for Role Conflict in Married Professional Women with Children', *Family Relations*, 33: 317–27.

Epstein, Cynthia F. (1971), 'Law Partners and Marital Partners: Strains and Solutions in the Dual-Career Family Enterprise', *Human Relations*, 24: 549–64.

Falkenberg, L. and M. Monachello (1990), 'Dual Career and Dual Income Families: Do They Have Different Needs?', *Journal of Business Ethics*, 9: 339–51.

Galambos, Nancy L., and Rainer K. Silbereisen (1989), 'Role Strain in West German Dual-Earner Households', *Journal of Marriage and the Family*, 51: 385–89.

Gilbert, L.A., C.K. Holahan and L. Manning (1981), 'Coping with Conflict Between Professional and Maternal Roles', *Family Relations*, 30: 419–26.

Gilbert, L.A. and C.K. Holahan (1982), 'Conflicts Between Student/Professional, Parental, and Self-Development Roles: A Comparison of High and Low Effective Copers', *Human Relations*, 35: 635–48.

Goode, William (1963), *World Revolution and Family Patterns*, New York: Free Press.

Goode, William (1964), 'A Theory of Role Strain', *American Sociological Review*, Vol. 25: 483–96.

Hall, D.T. (1972), 'A Model of Coping with Role Conflict: The Role Behavior of College Educated Women', *Administrative Science Quarterly*, 17: 471–86.

Herman, J.B. and K.K. Gyelstrom (1977), 'Working Men and Women: Inter- and Intra-role Conflict', *Psychology of Women Quarterly*, 1: 319–33.

Hill, Reuben (1958), 'Generic Features of Families Under Stress', *Social Casework*, 39: 139–50.

Hiller, Dana Vannoy and Janice Dyehouse (1987), 'A Case for Banishing Dual Career Marriages' from the research literature *Journal of Marriage and the Family*, 49: 787–95.

Holahan, C.K. and L.A. Gilbert (1979), 'Conflict Between Major Life Roles: Women and Men in Dual-Career Couples', *Human Relations*, 32: 451–67.

Huber, Joan, ed. (1973), *Changing Women in a Changing Society*, Chicago: University of Chicago Press.

Hutter, Mark (1981), *The Changing Family: Comparative Perspectives*, New York: John Wiley and Sons.

Johnson, C.L. and F.A. Johnson (1977), 'Attitudes Toward Parenting in Dual-Career Families', *American Journal of Psychiatry*, 134: 391–5.

Jordan, Cathleen, Norman Cobb and Rex McCully (1989), 'Clinical Issues of the Dual Career Couple', *Social Work*, 34: 29–32.

Kelly, Robert F., and Patricia Voydanoff (1985), 'Work/Family Role Strain Among Employed Parents', *Family Relations*, 34: 367–74.

Knaub, Patricia Kain (1986), 'Growing Up in a Dual Career Family: The Children's Perceptions', *Family Relations*, 35: 431–37.

Koos, Earl L. (1946), *Families in Trouble*, New York: Kings Crown Press.

Levitan, Sar A. and Richard Belous (1981), *What's Happening to the American Family*, Baltimore: John's Hopkins University Press.

McCubbin, H.I. and J.M. Patterson (1981), 'Family Stress Theory: The ABCX and Double ABCX Models' in *Systematic Assessment of Family Stress and Coping: Tools for Research, Education, and Clinical Intervention*, St. Paul: University of Minnesota, Family Social Science: 7–15.

McCubbin, H.I. and J.M. Patterson, et al. (1980), 'Family Stress, Coping and Social Support: Recent Research and Theory. An Expanded Version of Family Stress and Coping: A Decade Review', *Journal of Marriage and the Family*, 42(4): 855–71.

McNall, Scott and Sally McNall (1983), *Plains Families: Exploring Sociology through Social History*, New York: St. Martin's Press.

Ogburn, W. (1964), 'Technology and the Changing Family', Boston: Houghton Mifflin.

Olson, D.H. and H.I. McCubbin, et al. (1983), 'Family Coping Strategies' in *Families: What Makes Them Work*, Beverly Hills, CA: Sage Publications, Inc., chapter 8.

Pearlin, Leonard J. (1989), 'The Sociological Study of Stress', *Journal of Health and Social Behavior*, 30: 241–56.

Pearlin, Leonard and Carmi Schooler (1978), 'The Structure of Coping', *Journal of Health and Social Behavior*, 19: 2–21.

Poloma, Margaret M. (1972), 'Role Conflict and the Married Professional Woman' in *Toward a Sociology of Women*, Constantina Safilios-Rothschild, ed. Lexington, MA: Xerox College: 187–98.

Rapoport, R. and R. Rapoport (1969), 'The Dual-Career Family: A Variant Pattern and Social Change', *Human Relations*, 22: 3–30.

Reiss, David and Mary Ellen Oliveri (1980), 'Family Paradigm and Family Coping: A Proposal for Linking the Family's Intrinsic Adaptive Capacities to its Responses to Stress', *Family Relations*, 29: 431–44.

Rosin, Hazel M. (1990), 'The Effects of Dual Career Participation on Men: Some Determinants of Variation in Career and Personal Satisfaction', *Human Relations* 43: 169–82.

St. John-Parsons, D. (1978), 'Continuous Dual–Career Families: A Case Study' *Psychology of Women Quarterly*, 3: 30–42.

Schnittger, Maureen H. and Gloria W. Bird (1990), 'Coping Among Dual Career Men and Women Across the Family Life Cycle', *Family Relations*, 39: 199–205.

Sekaran, Uma (1989), 'Understanding the Dynamics of Self-Concept of Members in Dual Career Families', *Human Relations*, 42: 97–116.

Skinner, D. A. (1980), 'Dual-Career Family Stress and Coping: A Literature Review', *Family Relations*, 29: 473–80.

Spain, D. and S. Nock (1984), 'Two-Career Couples, A Portrait' *American Demographics*, 6(8): 25-7.

Stanfield, Jacqueline B. (1985), 'Research on Wife/mother Role Strain in Dual-Career Families', *American Journal of Economics and Sociology*, 44 (3): 355-63.

Stanfield, Jacqueline B. (1987), 'Dual Career Couple Styles of Coping With Role Strain', dissertation, Colorado State University.

Stanfield, Jacqueline B. (1991), 'Recent Perspectives in Dual Career Couple Research', paper presented at Western Social Science Association meetings, Reno.

Tucker, Robert C., ed. (1978), *The Marx-Engels Reader*, 2nd ed, New York: W. W. Norton and Co., Inc.

US Bureau of the Census, Current Population Reports, Series P-60, No. 165, *Earnings of Married-Couple Families: 1987*, Government Printing Office, Washington, DC, 1989.

Veblen, Thorstein (1934), *The Theory of the Leisure Class*, New York: Modern Library (originally published 1899).

Weingarten, K. (1978), 'The Employment Pattern of Professional Couples and Their Distribution of Involvement in the Family', *Psychology of Women Quarterly*, 3: 43-52.

Yorburg, Betty (1983), *Families and Societies: Survival or Extinction*, New York: Columbia University Press.

Zimmerman, Shirley (1988), *Understanding Family Policy: Theoretical Approaches*, Newbury Park, California: Sage Publications, Inc.

10. The Status of Women in Japan

Bernadette Lanciaux

Stories about the changing role of women in Japan appear frequently in the popular press. Stories have appeared about Japanese women becoming successful in traditionally male-dominated fields, choosing to continue working after they marry and have children and about the labor shortage pulling women into the workforce in record numbers. Japanese laws regarding women make it appear that women in Japan have advantages that women in the US do not. The Japanese Constitution of 1947 explicitly granted women equality under the law and outlawed discrimination on the basis of sex including wage discrimination. Japan has a legally mandated twelve-week maternity leave for women and offers working mothers nursing leave which allows two thirty-minute breaks per day for mothers to nurse babies under one year of age. Since 1986, Japan's Equal Opportunity Act has among other things, urged firms to equalize opportunities for men and women.

These laws and stories of Japanese women breaking with tradition offer evidence that Japanese women are gaining equality with men. An examination of the data on women's labor-force participation can leave the impression that women in Japan today are about where women were in the US in the 1950s. The similarities in the trends can suggest a convergence between the social position of Japanese and American women. But the evidence overstates the case. The fact that stories of Japanese women's success are newsworthy suggests that the reports are about the exceptions to the rule and not the norm. And although the position of women in Japan today may appear to be similar to that of Western women a few decades ago, the similarities are superficial. The categories used in the aggregated data do not necessarily have the same experiential meanings in different cultures.

Recognizing that the similarities may not be as great as they seem at first glance, it is tempting to use differences in the aggregates and differences in the coping strategies of Japanese and American women as evidence of the inferior position of women in Japan and a willingness among Japanese women to participate in their own exploitation. But such an analysis is ethnocentric and inappropriate. It is necessary to understand what lies behind the aggregate data and how Japanese women and men put their world together to understand the status of women in Japan.

Towards this end, this chapter begins with a discussion of the stereotypical roles of women in Japan both in the household and in the work place. While these stereotypes represent the norm, there is evidence that progress is being made in breaking out of the narrowly defined traditional boundaries. This evidence is presented along with a discussion of the institutions which reinforce stereotypical roles for women. This includes a brief discussion of the historical position of women in Japan, the educational and employment systems and relevant aspects of the legal system. The changes in these institutions affecting the status of women in Japan are discussed along with the forces stimulating change. The final section of this chapter is devoted to providing an interpretation of the information presented about women in Japan and some discussion of the likely direction of further change in the status of women in Japan.

The traditionally defined place for women in Japan is in the home as wife and mother. A woman's role in the family is seen as being her most important role and is her primary source of status. Wives typically manage everything including the finances within the Japanese household. Men hand over their paychecks to their wives and receive an allowance. Women do virtually all the housework, get the children off to school, oversee children's studies when they come home from school and assume responsibility for discipline of children. This presumption of woman as wife and mother heavily influences all other aspects of a woman's life, from her education, her labor-force participation pattern, her job choice and the number of hours she works. As evidence presented later in the chapter shows, the entire Japanese economy and social structure is based on this assumption as well.

Today, 60 percent of Japan's total female population holds wage-earning jobs and women comprise 37 percent of Japan's total labor-force.[1] The most distinguishing characteristic of Japanese women's work experience is the M-shaped pattern in the labor-force participation rate by age group. This pattern is the result of Japanese women following the societal expectation that a woman will work for a few years while she is young and single and then to 'retire' to take care of her family when she gets married or has children. Some young women even refer to their work as *koshikake*, which means chair that you sit on for just a little while (Condon 1985, 199). In 1988, the labor-force participation rate of women aged twenty to twenty-four was 73.6 percent for Japanese women compared to 72.3 percent for American women. While labor-force participation rates of American women stay above 70 percent until age fifty, this rate drops rapidly for Japanese women, falling to 56.9 percent for twenty-five to twenty-nine year olds and 50.5 percent for thirty to thirty-four year olds. Only 36.7 percent of the women surveyed by the Prime Minister's Office reported that they had continued working without interruption. Although Japanese women's participation rates rebound somewhat as their children enter school age, until women are age sixty, American women's participation continues to exceed the rate for Japanese women. Of Japanese working women surveyed, 60.8 percent indicated that they intend to work 'as long as I am able', while 11.1 percent responded 'until my children become financially independent', 7.5 percent said 'until retirement', and 6.6 percent said 'until I start receiving pension benefits'.

Women can get jobs as office ladies, factory workers, clerks in banks, supermarkets, in one of the many mom and pop type stores, and in farming. In 1989, 33.7 percent of working women in Japan were classified as working in clerical or related jobs; 21.2 percent in craft and production process jobs (factory work); 12.6 percent in sales, 10.7 percent as service workers and 5.6 percent as laborers. The percentage of female employees in professional and technical fields was only 14 percent in 1989, up from 9 percent in the 1960s. In 1989, 1.0 percent of female employees were classified as managers, and the remaining 1.2 percent in agricultural, forestry, fisheries, mines, transport and communications. In an effort to understand what lies behind this data, the following describes in some detail the typical jobs and work experiences of Japanese women in clerical, factory and professional jobs.

Many Japanese young women aspire to get work as an office lady (OL).[2] An office lady is typically a graduate of a junior college and does many of the clerical tasks done by secretaries in the US. She answers the phone, greets customers, makes copies, types and files. But an OL is also expected to serve tea and coffee and to arrive at work early to make the tea and clean the office, and is expected to be an 'office flower' herself, to 'decorate' the work space. The job of office lady offers no chance for advancement and has low pay. Office ladies typically live with their parents (if they live within commuting distance) or in company owned and operated dormitories. Office ladies do not tend to live in their own apartments in part because of the high cost of renting an apartment in Japan and also due to the impression that living in an unsupervised environment would make on prospective husbands. Japanese employers often see themselves as matchmakers since a salaryman's long working hours make it difficult to meet a potential spouse. The company tries to recruit the most marriageable young women for the job of OL and keeps a close watch on them during their off work hours to insure that they are 'nice' girls. This is achieved through the company dormitory within which the company assumes the parental role, supervising and restricting the activities of the young women.

Just over 21 percent of employed women in Japan work in factories. A typical female worker on Japanese assembly lines is a young high school graduate who has come to the city from a rural area. Some reasons for taking these jobs are so that she will not be a burden on her parents back home (called a *kuchiberashi*), so that she can meet a salaryman for a prospective husband, and so that she can save up money for a wedding. Young female factory workers usually live in company dormitories. The dormitories are advertised in the recruiting brochures sent to rural areas to assure the parents of the young women that the company will look out for their daughters.

The workday of the *kojo* or factory woman is long and hard, beginning at 7:55 with morning stretching exercises. The workday ordinarily ends at 5:00 p.m. although everyone is expected to work overtime if the company needs it — and most women do so without complaint. Women on the line also endure incidents of sexual harassment and are powerless to do anything about it.[3] Life in the factory and in the dormitory is sufficiently unpleasant to ensure that the option of marrying and leaving the company is an attractive one for most women. Few women continue to work in the factories beyond an age of thirty.

Women in professional jobs provide the stories so popular in the western press. They provide evidence that women are making in-roads into male-dominated fields in a way that is similar to American women of an earlier era. The percentage of female employees in professional and technical fields has increased from 9 percent in the 1960s to 14 percent in 1989. Still, only 6 percent of scientists are women. Most professional women have four-year degrees from a top Japanese university or an MBA from a top-flight American business school. The experience in the US can help the Japanese woman in her career by giving her role models not readily available in Japan and time to practice the necessary skills of assertiveness, etc. The proportion of female graduates of four-year colleges and universities (women most likely to get professional and technical jobs) who found employment in Japan increased from 65.7 percent in 1980 to 81 percent in 1990. For the first time, in 1990 the proportion of successful job seekers was the same for men and women graduates. Smaller companies in rural areas provide relatively good job prospects for Japanese women (because many men do not want to accept jobs there).

Anecdotal evidence of successful Japanese women, coupled with the Japanese equal rights law and equal opportunity law is used to convince western audiences that women are on the verge of achieving equality in Japan. And while it is true that progress is being made, the aggregate data camouflage the reality experienced by professional women in Japan. Getting a job with a large or a small company has been only part of the story. Women have traditionally had little control over the job to which they are assigned upon hire. In Japan employees are typically hired into the company and, after being hired, the company assigns the employee to what they view as an appropriate job-track. (This has been affected by the Equal Opportunity Law.) Even if a woman gets assigned to the same job-track as a man, unlike men, women do not tend to get the training to make them valuable lifetime employees. Nor do they tend to get the promotions and pay raises.

College educated women have the best professional career prospects with foreign subsidiaries in Japan. Jane Condon reported, 'More than 150,000 young women work with foreign firms where they tend to be treated with more respect and have a better chance at receiving promotions and more responsible work' (Condon 1985, 195). A growing number of professional women are starting their own businesses so that they can avoid the internal problems of working for a big company.

Regardless of the type of job held by the young woman, the societal expectation is that she will quit her job when she marries and has children. A Tokyo Metropolitan Government survey indicated that 44 percent of young working women want to marry before they are twenty-five, and 70 percent want to marry before they are twenty-seven. Half of the companies surveyed indicated that they 'believe women will quit work if they marry'. Until a 1966 court ruling, women could legally be forced to retire or be fired upon marriage. In spite of the change in the law, Japanese young women still tend to quit their full-time jobs to concentrate on domestic chores when they marry. The fact that it is not legal to force retirement does not eliminate subtle and not so subtle pressure to quit upon marriage. Subtle pressure is applied by the practice of giving women only unattractive, dead-end jobs at low pay that anyone would look forward to leaving. Pressure also comes in the form of disapproving comments from co-workers, superiors, family and friends. In a culture that values individuality this might not make much difference, but in Japan where the motto is, 'The nail that sticks out will be pounded down', this pressure is quite effective. Sixty-four percent of women report wanting to return to work after marriage and raising children.

Some Japanese women do remain employed after marriage. Of women in the non-agricultural workforce in 1989, 58.5 percent are married (up from 32.7 percent in 1960), 9 percent divorced or widowed and 32.5 percent never married. Married women in Japan who work tend to hold part-time jobs, defined as working less than thirty-five hours a week. More than 60 percent of women surveyed report wanting to return to work on only a part-time basis after marriage and raising children. As of February 1988, 53.7 percent of all Japanese mothers worked. Mothers whose youngest child is between fifteen and seventeen years old, have a labor-force participation rate of 70.6 percent compared to 72.9 percent for comparable American women. Of mothers whose children are of school age, 65-70 percent have jobs. Overall, Japanese women cite raising children and taking care of the sick or elderly as their greatest problems associated with working. As of February 1988, 31 percent of Japanese mothers held part-time jobs while 22.7 percent held full-time jobs. The number of women re-entering the workforce has increased in part due to the decline in the fertility rate in Japan which has dropped to 1.53 births expected per woman during her reproductive lifetime. The rising costs of children's educations, mortgage payments, other necessities of life as well as the expanding definition of what is a necessity have also provided incentives for Japanese mothers to re-enter the workforce. In addition many women report being bored by their married lives and seek to relieve the monotony by re-entering the workforce. When asked why they work, 41.1 percent of Japanese women responded, 'to supplement the family income', 33.4 percent responded, 'to maintain a livelihood' and 'to earn money that can be used freely', and 31.4 percent said 'to save money for the future'. Increasing numbers of women also indicated that they work 'to broaden my perspective and make friends' and 'to fill up free time'.

Part-time workers, or *furiitaa*, are the fastest growing segment of the female labor-force in Japan. Women report that they like part-time work because it allows them the ability to work while not requiring them to neglect their domestic responsibilities. In the survey conducted by the Prime Minister's Office, women were asked to identify what working conditions were 'desirable to allow women with infants and small children to continue working'. 'Being able to take days off to nurse children when they get sick' was the primary response given with 55.2 percent in agreement, followed in popularity by 'being able to take an extended child-rearing leave', with 41.5 percent. 'Being able to take special breaks during the working day for child-care' drew 35.8 percent approval, and 'being able to select convenient working hours' was cited by 28 percent of respondents.

Part-time work is also attractive to employers who use part-time employees as an economic buffer, hiring them for the maximum hours when times are good and severely cutting hours or letting them go when economic conditions dictate. Part-timers are also attractive to employers because they seldom receive the standard fringe benefits of full-time employees (paid vacations, social security, housing loans, and family allowances). Part-timers who work at home doing piece work are overlooked by the government and receive very low pay for their work.

The deep historical roots of the current status of women in Japan is one of the most important impediments to progress improving women's status. An inferior position for women can be traced back to the Kamakura period (1185–1333 AD) with the development of the samurai ideal out of feudalism. The samurai code, or *bushido*, incorporated Chinese-Confucian ideals of control of emotions, strict hierarchy, and loyalty to one's *daimyo* or lord. The samurai wife was expected to take orders from her husband. The husband's first loyalty was to his daimyo and the wife came second. By the Tokugawa period (1603–1867 AD) the adoption of Chinese-Confucianism had brought women's rights to a low point in Japan. Confucian ideas, introduced around 700 AD, had competed with ancient Japanese ideas for several centuries and were not widely adopted until the Tokugawa era. The Tokugawa government wished to unite the various regional factions into a nation/state under its direction and found the Confucian system of strict hierarchy to be useful in achieving this end. Establishing the inferiority of women in Japan was part of establishing this social hierarchy.

An influential book during this period entitled *Greater Learning for Women*, written by Kaibara Ekken, outlined the neo-Confucian code of behavior for women and reasons for women's inferiority. Women were said to be silly, indocile, discontent, slanderous, jealous and stupid. Silliness and stupidity also meant 'fostering rebellion or refusing to work for the lord' (Bingham and Gross 1987, 93–104). *Greater Learning for Women* established the definition of the ideal woman. Women were supposed to be obedient to their fathers when they were young, to their husbands in marriage, and to their sons in old age. Love was not considered important in marriage. In public, wives were expected to walk behind their husbands. Tokens of affection were interpreted as signs of masculine weakness and were seen as a potential source of power for women. The Tokugawa government feared rebellion and worried that women could use their wiles to lead good men astray. During this period, women were trained in household skills but formal education for women was discouraged as was reading of the classics of Japanese literature by women such as *The Tale of Genji* which was considered too risqué and corrupting. For the security of the state, even women's physical freedom to move about was severely restricted during the Tokugawa era.

Repression of women lessened during the Meiji Era (1868–1911 AD) and with the opening of Japan to outsiders. A group of reformers referred to as the Meiji Six wrote extensively on changes Japan needed to make to modernize, including changes in the role and status of women. Japanese emissaries sent abroad to study western institutions were surprised at the treatment received by American and European women. Yanagawa Masakiyo, attendant to the chief envoy to the US wrote in 1860:

> In this country women are usually revered. When a man enters the room, he greets women first if there are women present, and men afterward. Also a man takes off his hat when he greets a woman, whereas he does not do so in greeting a man. If a man meets a woman in the street, he steps aside and lets her pass first. The way women are treated here is like the way parents are treated in our country.[4]

The exposure to the West did have an impact on the treatment of Japanese women because of concern that Japan would be seen as barbaric due to its treatment of women.

Fukuzawa Yukichi, social critic and one of the Meiji Six, wrote extensively of the place of women in Japan. He consistently criticized *Greater Learning for Women*. He was an advocate of movement towards equality for women and men. He wrote that movement towards equality would involve changes in the structure of marriage and the relationship between husband and wife, changes in the nutritional and physical conditioning of women, changes in the legal and economic rights of women and the initiation of formal education for girls. Fukuzawa's writings were widely read but did not lead to dramatic improvements for women. But as a result of the work of the Meiji Six and other male reformers, public education for young girls was encouraged although the curriculum was directed at making them 'good wives and wise mothers'. Higher education in christian schools became available to women also. Women also gained the right to a divorce during this era.

By the 1880s, Japan had the beginnings of a women's rights movement. Some outspoken Japanese women campaigned for women's right to vote, employment, education, divorce, and for other aspects of family law. This movement had little impact on the Meiji Constitution adopted in 1889. A second wave of feminist activism began in 1910 with the publication of *Bluestocking*, a journal particularly notable for its stand on women's rights.

Although women's rights did not expand significantly during the Meiji Era, women began to work outside the home in large numbers during this period. Women's employment in Japan did not mean progress towards equality or liberation, but has in a sense, been one more example of their exploitation. Girls and women from samurai or well-to-do peasant homes were urged by the government to work in government mills and silk reeling operations for the good of the nation. Quickly, the daughters of well-to-do families chose not to work in these factories and were replaced by workers from urban slums, suburban villages and tenant farms in far away villages. Girls and women were sent by their families to work in the mills often with their families receiving their earnings up front so that the women themselves did not receive a paycheck. As a result, by 1900, almost 80 percent of the workers in the Meiji factories were girls or women. Foreign exchange earnings from these and government-owned cotton-spinning mills provided much of the funding for the Meiji miracle. Thus, Japan's earliest industrialization was based on imperialism, colonialism and the labor of women.

Many of the aspects of women's lives in Japan today are heavily influenced by Japanese history. The educational system for girls and women in Japan is no exception although it may appear on the surface to be equivalent to education in the West. Most girls in Japan complete high school and almost as many women as men go on to higher education. In 1988, 36.2 percent of Japanese women and 37.1 percent of Japanese men advanced to junior colleges or four-year colleges and universities. Most of the young women going on to college enroll in junior colleges making up over 90 percent of the students enrolled at the two-year colleges in 1989. At junior colleges in Japan classes are geared towards preparing young women for jobs as office ladies and for their future roles as wives. Home economics was the most popular course of study for women at Japanese junior colleges in 1989, with 27.5 percent of women choosing home economics, down from 30 percent in 1980. Female students at junior colleges are typically involved in many extra-curricular activities including cooking, tea ceremony, flower arranging and other traditional Japanese arts. Only 14.4 percent of Japanese women advance to four-year colleges and universities, compared to 35.3 percent of men. Women made up only 26.9 percent of four-year college university students in Japan in 1989. Even at four-year colleges and universities, 6.8 percent of Japanese women chose home economics as their course of study in 1989. Humanities has been and continues to be the most popular major for women at four-year colleges and universities with 36.3 percent of women, where as 46.8 percent of men choose the social sciences. Thus while higher education is open to Japanese women, they are not getting the educational experience that aggregate college enrollment numbers might imply to a western audience.

The educational choices of Japanese women are a result of a variety of factors. The societal value structure will not encourage her to pursue academically oriented higher education. There is very little economic incentive for a woman to get a university education given realistic career expectations. Her college degree will not eliminate the barriers to good jobs in most cases and it may limit her job prospects because firms prefer to hire younger and more docile junior college graduates who will work for more years before they marry. Many companies do not even accept job applications from female university graduates. As a result, many Japanese women make decisions in a way that is consistent with Japanese history and reinforces the social stereotype.

The Japanese Constitution, the Labor Standards Act, Equal Opportunity Act, maternity leave and nursing leave make it appear that women have a firm legal basis for achieving equality. But these laws look far better on paper than in actual practice. While the Constitution granted women legal equality since 1947, they clearly do not have equality in reality. The impact of the Labor Standards Act prohibiting wage discrimination on the basis of sex was limited by the fact that women and men are segregated in the Japanese labor market. In addition this law did not cover promotion or retirement. The Equal Opportunity Act 'prohibits gender discrimination with respect to vocational training, fringe benefits, retirement and dismissal' (Edwards 1992, 1). The Act does not attempt to achieve 'equality of result', only 'equality of opportunity' and does not specify penalties for those found to be in violation, does not include a provision for private parties to file suit in a court of law (not that filing a suit would be a likely response to discrimination in Japan), or for the government on its own initiative to investigate and prosecute cases of systematic discrimination. Rather, enforcement rests on the strength of the administrative guidance provided by the Ministry of Labor. In addition, the law is not backed up by affirmative action programs.

In response to the passage of the Equal Opportunity Law firms have begun offering employees their 'choice' of career tracks rather than making the assignment arbitrarily. This has opened up more opportunities for women but the actual change in outcomes resulting from this apparent change in practice is not as dramatic as one might expect. Employers encourage women to take positions traditionally defined for women by suggesting things like 'If you are transferred tomorrow to a remote area, can you leave your husband and children here? Your family will fall apart'. One author describes 'The institution of the two-track system has allowed enterprises to eliminate the female threat without breaking the law — it makes corporate discrimination seem a matter of free choice' (Masuda 1990, 6). Survey results indicate that 'About 85% of female workers in Japan feel discriminated against in chances for promotion and 70% assert they are victims of bias in pay and positions'. Managers rationalize their behavior by saying that training women represents 'unjustified costs to the firm', that women have low commitment to their job and are inefficient (Carney and O'Kelly 1990, 136–8). In a recent survey, 57 percent of employers said that women lack a strong attachment to their jobs and will not work for a long period, 40 percent said women perform poorly in business, while 90 percent said they provide *proper* opportunities for women.[5]

The twelve-week maternity leave policy (six weeks leave before the baby comes and six weeks after) sounds good but it is not sufficient to keep young Japanese mothers in the workforce. As any new parents can tell you, six weeks to adjust to life with a new baby is not very much and going back to work when a baby is only six weeks old is extremely difficult even in the US where we have comparatively good support for working mothers. In the US extensions of maternity leaves are very common, whereas in Japan such extensions are not. If a Japanese woman takes more than six weeks off when her children are born, she will not find it easy to re-enter the workforce. Japanese men who go abroad to manage subsidiaries are confronting this problem also. This re-entry problem is in part a consequence of the Japanese lifetime employment system but also a result of age discrimination. The lifetime employment system has an internal career ladder structure with only one entry point for jobs — the bottom. Employees tend to move up the career ladder and pay-scale at Japanese companies by entering class. Because of the emphasis on hierarchy and the role of age in that hierarchy, it is difficult in the Japanese system as it currently operates, to accommodate people who leave the regular workforce for a few years and then seek to re-enter it. Japan's nursing leave policy is a positive step towards making the workplace hospitable for mothers of young children, but the policy is not as good in practice as it is on paper. Commuting distances make it difficult to take advantage of the nursing leave policy, and few Japanese firms have on-site child-care. While the changes in the institutions affecting Japanese women's lives are in the direction of greater opportunity for women, and on the surface, the progress looks significant, the changes are greater in appearance than in effect.

Rather than interpreting the status of women in Japan with western biases, the following section is an attempt to provide a basis for understanding the position of women in Japan from a Japanese perspective. The following presents evidence from attitudinal surveys, articles about individual women's struggles, personal interviews with Japanese women, and letters by Japanese women in a newspaper advice column. These give some insight about how Japanese people and women in particular view the position of women in Japan. A survey by the Prime Minister's Office in 1990 found that 41.5 percent of Japanese feel there is sexual equality in Japan, while 38.8 percent feel there is not. More than 50 percent of Japanese men feel that the sexes are on equal terms in the home in Japan. Of those surveyed, 45.9 percent said that they believed women should marry citing that it is 'natural for women to marry and have children', that 'a woman's happiness lies in marriage', and that 'marriage leads to both psychological and economic stability'. Over half of those surveyed (52.3 percent) said that they do not feel men and women are treated equally at work with only 18.8 percent saying that they are. Only 12.8 percent indicated that men and women have 'the same opportunities to realize their potential in society', while 51 percent said men have a clear advantage and 31.9 percent indicated that men have a slight advantage.

Letters written to *Jinsei Annai*, a popular advice column in Japan, suggest that some women are very dissatisfied with their lot in life and are at a loss for what to do about it.[6] Letters in the column describe dissatisfaction with: selfish husbands, husbands' ongoing extra-marital love affairs, the husbands' long hours at work and with colleagues after work, husbands' lack of involvement in the activities of the household, a lack of affection between marriage partners, and other problems between husbands and wives. Women complain about: feeling lonely after marriage, being overburdened by the demands of housework and child rearing, having difficult relationships with in-laws, and the inequality of part-time work. The complaints of Japanese women are not all that different from complaints one might hear from American women. The responses to the letters are quite surprising, however.

Thus results of the survey and the letters in the advice column seem to indicate that many Japanese people perceive a lack of equality between men and women in Japan. This fact could cause us to conclude that the Japanese recognize that there is a difference between 'what is' and 'what ought to be' and therefore the Japanese will try to address these inequalities. But it is not necessarily the case that the Japanese feel that inequality is wrong. The importance of the social hierarchy in Japan even suggests that inequality is seen as a worthwhile sacrifice for achieving and maintaining harmony and is essential to the smooth functioning of their society. Although Japan no longer strictly adheres to Confucian ideas and maintains a strict social hierarchy for the security of the state as in the Tokugawa era, Japan is still a hierarchical society with institutions dependent upon the maintenance of the hierarchy. Japan's entire economic system itself is dependent upon women accepting their lot in life. Japan has historically maintained an extraordinarily low unemployment rate (hovering around 2 percent) by having women enter and leave the labor-force as economic conditions dictate. During boom times, women take temporary and part-time work, at low wages and minimal benefits. Then, during a downturn, the women return to their place in the home. This pattern goes back to the Meiji Era.

Even institutions that appear to support women's liberation on the surface, in practice maintain the status quo. The Constitution, Equal Opportunity Law, maternity leave and nursing leave make it appear that Japan has structures to allow women to remain in the workforce following childbirth. But in reality the availability of day-care in Japan is even worse than in the US. An absolute shortage of day-care facilities in Japan has been identified as a cause for concern for dealing with the impending Japanese labor shortage by the Labor Ministry's, 'White Paper on Working Women'. Because societal values assume that women will stop working when they get married and have children, the institutional structures to support alternatives have not developed. Until recently, even babysitting was considered to be alien in Japan.

The responses to women writing for advice from the newspaper column also demonstrate the absence of societal support for equality between men and women. The advice columnists were unsympathetic to the problems described by the letter writers and even engaged in what could be called blaming the victim. Frequently the advice seeker was told to stop complaining and grin and bear it, so to speak. They were told to try to figure out how they were bringing these problems on themselves. To the extent that this is a reflection of contemporary Japanese social values, the advice given suggests that the institutional impediments to women gaining equality in Japan are very great indeed. There is very little support indicated for women standing up for themselves and demanding change, (or even meekly requesting change for that matter).

And in spite of the trends and institutional changes that I have outlined here, it is still the case that women are treated as inferior in Japan and do not strenuously object to this treatment. A few individual women attempt to break into career-track jobs traditionally reserved for men, remain working after they marry or return to paid employment when their children enter school, divorce abusive mates, write letters to an advice columnist, or file suit for discrimination. But the vast majority, (78.3 percent) of women said they were satisfied with their jobs. Divorce rates in Japan are not skyrocketing, the legal system is not overburdened with discrimination cases. The vast majority of women seem content with the current rate of progress or feel powerless to change the rate of progress.

There are several reasons why Japanese women may be willing to accept the status quo. Harmony, or *wa* has long been the backbone of Japanese society. Japanese people seek to avoid confrontation explaining that living together in harmony is a necessity because of their small crowded island living conditions. Few women or men for that matter buck the system. Individuality is not a valued trait in Japan. Unlike American parents who typically view their newborn baby as dependent and see their job as that of raising this child to be independent, Japanese parents typically view their new child as an outsider who has to be brought into the group. American parents seek to encourage independent thinking and individuality, whereas Japanese parents encourage consideration for the group and conformity with the group. Japanese women are members of a culture that values harmony and places great emphasis on the group. Being raised to be part of the group makes it unlikely that Japanese women will do anything but accept the position society has defined for them.

Japanese women are also willing to accept their position in Japanese society because they can see that women today have it better than their mothers did before them and they can be hopeful that things will be better for their children after them. In addition, Japanese women may accept their position in Japanese society simply because it is easier than taking on the system. Why would a young Japanese woman try to buck the system, to give up the 'advantages' of her traditionally defined role, with little likelihood of gaining any of the advantages of a career, and without the support of structures necessary to make a career possible? It is difficult to work on opening a door that you will probably never walk through on the understanding that you are opening it for those who come after you.

It could also be argued that women in Japan accept second-class status because they do not recognize their exploitation. Some young Japanese women studying in the US told me that they intend to go back to Japan and live with the societal constraints. They explained that it was easier to go back to Japan because they would not 'have to make so many choices'. They knew what their life would be like in Japan. The future was not a vast unknown. Understanding and accepting such an explanation requires a recognition of the place of 'freedom of choice' in the western value system and to recognize that in our society, we reject the notion that wants are culturally determined. We focus on the individual and assume that individuals just know what they want out of life and will insist on having freedom to make choices reflecting their own individuality. We marvel at the fact that great numbers of Americans individually make the same choices. We fail to recognize that the full range of choices is not really available to everyone. I do not mean to imply that choice is bad, but rather I hope to point out that this decision by Japanese women to go with the flow is a different way of handling the cultural forces at work. Japanese women seem to consciously recognize the obstacles they are up against. Young American women often believe that radical feminists have already won all the battles for them and are shocked when they confront the reality of working and family life.

Japanese women also explained to me that they are willing to accept the system in part because they have freedoms that Americans simply do not recognize. They pointed out that women have control of the family finances in Japan and complete control over their own personal lives. They have their own friends and do not have to give up their own personal lives for their husbands. This is reinforced by McKinstry and McKinstry, when they write:

> In the modern American middle-class marriage, husbands and wives take priority in almost all matters involving elective time. This tends to build a wall of commitment around couples that is extremely difficult for friends to break through...(whereas) women in Japan not only can have friends, but they really feel a great need for friends (McKinstry and Nakajima McKinstry 1991, 88).

Japanese women are not controlled by their husbands because their husbands tend to not be around very much.

A young Japanese woman also explained that the fact that they were expected to be deferential to men was in some way liberating. I was told that in the US, we are expected to display genuine emotion and we have a conflict if our true feelings do not correspond with what is socially acceptable to express. But in Japan, there is no expectation that you actually believe in the role you are playing. There are even two different words to express the 'two truths'. The Japanese word for 'true feeling' is *honne*, whereas *tatemae* represents the 'principle'. With explicit recognition that there are these 'two truths', a woman need feel no inner conflict when she defers to men even if it does not reflect her genuine feelings.

Another factor making it easier for Japanese women to accept their position in society, is the fact that women's roles in the family are actually valued in Japan. With society sending Japanese women a consistent message it is less likely that the women will feel the exploitation. We all want to feel like what we do is appreciated. Japanese society does tell women: We value your place in the home. As a result, in Japan, a woman can be a wife and mother, have respect from others and have respect for herself. Her contribution to the success of Japan is recognized.

American women are told that we can have it all if we are just willing to work for it. But the reality is that the vast majority of American women do not really have the economic opportunities society promises. We do not have adequate affordable child-care and women are constantly reminded that home and family related responsibilities really do belong to women. Society sends American women mixed messages. 'You really should stay home and take care of kids'. But if she does, she will have no control over her life, no money except what is doled out by her husband and will have low status because in our society, status is achieved only through work outside of the home in the marketplace. As a result, women who choose to stay at home feel inadequate because they are not bringing home a paycheck. Women who work outside the home feel inadequate because they are not taking care of their families. Women who try to do both are under incredible stress, getting the worst of both worlds in many instances. In the US we expect women to accept the same inhumane working conditions as men rather than adjusting our economy to accommodate the lives of the real people the economy is supposed to be supporting. In the US, we have narrowly defined improvement in women's position in society as that of becoming more like men, to the detriment of all.

I would warn against taking the fact that many Japanese women work part-time as evidence of their exploitation. Surely there are problems associated with part-time employment but 'part-time' is not the problem. Low pay, low status, a lack of benefits, and little job security are the problem. Solve these problems and part-time work (or a re-definition of full-time work) for men and women might just provide a better quality of life for everyone. Full-time jobs with all the demands that go along with it, may have worse problems than are associated with part-time work. We must not forget that the economy is to support the ongoing life process and a significant part of that LIFE goes on in the home, not in the workplace. The workplace is supposed to support the household, not vice versa. Part-time work, particularly for married people with children, may be humane for everyone, not just for women. This is not to say that part-time work should be the only option for women in Japan. Women and men need options, and part-time work may be a good option.

It is clear that the choices open to women in Japan are widening and the position of women is improving although at a very slow pace. Clearly, women's status in Japan needs to continue to improve. But it is not valid to measure the progress of Japanese women by how much they are like western women, or even how much Japanese women are like Japanese men. Japanese women must define for themselves just what constitutes improvement. Rather than mimicking the western approach to women's liberation, they could learn from our mistakes and avoid some of the problems that we encounter as a result of the way we have defined 'improvement' and liberation. We can hope they devise innovative solutions to their problems that avoid some of the problems that we neglected to address.

Public opinion in Japan seems to support change however slow. A large majority of those surveyed (77.8 percent) indicated that 'women should be encouraged to participate more widely in society' with only 6.5 percent disagreeing with this statement. To achieve this end, 38.4 percent indicated that 'women must be given greater educational and training opportunities', 36.2 percent said that 'institutional reforms aimed at both men and women should be implemented so as to make balancing work and raising children possible', 27.5 percent said that 'information concerning women's participation in society should be made more readily available', and 25.2 percent said that 'men should take on more domestic responsibilities'. The Japanese Economic Planning Agency has even issued a White Paper on National Life indicating that expanding employment opportunities for women is necessary for Japan to successfully confront the challenge represented by the labor shortage.

Perhaps we as a society could learn from the Japanese and recognize the importance of group and family and harmony. Rather than building a system on the assumption that we all make it on our own, perhaps like the Japanese we could recognize that we are all dependent upon one another. We are all part of the economic and social system and these systems require that certain jobs be performed by someone in our midst and all these contributions are valuable. And perhaps in addition to offering suggestions for radicalizing Japanese women, we could learn from Japanese women.

Notes

1. The data reported in this chapter comes from a variety of sources which are listed in the references. The author would be happy to identify the sources of any individual statistics to interested readers.

2. Much of this and the following section is based on Jeannie Lo's wonderful account of life as an office lady and as a factory worker based on her experiences and her interviews of young Japanese women at Brother Industries in Japan. See *Office Ladies, Factory Women* (1991).

3. Lo (1991, 32–3). A recent issue of the *Japan Times Weekly International,* told of an incident where a metropolitan assemblywoman with a reputation as a women's rights advocate was grabbed by a politician who justified his action by saying 'he was tantalized by her comely hips'. The article also points out that there are no laws defining sexual harassment in Japan. See Jocelyn Ford (1992, 4).

4. Quoted in Sievers (1983, *Flowers in Salt,* 1). This quote demonstrates how cultural definitions influence one's perceptions of another culture.

5. 'Women Feel Bias in Japan', *The Wall Street Journal,* August 8, 1991, page A9. Emphasis added.

6. John A. McKinstry and Asako Nakajima McKinstry, (1991), *Jinsei Annai — 'Life's Guide': Glimpses of Japan Through a Popular Advice Column.* While an advice column gives an imperfect picture of a society, it does shed additional light on the subject of this chapter.

References

Bingham, Marjorie Wall and Susan Hill Gross (1987), *Women in Japan: From Ancient Times to Present,* St. Louis Park, MN: Glenhurst Publications, Inc.

Brinton, Mary C. (1988), 'The Social-Institutional Bases of Gender Stratification: Japan as an Illustrative Case', *American Journal of Sociology,* 94 (2) September.

Brinton, Mary C. (1989), 'Gender Stratification in Contemporary Urban Japan', *American Sociological Review,* 54 (4), August.

'The "Mommy Track", Japanese-Style: A Tight Labor Market Means New Status for Women Workers'(1991), *Business Week,* 11 March.

Carney, Larry S. and Charlotte G. O'Kelly (1990), 'Women's Work and Women's Place in the Japanese Economic Miracle' in Kathryn Ward, ed., *Women Workers and Global Restructuring,* Ithaca, NY: ILR Press of Cornell University.

Condon, Jane (1985), *A Half Step Behind,* New York: Dodd, Mead and Company, Inc.

Cook, Alice and Hiroko Hayashi (1980), *Working Women in Japan,* New York: Cornell University.

Edwards, Linda N. (1988), 'Equal Employment Opportunity in Japan: A View from the West', *Industrial and Labor Relations Review,* 41, January.

Edwards, Linda N. (1992), 'The Status of Women in Japan: Has the Equal Employment Opportunity Law Made a Difference?' paper presented at the meetings of the American Economic Association, January.

Ford, Jocelyn (1992), 'Sexual Harassment Taken For Granted', *The Japan Times Weekly International Edition,* 32 (6) February: 10–16.

Holstein, William J. (1990), *The Japanese Power Game: What it Means for America,* New York: Charles Scribner's Sons.

Kawahara, Junko (1990), 'Women Scientists: Achieving Recognition, The Science of Equality', *Look Japan*, 36 (414) September.

Kiyooka, Eiichi (1988), *Fukuzawa Yukichi on Japanese Women: Selected Works*, Tokyo, Japan: University of Tokyo Press.

Kodansha Encyclopedia of Japan (1983), Tokyo, Japan: Kodansha International, Ltd.

Lebra, Takie Sugiyama (1984), *Japanese Women: Constraint and Fulfillment*, Hawaii: University of Hawaii Press.

Lo, Jeannie (1991), *Office Ladies, Factory Women: Life and Work at a Japanese Company*, Armonk, NY: M.E. Sharpe.

Mackie, Vera (1988), 'Feminist Politics in Japan', *New Left Review*, January/February.

McKinstry John A. and Asako Nakajima McKinstry (1991), *Jinsei Annai, 'Life's Guide': Glimpses of Japan Through a Popular Advice Column*, Armonk, New York: M. E. Sharpe, Inc.

Masakiyo, Yanagawa (1938), *The First Japanese Mission to America*, trans. Junichi Fukuyama and Roderick H. Jackson, New York: Fred H. Stokes Co.

Masuda, Reiko (1990), 'Nice Try, But...: Women and Work, The Equal Employment Opportunity Law', *Look Japan*, 36 (414) September.

Myers, Frederick Shaw (1992), 'Women Architects Build Dreams into Creative Reality', *The Japan Times Weekly International Edition*, 32 (7) February: 17–23.

Neale, Walter C. (1990), 'Absolute Cultural Relativism: Firm Foundation For Valuing and Policy', *Journal of Economic Issues*, 24, June.

Osako, Masako Murakami (1978), 'Dilemmas of Japanese Professional Women', *Social Problems*, 26.

Reischauer, Edwin (1988), *The Japanese Today: Change and Continuity*, Cambridge, MA: Belknap Press of Harvard University Press.

Robins-Mowry, Dorothy (1983), *The Hidden Sun*, Stanford, CA: Stanford University Press.

Rudolph, Ellen (1991), 'On Language: Women's Talk', *The New York Times Magazine*, 1 September.

Seo, Akwi (1990), 'One for All, All for One', *Look Japan*, 36 (414) September.

Shibayama, Emiko (1990), 'Women Get On the Job: Women and Work, The Facts and Figures', *Look Japan*, 36 (414) September.

Sievers, Sharon L. (1983), *Flowers in Salt: The Beginnings of Feminist Consciousness in Modern Japan*, Stanford, CA: Stanford University Press.

Sundstrom, Marianne (1991), 'Part-Time Work in Sweden: Trends and Equality Effects', *Journal of Economic Issues*, 25, March.

Takagi, Haruo (1989), 'Aspirations of Women Executives: A US–Japan Comparison', *Japanese Economic Studies*, 17, Winter: 88-9.

Tsurumi, E. Patricia (1990), *Factory Girls: Women in the Thread Mills of Meiji Japan*, Princeton, NJ: Princeton University Press.

Ueno, Chizuko (1987), 'The Position of Japanese Women Reconsidered', *Current Anthropology*, 28 (4).

Weisman, Steven R. (1991), 'In Crowded Japan, A Bonus For Babies Angers Women', *New York Times: International Section*, Sunday, 17 February.

Japan Labor Bulletin, (1990), Japan Institute of Labour, 29 (10) October.

Japan Report (1989), 'Baby-sitting Becomes a Booming Industry', 35 (6) June.

Japan Report (1989), 'Promoting Increased Job Opportunities for Women and the Elderly', 35 (12) December.

Japan Report (1990), 'Tokyo Survey Finds Women Want to Keep Working After Marriage', 36 (2) February.

Japan Report (1990), 'Employment of Women Graduates Outpaces Men', 36 (4) April.

Japan Report (1990), 'With More Women in the Work Force, Child Care Facilities Feel the Strain', 36 (5) May.

Japan Report, (1990), 'Women to be Admitted to Japan's Defense Academy', 36 (5) May.

Japan Report, (1990), 'Poll Finds that Mothers are in Charge', 36 (11) December.

Japan Report (1990), 'Japanese Consumers Focusing on Luxury Durables', 36 (10) November.

Japan Report (1990), 'PM's Office Looks at Women in the Work Place', 36 (10) November.

Japan Report (1991), 'Experts Think Japan's Low Birthrate Could Decline Further', 37 (1) April.

Japan Report (1991), 'Support for Women's Equality and Freedom Gains in Japan', 37 (1) April.

Japan Report (1991), 'Survey Compares Life in Japan and Elsewhere', 37 (6) June.

Japan Report (1991), 'Japan's Working Mothers', 37 (5) August.

Japan Report (1991), 'Japan's Fertility Rate Set Record Low in 1990', 37 (5) August.

Japan Report (1991), 'Dealing with the Labor Shortage', 37 (6) September.

Japanese Working Life Profile: Statistical Aspects (1990), Tokyo, Japan: The Japan Institute of Labor.

The Wall Street Journal (1991), 'Women Feel Bias in Japan', 8 August.

Conclusion

Doug Brown

Conclusions to volumes such as this usually provide the editor(s) with that special opportunity to summarize, reflect and offer hope and optimism for the future prospects of their project. In that respect this conclusion is no different. The articles we have assembled here are the product of a conscientious group effort in which all of us gathered for a summer conference with the common understanding that radical institutionalism is meaningless if it does not further the cause of women's emancipation.

Our institutionalist heritage as described in these pages and our lineage traceable to Thorstein Veblen are not merely concerned with ending *economic* forms of injustice. To state our concern in this way is to mistakenly narrow the focus of radical institutionalism and misrepresent what this book is about. What, in part, makes our institutional economics radical is *not* that we focus on economic types of injustice, but more broadly, that we focus on injustice in general and the ways in which the economy, as a social provisioning process, may hinder or help the cause of a more socially just world.

In the case of this volume, the specific issue is gender-based injustice. At the same time, institutional economics does not view 'the economy' as an isolable, reified entity that can be studied (with respect to any number of injustices) independently of other social and cultural spheres of activity. As virtually all of the preceding essays mention, either explicitly or otherwise, institutional economics views economic activity as immersed within both a cultural context of meanings and ideologies, and immersed within the broader social reproductive process including politics, the family, religion and a host of other institutions.

Perhaps as radical institutionalists we are concerned first with injustice (and in this case, sexism) and second with economics. As the last set of articles in Part III suggests, we are multidisciplinary in character, and in examining a problem like sexism, are willing to become, temporarily and in a most humble and modest fashion, sociologists, political scientists, psychologists and anthropologists.

Thus, institutional economics considered as an approach or method, is eclectic in that it eschews economic essentialism, determinism and reductionism. Of course, because it searches for a global picture of reality, yet is eclectic and condemns social injustice, it shares much with Marxism. Like many institutionalists today, Marx was willing to draw on a variety of disciplines. Marxism has deeply influenced sociology, political science, philosophy and economics, and to a certain extent Marx practiced all of these academic disciplines.

This is precisely because Marx, and many of those in the Marxist tradition that succeeded him, was in search of a 'global theory of society'. In other words, Marxism has been about the quest for a 'grand narrative', or a 'meta-narrative', as the postmodernists contend. The 'grand narrative' is therefore (if it were to truly exist) capable of explaining who we are, where we have come from, and where we are going.

Unfortunately, whenever the search for a global theory of society tends to overshadow the details of trying to explain society, the approach runs the risk of becoming reductionist, essentialist and determinist. This apparently has happened with Marxism in the last century despite various efforts to rescue the 'real Marx'. This does not have to force the conclusion that Marxism must be completely abandoned, but perhaps the quest for a global theory must be reassessed as we move into the next century and the third millenium, humbled by what we increasingly cannot explain and continuously fail to understand.

But what about institutional economics? If it does share so much with the Marxist tradition, is it also at this point a dated 'grand narrative'? Is it also a search for a global theory of society that has (or will) eclipse its explanatory power? This is where the issue of gender and sexism enter. As should be clear to the reader upon concluding this volume, what institutional economics and the issue of gender-based injustice have in common is *diversity*. It is this diversity in both the institutional approach and in the multi-layered, overlapping character of sexist injustice that may very well prevent institutional economics from going the way of orthodox Marxism.

In fact Thorstein Veblen did not embrace Marxism because of the fact that it seemed to him to be excessively concerned with the derivation of a global explanatory theory. As most of the preceding essays conclude, institutionalists are different precisely because they want to theorize, explain problems, contribute to the elimination of these problems, but want to do so without subscribing to or drafting a specific global theory.

The issue of sexism presents a special problem here. In some respects it represents a test for institutionalists who want to theorize and explain as best as possible without succumbing to essentialism, reductionism or economic determinism. As the comments by the authors in this volume indicate, sexist injustice is an unusual type of injustice because it is not reducible to any one sphere of activity, nor is it manifested in any one particular fashion.

Undoubtedly the most fundamental theme in this book is that the multidimensional character of sexist injustice, if it is to be theorized about at all, requires a multidimensional approach that is perhaps well suited to the radical institutionalism of these authors. Or conversely, the multidimensional approach of institutional economics is well suited to the diversity and complexity inherent in the very nature of sexism (as the Whalens' essay argues). The chapters in Part I all seem to suggest this.

On the other hand, as the foregoing essays demonstrate, all of us as feminist institutionalists *and* institutional feminists are unwilling to give up completely on trying to describe, explain and arrive at, some conclusion about what sexist injustice is and how we can get rid of it. We have all found it to be a messy problem, irreducible to one of simple exploitation, biological difference or family structure. We continue to struggle to come to terms with this most pernicious and pervasive inequality, and have tried to consider it from diverse angles as well: from Veblen's perspective; from 'insights from the margin'; from the cultural context of Japanese life; from the Soviet case after the Bolshevik Revolution; and from various feminist theories.

Each article, in effect, presents a different angle focused on a monstrous problem that seems to stretch beyond the limits of patriarchy in general. As Bill Dugger states in his essay, we are institutionalists inspired by a vision of a socially-just world of *equality* in *full participation*. Consequently, we realize that an eclectic problem requires an eclectic approach. This is where radical institutionalism and gender connect and converge.

So all efforts of the sort presented in this volume must end with a statement about hopes for the future. This collection appears to offer both optimism and pessimism simultaneously. The optimism results from the fact that we are radical institutionalists, while the pessimism most likely results from the character of sexist injustice itself.

First, with respect to the bad news and the difficulties that the future presents, the preceding chapters emphasize the fact that although most of the world's female population has the problem of gender injustice in common, there is no clear evolutionary or teleological process at work that is automatically going to unite them in common cause and a common agenda. It looks as though unity-through-diversity is getting harder to achieve. The united front and majoritarian policy consensus is going to be harder to forge; not easier. It will take more work in organizing and building solidarity than ever before.

The nature of capitalism, as it becomes ever more globalized and integrated while paradoxically ever more fragmented and decentralized, seems to be working against the growth of organic and spontaneous solidarity. This is certainly not a new development, but the Marxian prospect of a drift towards increasing victim-solidarity is now remote. *The means and mechanisms by and through which women and other victims are able to define themselves differently is increasing as the technological changes in global capitalism proceed.*

The unification is becoming more difficult to forge, *not* because victims of sexist injustice are increasingly being duped by ideology, enabling myths, reification of consciousness or other means whereby awareness of the problem at hand is nullified or reduced. Women are more than ever aware of their plight, but the process of unification for strategic political action is more difficult.

In this respect the situation is different and less pessimistic than thirty years ago when Herbert Marcuse concluded his classic piece, *One-Dimensional Man*. Marcuse believed that high-tech, consumerist capitalism, that is the 'administered society', was on the verge of administering consciousness-of-problems out of existence. He stated that the only hope left was for the hopeless, and that nothing indicates that it will be a good end. 'The critical theory of society possesses no concepts which could bridge the gap between the present and its future; holding no promise and showing no success, it remains negative'. For him, life was becoming so one-dimensional that our ability to actually think about our problems was being eliminated. I believe that this is also what John Kenneth Galbraith had in mind when he published the *New Industrial State* at approximately the same time as Marcuse's *One-Dimensional Man*. The capabilities of advanced capitalism were so great that the system could not only deliver the goods, but all boredoms would be amused, all anxieties tranquilized, and all needs fulfilled. Thus, women, like other victims of injustice, would no longer view themselves as victims of anything more than what was natural to their condition.

The good news is that the multidimensionality of sexist injustice today, coupled with the continued growth in self- and collective-awareness of and by women, seems to dispute Marcuse's thesis and pessimism. Additionally, our optimism comes, in part, from the institutionalist perspective that informs these essays. Contrary to Marcuse's fears, we do not foresee women either giving up the struggle to end sexism, nor being led to believe that no problems of injustice exist. Marcuse might have concluded that the power of the system to engineer needs might well have led to women's acceptance that they were 'born to shop'. Yet the administration of consciousness that Marcuse and Galbraith warned us about did not materialize as anticipated. In this we are grateful.

As institutionalists we view the economy and the broader society as a set of institutions which are nothing more than relationships between people. As Marx so rightly stated, capitalism is nothing more than an 'ensemble of social relations'. Generally, if people either embrace or at least acquiesce with the institutions in which they are enmeshed then the system will work fairly well. However, if people do not like their institutions then the system will dysfunction and continually falter. This does not mean that progress is inevitable. It simply means that as long as people are not happy with the way things are, the way things are will not be so good. There are going to be problems, the outcomes of which we are not sure.

In this case, all of the authors in this volume do not think it likely that women will acquiesce; thus the overall functioning of the society and economy will continue to be a problem. Capitalism does not work well unless people accept it. Women have not accepted it. The reader should realize that in all of the previous essays, there is no question by any of the authors of whether there *should* be a feminist movement. It simply exists and we struggle to help it along in whatever modest manner we can. As long as women and all who are victims are aware of injustice and struggle against it, the economy will evolve and change. We can only choose and work to be on the progressive side. As Albert Camus once said, there is simply pestilence and victims — all we can do is choose which side to be on.

Index

Acker, Joan 118-9, 126
Aid to Families with Dependent
   Children (AFDC) 96–7, 134–7
Aldous, Joan 146, 153
Allot, Susan 121, 126
Anazaldua, Gloria 79, 94
androcentric (androcentrism) 23, 45, 63,
   68, 72, 78, 87, 100
Ardzrooni, Leon 17
Aronowitz, Stanley 39–40
Ashley, David 142, 153
axiology xiv, 19, 24–6, 30
Ayres, Clarence E 59, 67–9, 73, 142,
   153

Becker, G 103, 109
Bell, Carolyn Shaw 132, 139
Belous, Richard 144, 146, 155
Benhabib, Seyla 41
Berch, Bettina 133, 137, 139
Bergmann, Barbara R 133, 139–40
Berman, E 148, 154
Bernstein, Aaron 116, 126
Bielby, William T 150–1, 154
Bielby, Denise 150–1, 154
Bingham, Marjorie Wall 163, 174
Bird, Gloria W 151–2, 155
Blank, Rebecca 117–8, 126
Blau, Francine 115, 125–6
Bleier, Ruth 31
Bordo, Susan 35, 41, 47, 64
Braudel, Fernand 65
Brinton, Mary 174
Brown, E B 107, 109
Brue, Stanley L 22
Bryson, J and R 148, 154
Buckley, Mary 120–2, 126
Burgess, Ernest 145, 154

Bush, Corlann 70
Bush, Paul 70
bushido 163
Butler, Judith 47

capitalism 24, 35–9, 40–2, 48–9, 50, 78,
   109, 114, 117–9
Carney, Larry S 167, 174
Carper, L 97, 109
cartesian, noncartesian xi, 19, 36, 41,
   43–4, 46, 63, 101
Caulfield, M D 107, 109
ceremonial-instrumental   dichotomy
   28–9
Chafe, William H 128, 130, 140
Chicago School 144
child-care 11, 118, 120–4, 132–9, 153,
   162, 172
Childe, V Gordon 56, 63, 65
children vxi, 3, 5–9, 10–12, 16, 71,
   99–100, 103, 105, 114, 119, 128,
   130–9, 144, 146, 151–52, 157–9,
   161–2, 166–73
children's allowance 139
Christensen, Kathleen 117, 126
Cipolla, Carlo 65
civil rights 81, 96
class, (classism) 6, 36–7, 46–7, 77, 79,
   93–100, 102–6, 142, 167
Cobb, Norman 151–2, 155
Collier, J 99, 100, 109
Condon, Jane 158, 161, 174
conflict theory 145–6
Confucian(ism) 163, 169
Cook, Alice 174
coping 148–54
Cox, O 103, 109
Cronin, Jim 37

culture (cultural) xi, xii, xvii, 4, 6–8, 23, 32, 41, 43, 46, 56, 59–60, 62, 64–7, 72–3, 77, 79–80, 83, 88, 90–1, 93–4, 100–1, 107–9 129, 131, 143, 145–6

daimyo 163
Dally, Ann 10–11, 132, 136, 139–40
day-care 117, 123, 169
de Courtivron, Isabella 45
de Groot, Joanna 84, 93
De Beauvoir, Simone 5, 9, 14
Deckard, Barbara S 147, 154
deconstructive 67, 78, 85, 93
democracy 49–50
Diamond, Irene 93–4
Dill, B 108–9
DiStefano, Christine 46, 50
divorce 8, 162, 164, 170
Dornbusch, Sanford M 20–1, 31
dual career couple xvi, 142–156
dualism (public–private), dualistic 23, 28, 32, 36, 41, 63–4, 79, 82, 89–91, 100–2, 106–7
Dugger, William M xi, xiv, xvii, 4, 12, 15, 129, 133, 139–40, 142, 153–4
Dyehouse, Janice 154

ecofeminism 93–4
economic development 31, 93
Edwards, Linda N 166, 174
Ehrlich, Elizabeth 118, 126
Eisenstein, Zillah R 130–1, 140
Ekken, Kaibara 163
Elman, Margaret R 150, 154
Engels, Friedrich 103, 109, 119, 121, 123–4, 126
England Paula 133, 140
epistemology xiv, 19, 21, 23–7 30, 35–6, 39–49, 57, 73, 94
Epstein, Cynthia F 148, 154
equality xi, xiii, xvi, xvii, 128–41, 145, 179
equational theory of justice 129–30
eurocentric, eurocentrism 80, 100, 105
evolutionary economics 21, 23, 26, 28, 30, 74, 110

exploitation; exploitative xiii, 82, 90, 118–9, 132, 158, 165, 170, 172, 179
Falkenberg, L 151, 153–4
family, familial xv, xvi, xvii, 6–10, 15, 21, 25, 30, 61, 82, 88, 90, 95–108, 113–24, 131–9, 143–53, 158–66, 171–3, 177, 179
Feher, Ferenc 40, 47, 51
feminism (feminism) x–xvii, 3, 6, 12, 19, 22, 27–9, 31–2, 35, 43–8, 64, 66, 77, 87, 95, 102–6, 108, 128
feminist, black scholars xvi, 96
feminist empiricism 46
feminist standpoint 46
Ferber, Marianne 115, 125
Ferguson, Ann 20, 32
Firestone, S 103, 109
Flax, Jane 31, 41, 51
Folbre, Nancy 116, 119, 126
Ford, Jocelyn 174
Fordism, (post-Fordism) 38
Foster, J Fagg 128, 130, 140
Fraiberg, Selma 135, 150
Frankel, David 116, 118, 127
Fraser, Nancy 42, 45, 48, 51
Friedan, Betty 9, 10, 16–7
Friedman, Milton 22, 32
Fuchs, Victor, R 133, 139–40
functionalism, functionalist xv, 95–109, 144–7, 149
furiitaa 162

Galambos, Nancy L 149, 154
gender 4–7, 13, 16–7, 22–8, 31, 35–7, 46–7, 55–8, 61, 64–5, 68, 70–3, 77–9, 84, 87–90, 95–108, 113–4, 124–5, 152, 162, 178–80
gender based 19, 28, 35, 46, 177–8
gender biased 87
George, Susan 86, 94
Giddings, P 96, 105, 108–9
Gilbert, Lucia A 148, 150–1, 154
Goode, William 148, 154
grand narratives 48
Gray, Francine Du Plessix 121, 123, 126

Greenwood, Daphne 32, 35, 51, 66, 68, 74, 137, 140
Grimshaw, Jean 47, 51
Gross, Susan Hill 163, 174
Gruchy, Allan G 23–4, 32

Hall, D T 148, 151, 154
Hamilton, David 55, 74
Haraway, Donna 37, 51
Harding, Sandra 20, 22–9, 31–2, 36, 46, 48–9, 51, 64–5, 68, 74, 93–4
Harley, S 107, 109
Harrison, Robert S 21, 34
Hartmann, Heidi 66, 75, 103, 109, 119, 126
Harvey, David 37–41, 51
Hayashi, Hiroko 174
Hayes, Cheryl D 132, 134–5, 138, 140
Head Start 139
Helburn, S 134, 140
Herman, J B 148, 154
Hickerson, Steven R 131–2, 140
hierarchy, hierarchial xii, xv, 64, 99, 101–3, 106–8, 163, 167–9
Hill Collins, P 106–9
Hill, Reuben 150, 154
Hiller, Dana Vannoy 154
Hintikka, Merrill 79, 94
Hochschild, Arlie 116, 126
Holahan, C K 148, 150–1, 154
holistic, holism xiv, 19–21, 26–7, 55, 63, 106–8
Holstein, William J 174
hooks, bell 79, 94, 108–9
Huber, Joan 146, 154
human capital 103, 132
humanism, humanist xv, 42, 44–5, 77–82, 87, 93
Hunt, Diana 85, 94
Hutter, Mark 144, 145, 154
Huyssen, Andreas 40, 42, 51
Hymowitz, Carol 6, 17

imperialism 78, 81, 83, 90, 165
industrial policy 138
industrial revolution xvi, 144, 146–7, 153

inequality xiv–xvi, 4–7, 13–7, 27, 77, 79, 98–9, 102, 114, 118–9, 122, 125, 127
instinct of workmanship 3, 17, 62, 75, 142
institutional economics 35, 42, 55, 58, 62, 68, 128–9, 131–2, 177
institutionalism (radical) xiv, 3–4, 17, 29, 35, 74, 77–8
instrumental (valuation, value theory) 57, 59–61, 70
instrumentalism 24, 59
invidious distinction, invidiousness 5, 70, 96, 98–101, 107, 131
Irigaray, Luce 45, 51

Jaggar, Allison M 93–4, 103–4, 109, 119, 125–6, 130, 133, 140
Jameson, Fredric 37, 39, 51
Japan xvii, 133, 157–74, 179
Japan Report 175, 176
Japan's Equal Opportunity Act 157
Japanese women xvii, 157–74
Jefferson, Thomas 129, 131
Jennings, Ann 19–23, 25, 27–8, 31–2, 35, 43–4, 51, 61, 63–8, 71, 75, 95–6, 100–1, 103–4, 109, 113, 127, 129, 140–1
Johnson, M 148, 155
Johnson, C L and F A 148, 155
Johnson, Ian 123
Jones, G S 95, 109
Jordan, Cathleen 151–2, 155
Joseph, George 86, 94, 107–8, 110
Junker, Louis 66, 75

Kahn, Alfred J 134–5, 137, 140
Kamakura period (in Japan) 163
Kamerman, Sheila B 134–5,137
Kawahara, Junko 175
Kelly, Robert F 148–9, 155
Kessler–Harris, A 100, 110
King, D 107, 110
Kiyooka, Eiichi 175
Knaub, Patricia Kain 151–2, 155
kojo 160
Koos, Earl L 150, 155

Kruks, Sonia 118, 126
Kuchiberashi 160

labor force participation 15
Laclau, Ernesto 41, 49, 51
laissez-faire 128, 130, 132
Lanciaux, Bernadette 32, 33, 133, 157
Lapidus, Gail Warshofsky 120–2, 126
Lebra, Taki Sugiyama 175
Levitan, Sar A 144, 146, 155
Lewis, J 107, 110
liberalism 42, 130
Liebhafsky, Herbert Hugo 30, 33
Lief, L 148, 154
Lo, Jeannie 174, 175
Locke, Harvey J 145, 154
Lorde, A 108, 110
Lyotard, Jean–Francois 40–1, 43, 45, 50–1

Mackie, Vera 175
MacKinnon, C 103, 110
male–dominated 7, 12, 35, 136, 157
Malson, M 108–10
Manning L 151, 154
Marks, Elaine 45, 51
marriage 3, 14, 25, 90, 105, 119, 130
Marxism xi, xvi, 4, 16, 29, 31, 35–6, 41–40, 47–8, 50, 93, 102, 110, 119, 124–5, 178
Masakiyo, Hanagawa 164, 175
mass customization 38, 49
Masuda, Reiko 167, 175
matriarchy 97
Matthaei, J 100, 110
Mayhew, Ann 60, 75
McConnell, Campbell R 22, 24, 33
McCubbin, H I 149–50, 155
McCully, Rex 151–2, 155
McKinstry, John A and Asako Nakajima McKinstry 171, 174
McNall, Scott and Sally 144, 146, 155
Mead, Margaret 140
Meese, Elizabeth 47, 51
Meiji era (in Japan) 164–5, 169
Merchant, Carol 79, 94
Mervosh, Edward 116–7, 127

methodology xi, xiv, 19, 24, 27–31, 35, 42, 57, 77, 80
Miller, Edythe S 140
Mishel, Lawrence 116, 118, 127
modernism 36, 40, 42, 50
modernism (post) 35–9, 40–2, 45–9, 50
Mohanty, Chandra 87–91, 93–4
Monachello, M 151, 153–4
Montagu, Ashley 3, 17, 140
Moraga, Cherrie 79, 94
Morris, J 134, 140
Moses, Joel 122, 127
Moynihan report 96
Moynihan, D P 95–104, 109
Mumford, Lewis 62–3, 75
Myers, Frederick Shaw 175
myth (cultural) xi, xiv, xv, 5, 9, 10–17, 41, 46, 70, 78, 100–1
myth (enabling) 4, 180

Neale, Walter C 175
negative income tax 138
neoclassical economics xi, xvi, 5, 17, 28, 41, 50, 101–3, 113, 117
neoclassical, neoclassicism xi, 19, 24–6, 31, 42–3, 67, 113–4, 125, 130, 132
Nicholson, Linda 41–2, 48, 50–1, 100, 110
Nock, S 148, 156
nuclear family 117, 144–5

O'Kelly, Charlotte G 167, 174
occupational segregation 114
office ladies (in Japan) 159, 165, 174
Oliveri, Mary Ellen 150, 155
Olson, D H 150, 155
Olson, Paulette I 32–3, 77, 140
Omi, M 96, 110
ontology xiv, 19, 21–4, 27, 30, 56
Orenstein, Gloria Feman 43, 94
Orenstein, David 142, 153
Orientalism 8, 81, 84–7, 92
orthodox economics xiv, 24, 29, 66, 77
Osako, Masako Murakami 175
Owens, Craig 47, 51

Palmer, John L 140

part–time work (employment, jobs) 117–8, 122–3, 162–3, 168–9, 172–3
patriarchy, patriarchal 6, 9, 13–6, 32, 35, 45–6, 90–1, 97–8, 103, 119–20, 131, 153, 179
Patterson, J M 150, 155
Pearlin, Leonard 149–50, 155
Peattie, Lisa 86, 94
Peers, Jo 120–2, 127
Pennar, Karen 116–7, 127
Perlich, Pam 93–4
Peterson, Janice 30, 32–3, 108, 110, 113, 123, 127, 133, 141
Petr, Jerry xvii
pluralism 49–50
politics of difference 49–50
Poloma, Margaret N 155
positive economics 22
postcolonial xv, 7, 80–1, 85–6, 92
postmodern xiv, 35, 50, 93, 178
poverty xv, 11, 86, 97–8, 128, 133, 135, 137–9
pragmatic (-ism) xiv, 22–4, 27, 31, 44, 66

race relations xi, xv, 95, 105, 108
racism 6, 79, 90, 95, 107
Rainwater, L 96, 109, 110
Ramstad, Yngve 19–20, 31, 33
Rapoport, R 147–8, 155
Rapp, Rayna 118, 126
Reddy, Vasu 94
reductionism, reductionistic 16, 44, 77, 86–7, 92, 98, 102, 104, 108, 178
Reischauer, Edwin 175
Reiss, David 150, 155
relative earnings 114, 116
Robertson, Linda 60, 76
Robins-Mowry, Dorothy 175
Robinson, Joan 24, 33, 129, 131, 141
role strain 148–9, 151, 153
Rorty, Richard 40, 42, 52
Rosaldo, M 99, 100–1, 109
Rosenthal, Pam 38, 52
Rosin, Hazel M 151–2, 155
Ross, Andrew 49, 52
Rothenberg, Paula S 93–4

Rothschild, Joan 62–3, 68, 75
Rudolph, Ellen 175
Russo, Ann 93–4

Sacks, S 148, 154
Said, Edward 94
Samuels, Warren 75
Schnittger, Maureen H 151–2, 155
Schooler, Carmi 149–50, 155
Scott, Joan W 141
Searle-Chatterjee, Mary 94
second shift 116–7
Sekaran, Uma 155
Seo, Akwi 175
sexism x, xi, 8, 21–2, 35, 46, 79, 177–9, 8181
sexual equality 131, 168
Shanley, Mary Lyndon 30, 33
Shibayama, Emiko 175
Shiva, Vandana 93–4
Sidel, Ruth 141
Sievers, Sharon L 175
Silbereisen, Rainer K 149–54
Simpson, Peggy 123, 127
Skinner, D A 151, 155
slavery 83, 96–7, 104–5
socialism xii, 4, 50, 120, 124
sociology xvii, 66, 80, 142–4, 147, 153, 178
Soviet economy 114, 118, 120, 125
Soviet Union (former) 113–4, 118, 120–5, 133
Spain, D 156
Spelman, E 104, 110
Spitz, Glenna 115–6, 127
Spivac, Gayatri Chakravorty 94
St John-Parsons, D 148, 155
Stanfield, Jacqueline B 156
Stanley, Autumn 75
Strober, Myra H 20, 31–2
Sundstrom, Marianne 175
Swaney, James 57, 75

Takagi, Haruo 175
technology 38, 48, 55–73, 143–6
Terborg-Penn, R 108, 110
Tilly, Louise A 141

Third World women 78, 85–93
Tinker, Irene 87, 94
Tokygawa Period (in Japan)
Tool, Marc R 31, 33, 60, 75–6, 131, 141
Torres, Lourdes 93–4
Trescott, Martha Moore 65, 75
Tsurumi, E Patricia 175
Tuana, Nancy 68, 75
Tucker, Robert C 145, 156

Ueno, Chizuko 175
US Bureau of the Census 15, 17, 133–4, 139, 141, 147, 156

Veblen, Thorstein xi, xiii, xvi, xvii, 3–4, 17, 27–8, 32, 37, 43–4, 47, 52, 58–63, 66, 70, 73–5, 96, 100, 106–8, 129, 131, 140–2, 145, 153, 156, 177–9
Veblenian dichotomy 3, 27–9, 58–9, 732–4, 76
Verhelst, Thierry G 86, 94
Voydanoff, Patricia 148–9, 155

wages 100, 108, 115–7, 123, 125, 169
Wagman, Barnett 116, 127
Waller, William T, Jr xi, xii, xv, xvii, 17, 19, 20–3, 28–9, 31–5, 43–4, 51, 55, 59–64, 66, 68, 75–6, 100, 103–4, 109, 113, 127, 129, 140–1
Waring, Marilyn 87, 94, 141
Waugh, Patricia 45–6, 52
Weingarten, K 148, 156
Weisman, Steven R 175
Weissman, Michaele 6, 17
West, Cornel 44–5, 52
Whalen Charles J 19, 30–2, 34, 129, 179
White, Lynn, Jr 57, 62–3, 76
Wilber, Charles K 21, 34
Winant, H 96, 110
Wittgenstein, Ludwig 42, 52

Yanagisako, S 99, 109
Yancey, W 96, 109
Yeatman, Anna 37, 48, 52

Yorburg, Betty 144–7, 157
Young, Iris 49, 52
Young, Marilyn 118, 126

Zaretsky, E 103, 110
Zaslow, Martha J 140
Zimmerman, Shirley 144, 156